1981

THE POLITICS
OF
PUNISHMENT

the text of this book is printed
on 100% recycled paper

HARPER TORCHBOOKS
Harper & Row, Publishers
New York, Hagerstown, San Francisco, London

The Politics of Punishment

A CRITICAL ANALYSIS OF PRISONS IN AMERICA

By Erik Olin Wright

WITH CONTRIBUTIONS BY

Robert Barber
Brian Glick
Thomas Lopez Meneweather
John Pallas
Eve Pell
Frank L. Rundle
James F. Smith
Fay Stender

THE POLITICS OF PUNISHMENT

FIRST EDITION: HARPER COLOPHON BOOKS 1973

LIBRARY OF CONGRESS CATALOG CARD NUMBER: 72–12243

STANDARD BOOK NUMBER: 06-131904-X

A hardcover edition of this book is published by Harper & Row.

Designed by Yvette A. Vogel

79 80   12 11 10 9 8

CONTENTS

TABLES

PREFACE

In the fall of 1970, after studying history at Oxford for two years, I returned to the United States and entered the Starr King School for the Ministry, a Unitarian-Universalist seminary in Berkeley, California. One of the programs in the school is called an "in-field assignment," the idea of which is to give students the opportunity to experience a wide variety of settings for ministerial work. I wanted to pick an activity that would be as removed from my past experience as possible, that would put me in contact with new kinds of people and new kinds of human problems. After exploring a number of possibilities, I decided to be a student chaplain at San Quentin.

It would be wrong to say that I had no particular expectations when I first began working at San Quentin. I was prepared for it to be a gruesome place. I expected prison conditions to be harsh and oppressive, the prisoners to be tough and resentful, and prison officials to be conservative and authoritarian. In the course of the next nine months, some of these expectations were confirmed; others were shown to be naïve and simplistic.

In November, 1970, I wrote a paper on my experiences at San Quentin. The paper was based largely on my observations of prison life, along with a few formal interviews with prison officials. Two months later I was invited to attend a weekend con-

ference on prisons. One of the issues discussed at the conference was the problem of educating the general public about
conditions in prison. A general feeling prevailed that one of the
biggest obstacles to changing the prison system was widespread
ignorance about prisons and prisoners. In particular, many people felt that there was a serious need for a systematic critical
analysis of the prison system as a whole. Several of the lawyers
at the conference looked through the paper which I had written
on San Quentin and suggested that I expand it into a book on
prisons. *The Politics of Punishment* is the result of that sugges-
tion.

Following the conference, I began taking thorough notes on
my experiences at San Quentin. As a student chaplain, I was in
a position to observe many activities, such as disciplinary hearings and parole board sessions, which outsiders are not normally
allowed to attend. I could not take notes during such activities,
but I retained as much as possible by memory and recorded my
observations immediately after I left the prison each day. In
addition, I interviewed more than 150 prisoners and had both
formal and informal conversations with most of the top officials
of the prison. These observations and interviews form the basis
of Part II of the book: "San Quentin Prison: A Portrait of Contradictions."

In the course of working on the book I met a number of
people who agreed to make various contributions. They include
two prisoners, a number of lawyers, and a former prison psychiatrist, among others. No effort was made to create a completely homogeneous perspective in all the chapters, although
each contributor shares a commitment to fundamentally changing the prison system.

The book revolves around two broad issues: the internal operation of prisons in the United States, and the political reality of
prisons with respect to society at large. Certain chapters discuss
these issues in theoretical terms; others are descriptive and
concrete. I have attempted to construct a book which will be

useful both to students who are interested in the conceptual issues of punishment and to general readers who are more interested in learning about what goes on inside American prisons.

Three interrelated themes are explored in the discussion of the internal operations of prisons:

Rehabilitation as manipulation. Most American prisons have adopted, or are in the process of adopting, a "rehabilitation" ideology. Officially, prison administrators proclaim that the prison is trying to transform prisoners into useful, responsible, law-abiding citizens. This is the theory; the practice is quite different. In many ways the rehabilitation ideology simply serves as a façade for the traditional punitive custodial practices of the prison. Frequently, in fact, rehabilitation is used to manipulate and control the prison population (see Chapters 3, 4–7, and 15).

The lawlessness and totalitarianism of prison. To a significant extent, prisons operate outside the law. Prison officials have enormous discretionary power, and the prisoner is almost totally helpless to protect himself against arbitrary and unjust treatment. Prisons are totalitarian institutions which, in the name of upholding the law, violate the very precepts of legality (see Chapters 5–7, 8, 10, 11, and 15).

The prisoners' response to prison conditions. The experience of prison is dehumanizing and frustrating. Prisoners react in many ways: some try to adapt to prison and conform to every demand by prison officials; others are broken by the prison experience; and some resist. In the late 1960s and early 1970s prisoners increasingly moved toward open resistance to prison authorities (see Chapters 6, 9, 11, and 12).

The book's analysis of the political reality of punishment centers on two basic issues:

The political meaning of crime and punishment. I have adopted an explicitly political notion of both crime and punishment. I do this not because I feel these phenomena are solely political, but because the political implications of crime and punishment are crucial to an understanding of how to change the prison system, and because those implications have received too little attention in the literature on prisons. Crime in the United States is discussed as a consequence of certain implicitly political choices in American society concerning the distribution of wealth and power, the pattern of opportunities open to various social groups, and the kinds of problems which people confront in their lives. Punishment is viewed as a political response to certain actions which threaten the stability of the existing social order (see Chapters 1, 2, and 15).

The politics of changing the system. It is not enough merely to attack the prison system, to analyze its oppressiveness and its political meaning. It is also necessary to explore how the system can be changed. The book examines three general approaches to challenging the system: direct action by prisoners, legislative reform, and court action. It concludes that although some changes are possible by working "through the system," ultimately it is necessary to restructure fundamental aspects of the society itself before prisons can be significantly humanized (see Chapters 12–15).

ERIK OLIN WRIGHT

Berkeley, California
June, 1972.

PART I

Crime and Its Punishment

by Erik Olin Wright

CHAPTER 1

The Meaning of Crime

If you are a typical American citizen, chances are that in your life you have committed some crime for which you could have been sent to jail or prison. In all probability, you have stolen something from a store, cheated on your income tax, or committed some other punishable offense.[1] Similarly, as a typical American citizen, chances are that you have been the victim of crime. Your house has been burglarized, your car has been stolen, or you have been cheated by a fraudulent repairman. If you are an American citizen who is poor, chances are that you have been the victim of crime many times.[2]

More than 2 million burglaries, 300,000 robberies, and 15,000 murders are committed each year in the United States.[3] Hun-

1. Very few studies have attempted to measure the proportion of the general population which has committed one form of crime or another. Such a study obviously faces serious methodological problems. One of the few studies which has attempted this produced some startling results. Based on a sample of 1,020 randomly selected males, it was found that 26 percent admitted to auto theft, 17 percent to burglary, and 13 percent to grand larceny. Overall, 91 percent of the respondents had committed one or more offenses for which they might have received jail or prison sentences. Cited in the report of the President's Commission on Law Enforcement and the Administration of Justice, *The Challenge of Crime in a Free Society.* (New York: Avon Books, 1968), pp. 147–148.
2. For a discussion of victimization from crime, see pp. 38 ff. below.
3. *Uniform Crime Reports,* 1971, published by the FBI.

dreds of millions of dollars are stolen from consumers through criminal consumer fraud. Nobody deliberately designed this pattern; nobody says that it is desirable to have this much crime. Yet, the level of crime in American society and the forms which it takes are substantially the result of *political choices.*[4] Although the state does not desire this pattern of crime, it chooses courses of action which make such high levels of crime inevitable.

In certain situations, the relationship of crime to political decisions is very direct: the extremely high homicide rate in the United States, for example, is due in part to the absence of any real control on guns. More often, though, the relationship of crime to political decisions is less obvious. A high level of "street crime" is one of the prices the society pays for creating high levels of urban poverty and systematically discriminating against certain groups of people. Broadly speaking, the pattern of crime in America is a product of the basic political choice to maintain the existing structure of wealth and power in this society.

The political nature of crime can be clarified by looking at such problems as traffic fatalities and unemployment. In the case of traffic accidents, the unwillingness of the government to impose strict safety standards on automobiles or systematically to enforce the laws against drunken driving contributes substantially to the death rate on American highways. High profits from automobile sales and repairs, and the individual's "right" to drink when and where he pleases, have been considered more important than the lives lost on the roads each year. While it cannot be said that the government, the automobile manufacturers, and the voters and consumers who support them want

4. I will use the word "political" to refer to aspects of a system that center on power and power relationships, especially power that is connected with the state. A "political choice" refers to a course of action (or inaction) adopted when alternative courses of action are available. For example, in a wealthy country such as the United States the existence of poverty is a political choice in the sense that alternative choices are available which would eliminate poverty.

50,000 people to die each year in automobile accidents, they refuse to take necessary steps to reduce the number of those deaths. This refusal is a political choice, and the ensuing fatalities are its consequence.

The case of unemployment is even clearer. It is standard economic policy that under certain circumstances unemployment should be deliberately increased in order to "cool off " the economy. Rather than deal with problems of the economy by reducing profits or by fundamentally restructuring the economy itself, the political decision is made to increase the number of people without work. Again, it is not that the government likes to see people without work, but rather that it feels it is more advantageous to increase the unemployment rate than deal with economic problems in other ways.

To say that traffic fatalities, unemployment, and crime are products of political choices does not mean that they are purely political phenomena. Individual characteristics obviously play an important role. But it is important that these individual factors always be placed in a social and political context.

The relationship between individual and social-political factors is especially clear in the case of traffic accidents and unemployment. In any traffic accident individual explanations are always available: the driver was incompetent; there was ice on the road; the driver was depressed about his job and not paying attention. Similarly, there are always individual explanations for why a worker is unemployed: he has a bad work record; he is too lazy to look for a job; his firm lost a great deal of money and had to lay off many employees. These sorts of explanations may be useful for understanding why a particular accident occurred or why a particular worker is out of a job. But they are not particularly useful in understanding the *rate* of accidents or of unemployment. To explain the rates, it is necessary to look for factors which affect the system as a whole and influence the outcome of many individual situations. In the case of traffic accidents, issues such as the absence of good, inexpensive public transportation and the safety of cars need to be examined. In the case of unemployment, it is necessary to look at such things as the policies which influence the job market and the kinds of incentives which exist for finding new jobs.

If in the study of crime, a main concern is to explain why one particular individual commits a crime while another individual, in roughly the same social position, does not, then broad social issues may be relatively unimportant. The emphasis in such an analysis would be more on individual psychological characteristics, differential associations with various kinds of peer groups, and so on. Here, however, our basic interest is in explaining broad patterns of crime, and the analysis shifts to the sociopolitical forces at work. Although the individual is not ignored in this analysis, the focus is on the social reality which impinges on his life, and the political forces which sustain that social reality.

The following discussion will examine how patterns of crime in America emerge out of the social forces which confront people in the society. Social structure influences the pattern of crime in three essential ways: by creating *problems*, especially economic problems, which confront individuals in various positions of the society; by creating a particular pattern of *options* available to individuals for solving those problems; and by creating constraints which influence the *decision* to adopt a particular option for solving problems.[5]

5. Much of the sociological writing on crime involves some variant of the general perspective that crime should be seen as an outcome of the problems faced by individuals and the opportunities available for solving them. The classical statement of this viewpoint is made by Robert K. Merton in his article "Social Structure and Anomie," *American Sociological Review*, Oct., 1938: "It is only when a system of cultural values extols virtually above all else certain common success goals *for the population at large* while the social structure rigorously restricts or completely closes access to approved modes of reaching these goals *for a considerable part of the same population* that deviant behavior ensues on a large scale." In American society Merton saw this as meaning that the poor accept the values of individual wealth and success but lack access to legitimate means of fulfilling their aspirations, and thus they turn to illicit means. The analysis of this chapter, however, suggests that crime is a consequence of the problems and options of all social classes, not just the poor.

A variant of Merton's thesis is what has been called the theory of delinquent

PROBLEMS

The problems which confront an individual are to a large extent the result of the society in which he lives and of his particular place in it. Many of these problems are bound up with economic issues: how to acquire the resources for food, clothing, shelter, recreation.[6] In American society, the intensity and concrete forms of such problems vary considerably with class, race, sex, and age. A corporation executive, for example, never faces the problem of how to cope with the rats in a tenement or where to get money to pay the rent. A worker, on the other hand, never faces the problem of how to get promoted to a top managerial position or how to get a favorable ruling from the government on an antitrust case.

subcultures. While accepting that crime is a response to blocked opportunities, this perspective sees crime as a repudiation of middle-class values rather than as an attempt to realize those values through criminal means. For two different versions of this general approach, see Albert K. Cohen, *Delinquent Boys* (New York: Free Press, 1955) and Richard Cloward and Lloyd Ohlin, *Delinquency and Opportunity* (New York: Free Press, 1961).

Without denying that the subcultural approach may be useful for the study of certain questions, I will use a narrower problem-opportunity model of crime. I do this for several reasons. First of all, most of the literature concerning delinquent subcultures has focused on juvenile offenders, not on the adult criminal. The subcultural perspective may be quite useful in understanding youthful vandalism, but it is really unnecessary in explaining theft. The vast majority of crimes are economic. They represent the illegal appropriation of the property of others. It is unnecessary to postulate a subculture of vice or crime to explain why people turn to illegal activities to acquire material wealth. Second, the view that crime represents a natural, adaptive solution to problems stresses the essential continuity of working-class crime, middle-class crime, and crimes of the very rich. The problem-opportunity model of crime highlights the fact that criminality is not a special characteristic of the poor, but rather that the available criminal options of the poor and the rich are very different. The subcultural model of crime sees working-class crime as a fundamentally different phenomenon from white-collar and business crime; the problem-opportunity model stresses that they are all efforts to solve problems through illegal means.

6. Throughout this discussion the emphasis will be on economic problems because most crime is associated with the economic difficulties people face in their lives (see p. 19 below).

Many of the problems which individuals face are intensified by the consumption values of American society. People are constantly told that their status is defined in large part by the level of their private wealth and that happiness is dependent upon ever-increasing levels of consumption. Because they have accepted these individualistic consumption values, even the relatively affluent face the "problem" of how to acquire more wealth. When the poor accept these values they are placed in an especially difficult situation, since they have the most limited opportunities for such consumption.

Not only does the society determine the problems the individual faces (or feels he faces) but it also influences the way the individual analyzes his problems. The ideology of competitive individualism, which is such an important element of American culture, tends to make people see their problems in highly individualistic terms. Even when there is a realization that their problems are shared by others, many people still fail to see the problem as stemming from the structure of the society itself, and so they seek individualistic solutions.

OPTIONS

The options available to the individual for solving his problems are, like the problems themselves, closely bound up with the society in which he lives. The individual's position in the society defines to a significant extent what alternative actions are realistically open to him. The options available to a twenty-five-year-old unemployed black for solving his economic problems are more limited than those of a twenty-five-year-old white with a college degree, or those of a fifty-year-old wealthy doctor. They may all have certain economic problems in the sense of having limited resources to satisfy their needs and desires. However, the ghetto black rarely has the option of getting a job that pays well or of taking out a mortgage on a home.

The way the individual perceives and analyzes his options is also strongly influenced by the society. The competitive individualism which defines economic problems in individualistic terms also defines solutions in individualistic terms. Success is seen as the result of individual competitive effort, rather than of collective cooperation. When the individual seeks ways to cope with the problems which confront him, his socialization directs him toward individualistic forms of action. Most crime represents this type of individualistic solution to problems.

Frequently, some of the significant options available to the individual are illegal.[7] Like legal options, the illegal ones are often closely tied to the individual's social situation. An unemployed worker cannot embezzle cash from the till of a bank or claim illegal business deductions on his income tax returns. Similarly, a bank president never needs to consider the option of holding up a bank; a wealthy home owner never needs to consider the option of burglarizing wealthy homes. Given the competitive individualistic outlook on solving problems which is so pervasive in American society, it is not surprising that under certain circumstances individuals at all levels of the society should turn to illegal options.

A significant difference between the illegal options available to the poor and those available to the more affluent is the question of violence. Most violent crimes, especially robbery, are committed by the poor. Middle-class and upper-class property crimes are characteristically nonviolent. Rather than taking

7. There has been much discussion in the field of criminology over what is the most useful definition of "crime." In general, criminologists have increasingly tended to adopt a somewhat narrow legal definition of criminal behavior. That is the definition that will be used throughout this discussion: a crime is an action which violates the criminal law. There is no necessary implication in this definition that a particular crime is immoral or antisocial. For a good general discussion of the problems of defining crime, see Edwin M. Schur, *Our Criminal Society: The Social and Legal Sources of Crime in America* (Englewood Cliffs, N.J.: Prentice-Hall, 1968), especially the introduction. For specific discussions of the legal definitions of crime, see: "The Legal Definition of Crime and Criminals," by William L. Marshall and William L. Clark, and "Who Is the Criminal?" by Paul W. Tappan, in Marvin E. Wolfgang, et. al., *The Sociology of Crime and Delinquency* (New York: Wiley, 1970).

place in the street, they frequently occur in the privacy of the home while filling out income tax forms, or behind the closed doors of a corporation president's office. The poor lack this access to circumspect property crime. This means they are much more likely to confront the victim of their crimes, and violence is much more likely to be involved in the outcome.[8] This does not mean that the poor are necessarily more violent than the rest of the society. Rather, it means that the nature of the illegal options open to them tends to make violence more common in their crimes.

DECISIONS

In general, the problems an individual faces and the options open to him do not totally determine the particular course of action he follows. Two people can face roughly similar problems and have roughly similar options and still make entirely different decisions as to what to do. Specifically, one person can choose a legal option and another an illegal option for coping with the same problem.[9]

8. It is important to stress that even among the poor the vast majority of crime is still nonviolent. According to the FBI's *Uniform Crime Reports,* there were 2,169,300 burglaries (i.e., theft resulting from an illegal entry in which the criminal does not personally confront the victim) committed in the United States in 1970, 1,746,100 larcenies of over $50, and 921,400 automobile thefts, for a total of just over 5 million nonviolent serious property crimes. But there were only 348,380 robberies (i.e., theft in which the victim is confronted by the criminal). Thus, theft involving even the threat of violence amounts to less than 8 percent of all thefts. Furthermore, the President's Commission on Law Enforcement and the Administration of Justice estimates that physical injury occurs in 25 percent of all robberies at most, and death in fewer than .5 percent of all robberies. *(The Challenge of Crime in a Free Society,* p. 91.) Thus *actual* violence occurs in less than 2 percent of all serious thefts.

9. Throughout this discussion, the commission of a crime will be considered a *decision* on the part of the individual (i.e., an action that to some degree involves weighing alternatives and making a choice between them). David Matza, in *Delinquency and Drift* (New York: Wiley, 1964) and *Becoming Deviant* (Englewood Cliffs, N.J.: Prentice-Hall, 1967), sees criminal behavior in these terms as a positive choice. To say this does not imply any hard notion of "free will." Rather, it implies that human behavior is "choosing behavior" which

Many considerations enter into the actual decision to commit a crime, to choose an illegal option for solving problems. Four of these are particularly important: the crime's *effectiveness,* its *risk,* its *ethical implications,* and its *intrinsic satisfaction.* We will consider each in turn.

The effectiveness of illegal options in solving the problem (especially compared to legal options). In many cases an illegal option may be the only viable option for effectively solving a particular problem. For a person whose business is foundering avoiding bankruptcy may necessitate bribing a public official in order to obtain an advantageous government contract. For a ghetto youth, the *only* way that he can acquire the symbols of American affluence—a new car, flashy clothes, money to throw around, and so on—may be through illegal means. For a political activist, the only effective option for political action may be illegal. In the early 1960s this meant illegal sit-ins and other forms of nonviolent civil disobedience. In the labor movement it has meant illegal strikes. In each of these cases, legal means are not simply less effective or slower, but under the given circumstances, they will not work. In such situations the individual has the choice either of abandoning the goal—letting a business fail, becoming resigned to one's poverty, accepting the defeat of one's social and political goals—or of adopting the illegal, criminal option.

makes discriminations, weighs alternatives, evaluates consequences, and then makes a choice. It is a real question whether all criminal acts can be so described. Thomas Szasz, in his book *Law, Liberty and Psychiatry* (New York: Collier, 1968), argues that all human action, even the most apparently insane, involves elements of decision making. In his analysis, even the most compulsive, psychotic criminal chooses to commit his crimes: ". . . insofar as men are human beings, not machines, they always have some choice in how they act—hence, they are *always* responsible for their conduct. There is method in madness, no less than in sanity" (p. 135). Other writers draw a sharp distinction between the criminal who is "responsible" for his acts and the criminal who is driven by some "irresistible urge." As I will argue later, most crime can be considered relatively rational, adaptive behavior, and thus it is reasonable to assume that the substantial majority of criminal acts involve decisions (see pp. 17 ff. for a discussion of the mental-illness theory of crime).

Most situations are more ambiguous than this. Rarely is the choice between completely abandoning the goal on the one hand and accepting illegal courses of action on the other. Rather, the individual is faced with a variety of alternatives, some of which take longer than others, some of which are more certain, some of which are illegal. In such situations an important, although not necessarily decisive, consideration is the extent to which the illegal course of action is also the most effective course of action. If the most effective course of action is legal, then most people would adopt it; if the most effective course of action is illegal then other factors come into play.

The risk involved in the illegal option. There has been much debate about the extent to which punishment acts as a deterrent to crime. Obviously, the threat of punishment does not deter those individuals who actually commit crimes. And equally obviously, the threat of punishment is not a deterrent to those people who are never in the position to commit a particular crime.

The important question is whether the risk of punishment has an effect on those individuals who have to choose between legal and illegal actions. In certain instances it would seem that risk plays a decisive part. For example, in the case of draft evasion, the threat of three years' imprisonment for refusing induction is a significant issue. The risk in draft evasion is very high, in terms of both the likelihood of being caught and the likelihood of being punished. Many people are unwilling to take that risk. In a criminal action in which the risk is marginal, such as smoking marijuana or tax fraud, the fear of punishment plays a smaller role. In cases like robbery or burglary where the chances of getting caught are significant, but not high, the importance of the risk involved will depend upon the individual.[10] Some people are easily intimidated; some people are unrealistic

10. According to data presented by Ramsey Clark in his book *Crime in America* (New York: Pocket Books, 1971), pp. 101–102, the odds of being apprehended for burglary or robbery are still relatively low. A robber has only about a 1 in 12 chance of being caught; a burglar, a 1 in 50 chance.

in their assessment of risk; some people decide that the risk is irrelevant. Of course, even the experienced robber or burglar who is not deterred from committing a crime by the risk will choose the form and target of his crime in terms of minimizing his chances of being caught.[11]

Ethical implications. Two basic moral issues are involved in the commission of a crime: the morality of lawbreaking per se; and the intrinsic morality of the criminal act itself. Much of the conservative outcry against the desegregation sit-ins of the early 1960s focused on the first of these. People argued that it was wrong to break the law, even if the law was flagrantly unjust. If you feel that all lawbreaking is necessarily immoral, then the ethical implications of choosing illegal options become very simple.

The question of the intrinsic morality of criminal acts is considerably more complicated. Most people regard certain crimes, such as murder or rape, as immoral. However, for some criminal acts there is no such consensus. Possession of drugs, homosexuality, prostitution, and other so-called crimes without victims are regarded as morally reprehensible by people in America possessing one set of values, and as morally acceptable (although not necessarily desirable) by those possessing another.

In certain situations, ethical imperatives directly operate to encourage or to justify crime. This is most obviously the case in politically motivated crime in which the individual feels a moral obligation to commit certain criminal acts. The romantic image of the Robin Hood figure who robs from the rich to give to the poor also depicts crime as highly ethical. Ethical imperatives may also be involved when a poor black holds up a ghetto store and feels that his action is justified because of the way that store has treated him in the past. This is also the case in various middle-class forms of petty theft, such as flying youth-fare on

11. A more detailed discussion of the question of deterrence is presented in Chapter 2, especially pp. 34 ff.

airplanes when the passenger is no longer legally eligible. Such actions are often justified by saying that no one is hurt by them and that it is all right to "rip off " capitalist businesses.

Even if the individual sees a criminal act as being intrinsically immoral, he may still feel that he is justified in committing it. The moral issues in human decisions are rarely so simple that one decision is all good and another all bad. An individual may face the ethical dilemma of being unable to provide a decent standard of living for his family if he does not commit a crime. In such a case it is not at all clear which choice is "moral." The individual may feel that stealing is still wrong, but that under extenuating circumstances it is justified.

Finally, an individual can look at the society around him and feel that many profoundly immoral, exploitative activities are protected by the law. A black in Harlem experiences the law as supporting the collapsing tenements of the ghetto. A migrant farm worker experiences the law as supporting intolerable working conditions and miserable wages. As a result of such experiences many people, especially the poor, feel a profound disrespect for the law and a pervasive alienation from the institutions which the law protects. An individual can easily come to the conclusion that crime is no more exploitative and vicious than many legal and respected activities. Without necessarily going through a conscious process of analysis, he can rationalize his own behavior by saying that he is merely doing on a small scale what big business and the government do on a large scale. It is not so much that he feels his criminal activity to be ethically justified, but rather that the issue of morality has become largely irrelevant.

This view of crime and morality is articulately expressed by Alfred Hassan, a former prisoner of the California Prison System:

> Don't be telling me what is right. You talk that right jive,
> but where was you when my old man and the neighbors

was teaching me how to steal and shoot dope? Where was you when me and my brothers and sisters was crazy and blind from hunger? Where was you when my mama was gambling away the welfare check? Where was you when the World was calling me a dirty nigger and a greasy Mexican and a poor white peckawood? Where was you when the cops was whipping me upside my head just because my skin was dark? Where was you when I was losing respect for your law and your order? Where was you when Wrong was my salvation? I'll tell you where you was. You was clear across town—Y'know, over there living in them big, fine houses—talking that trash about right and wrong. But check this out: There ain't no such thing as right or wrong in my world. Can you dig? Right or wrong is what a chump chooses to tell himself. And I choose to tell myself that stealing is right. I had a choice: to be a poor-assed, raggedy-ass mothafukker all my life or to go out into the streets and steal me some money so I could buy me a decent pair of shoes to wear, or shoot me some dope so I could forget about the rat-and-roach infested dump I live in. Yeah, I got a chip on my shoulder. But it didn't get there by itself. And it's gonna stay up there until you eliminate the funky conditions that breed cats like me.[12]

Intrinsic satisfaction in the illegal option. A crime may not simply be a means to some other end; it may also be an end in and of itself. It can provide the perpetrator of the crime with a variety of intrinsic satisfactions. This is most clearly the case in crimes without victims, but it is also the case in other kinds of crime as well. A study of white-collar embezzlement conducted by Lawrence Zeitlin found that one of the main reasons for such crime by retail store employees was the boredom of the job itself:

> When the average retail employee becomes dissatisfied with his job, if he doesn't quit, he starts stealing from his employer. He gets back at the system. In a sense, the intel-

12. Quoted in Eve Pell (ed.), *Maximum Security* (New York: Dutton, 1972) p. 2.

lectual and physical challenges provided by opportunities to steal represent a significant enrichment of the individual's job. He can take matters into his own hands, assume responsibility, make decisions, and face challenges. The amount he gets away with is determined solely by his own initiative. He is in business for himself.[13]

The same issues are involved in "street crime." Various forms of theft, rackets, drug pushing, and so on may offer the individual a greater realm of personal initiative, of individual responsibility, of excitement and challenge, than any alternative employment available to him.

Undoubtedly, for some people the emotional satisfaction of crime stems from its exploitative, manipulative character. Crime, like police work, can offer outlets for sadistic urges. It can also satisfy needs for power and domination. In the act of committing a crime, an individual who is otherwise powerless can, for a moment at least, hold considerable power in his own hands. This is especially true for a crime like armed robbery in which the robber directly confronts his victim.

Crime can also be a significant outlet for rage. It can be a form of primitive rebellion against what is experienced as a hostile, oppressive society. But unlike revolutionary militancy, most crime is an apolitical response to oppression. It is a highly individualistic form of revenge against "the system" and is generally not connected to any broad conception of social and political change.

The extent and nature of the intrinsic satisfaction of a crime will, of course, vary considerably. For some individuals the specific material gains of a crime are secondary to the satisfaction gained from the *process* of the crime itself. To others, there may be very little satisfaction in the criminal act itself and even a great deal of guilt. For most individuals the situation is undoubtedly somewhere in between.

13. Lawrence Zeitlin, "A Little Larceny Can Do a Lot for Employee Morale," *Psychology Today*, June, 1971, p. 24.

The decision to follow an illegal course of action to solve one's problems is, then, not unlike the decision to adopt a legal course of action. In both cases the individual makes some assessment of the effectiveness of his action, of the risks involved, of the moral implications of what he is doing, and of the intrinsic satisfaction to be gained from the action. This assessment is not necessarily systematic or even completely conscious, but it is common to both criminal and law-abiding behavior. What is distinctive about the decision to commit a crime is the particular risks involved and the specific moral question of breaking the law.

This view of crime is very different from that of most American prison administrators and many criminologists who view criminality as a form or symptom of emotional disturbance on the part of the criminal rather than a more or less rational, natural way of solving problems.[14] The conception of crime as pathological includes a wide range of specific hypotheses. At one extreme is the view that crime is primarily the result of genetic factors. At the other extreme is the sophisticated notion that emotional disturbances which lead to crime are the result of poverty, alcoholism, family disorganization, and so on.[15]

In all these notions, crime is seen as basically *irrational*, caused by emotional problems in the individual. However, irrationalities and emotional problems enter into virtually all human decisions. Crime, while in general no more rational, adaptive, or sane than law-abiding behavior, is not necessarily less so.

14. I am referring to crime as "rational" behavior in the sense of being an effective means to some end. There is no implication that it is necessarily an ethically desirable means to that end, or that it is always the most effective means to that end.

15. Although the subcultural theories of crime and delinquency (discussed in footnote 5) formally reject the conception of crime as a symptom of emotional disturbance, an implicit image of criminal behavior as illness often persists. While the individual is not seen as individually sick, he is seen as accepting and participating in a "sick" subculture. Criminal behavior thus becomes the active manifestation of this deformed subculture, rather than a rational, adaptive action by the individual.

Furthermore, in some situations the "normal," rational, sane response is to commit a crime rather than to obey the law.

Much of the argument that crime is a form of mental disturbance is, in the final analysis, simply a matter of formal definition. If "respect for authority" is seen as a necessary element of sanity and rationality then the criminal becomes a priori emotionally unbalanced. If the unwillingness to "delay gratification" of material desires (which in the case of most poor people would mean to delay gratification permanently) is taken as an indication of immaturity, impulsiveness, and emotional maladjustment, then many criminals are, again by definition, sick. While the idea that crime is a form of inherent "wickedness" has generally been rejected, many people are unwilling to accept the indictment of the social order implied by the view that crime is a more or less rational means of solving real problems. Instead they have developed the notion that crime is a form of emotional illness, and they have defined illness and sanity in such a way as to support the conclusion.[16]

Aside from the issue of what "sanity" is, two basic objections can be leveled against explanations of crime in terms of mental illness. First of all, even if most criminals were incapable of "controlling their impulses," or were in other ways emotionally

16. It is, of course, very difficult to find data that would clearly support either the problem-solving or the mental-illness view of crime. It is not possible to get hard data on the total population of "criminals" per se, but only on individuals who have been caught, convicted, and incarcerated for crimes. Data on prisoners, especially psychological data, cannot be considered a reliable indication of the characteristics of criminals in general. The experience of imprisonment itself has an enormous impact on the individual; it is a frustrating, oppressive, degrading experience. Any data will, therefore, be distorted by the fact of imprisonment. Since reliable information on criminals cannot be obtained by asking prisoners questions, and since it is not feasible to give personality tests to criminals at large, the next best thing is to look at the criminal act itself in order to see whether it is more consistent with the problem-solving view of crime or the mental-illness view of crime. For a good discussion of the issue of whether or not crime should be considered a form of illness, see Nettler, "Good Men, Bad Men and the Perception of Reality," in Wolfgang, *The Sociology of Crime and Delinquency*, pp. 49–60, and Szasz, *Law, Liberty and Psychiatry*, pp. 91–146.

disturbed, this would not explain the overall *pattern* of crime. It might help to explain why one brother in a family became a burglar while another did not, but it would not explain why a poor criminal is likely to commit burglary whereas a rich criminal is likely to commit fraud. It does not explain why a poor man who cannot "delay gratification" or "control his impulses" may commit a crime to obtain possessions, whereas a rich man with the same "emotional problems" may simply spend his money impulsively. And it doesn't go very far in explaining the extremely high levels of crime in American society among all social groups. To understand these patterns, it is necessary to look at structural forces, rather than simply at individual pathologies.

A second objection to the mental-illness theory of crime concerns the nature of the criminal act itself. There are, of course, some criminal acts which clearly indicate mental disturbance. Crimes such as rape, child molesting, or mass murders cannot be considered rational, adaptive behavior. However, such acts are a very small proportion of the crimes committed in the United States. The vast majority of crimes are economic. According to the FBI's *Uniform Crime Reports,* approximately 5,600,000 Index Crimes (homocide, forcible rape, robbery, aggravated assault, burglary, larceny over $50, auto theft) were committed in the United States in 1970. Of these, just over 4,800,000 (87 percent) were property crimes, and only 700,000 were crimes against persons. In these statistics the 350,000 robberies were regarded as crimes against persons, not as property crimes, even though robberies are essentially crimes for economic gain. Moreover, these figures only include crimes designated as "serious" by the FBI; they do not include the vast realm of white-collar crime, nearly all of which is economic.

Crimes are thus overwhelmingly committed in the pursuit of property. Given the economic realities of most people's lives, such behavior does not need to be explained in psychiatric terms. Many problems in people's lives center on economic difficulties of various sorts, and crime is an effective way to solve many of those problems. This is true not only of the poor, whose economic problems are particularly oppressive, but of the middle class and the rich as well. In a society which places such emphasis on consumption, moving up the economic ladder simply means that one's needs increase and one's economic difficulties change form. Moving up the ladder also means that the opportunities for illegal solutions to those difficulties change in character. Thus, the poor resort to robbery and burglary, the rich to bribery and fraud.

Crime can thus be broadly interpreted as a response by individuals to the problems which they face in their lives. The level of crime and the particular forms it takes in American society reflect the pattern of problems and the pattern of solutions available to different groups in the society. The "crime problem" is a problem of the social structure, not of individuals. This means that solutions to the problem of crime must involve political action to change the social structure itself.

The analogy between crime and traffic fatalities discussed earlier in this chapter will help to explain this point. Broadly speaking, two approaches can be taken to reduce the level of traffic fatalities: a massive campaign could be launched to convince people not to drink when they drive and to teach them to drive carefully; or there could be a radical change in the pattern of transportation, in the economic structure of the automobile industry, and in the enforcement of drunken-driving laws.[17]

Of these two approaches, change in the underlying social

17. All of these changes would involve political action in one form or another. Good public transportation could be created so that people did not have to rely on private cars. The automobile industry could be publically owned so that safety and durability replaced profits as the basic determinant of how cars are made. And there could be stringent enforcement of drunk-driving laws through devices such as the breathalizer test.

structure is likely to be more effective than efforts limited to trying to change individuals. For years attempts have been made on television, in schools, and in the press to improve the quality of the average motorist, but with little success. People are still in a hurry to get where they are going; they still drive when they are sleepy; they still feel that a few drinks won't hurt. Cars are still deadly, and inexpensive alternative forms of transportation are still largely unavailable. There will not be a significant change in the patterns until the structures which support the high levels of accidents are themselves changed.

The same is true for crime. As long as American society maintains a distribution of income and power which creates serious economic difficulties for the poor, and as long as it maintains an opportunity structure which makes legitimate solutions to those problems difficult, then crimes of the poor will continue at a high rate. And as long as the society continues to pose both problems and solutions in highly individualistic and competitive terms, the choice of illegal options will continue to be a natural response to the economic difficulties people of all social classes face.

No concerted political effort has been made to deal with the underlying causes of crime. To do so would be to threaten the established order. Instead, the political system has responded to the problem of crime in a way that leaves the structure of wealth and power untouched: by maintaining an elaborate system of *punishment*, in which prisons play a key role.

CHAPTER 2

The Punishment of Crime

The punishment of crime is a political act. It represents the use of physical force by the state to control the lives of people the state has defined as criminal. Whether the main purpose of imprisonment is the "rehabilitation" of the criminal, the deterrence of certain kinds of behavior, or simply the vengeful punishment of the wicked, it is a political act, for the organized power of the state is imprisoning the offender.

This notion that all imprisonment is political, whether the prisoner be a rapist, a bank robber, or a draft evader, is alien to American liberal philosophy.[1] In traditional American liberalism the term "political" is limited to reference to individuals who are imprisoned for explicitly political reasons. Thus an individual who is imprisoned for his political beliefs would generally be considered a political prisoner. This would include people who are convicted directly for those beliefs and people

1. Throughout this discussion I will be using the word "liberal" to describe the political perspective of liberalism, not a particular set of public policies or a particular kind of political party. In the American political tradition most "conservatives" still hold a basically liberal political philosophy, in the sense of viewing the world in individualistic rather than class terms, in believing in individual liberties and a pluralistic society, and in feeling that social and political change should be reformist and evolutionary. The specific public policies of both Republicans and Democrats fall easily within the general philosophical framework of this tradition of liberalism.

who are imprisoned under the pretext of some other offense such as "conspiracy to incite to riot." In many cases an individual who is imprisoned for breaking certain grossly unjust laws which are felt to be "political" in nature—such as segregation laws in the American South—would be considered a "political prisoner," especially if he broke the law out of political motives. And in certain circumstances, an individual who is convicted of a common law crime, but is felt to have been denied due process and unjustly convicted—such as a black convicted by an all-white jury of raping a white woman—might be considered a political prisoner. But beyond these rather special circumstances, prisoners are generally not considered "political prisoners" in American political theory.

The liberal distinction between persons who are imprisoned for their political beliefs or who have been unjustly imprisoned and those who have been imprisoned simply for breaking the criminal law is a valid one. But to call the former "political" prisoners and the latter simply "criminals" obscures the meaning of punishment and the political function it plays in society.[2] It will be the central theme of this chapter that the imprisonment of the criminal is no less political an act than the imprisonment of the political activist.

2. The liberal distinction between the "political" prisoner and the "criminal" prisoner is grounded in the notion of natural law, which plays an important part in liberal political theory. Basically the liberal theorist makes a distinction between two kinds of *positive laws* (i.e., statutes and practices on the books): those which are consonant with *natural law* and those which are not. Laws which are unjust, arbitrary, oppressive, which violate due process and so forth, are seen as "political" laws. They are laws which owe their existence to the particular political realities of the time rather than to the exigencies of eternal natural law, and they sometimes are not considered laws at all. An individual who is imprisoned for breaking natural laws (i.e., just and good laws) is not a political prisoner because he has violated laws which are "natural" rather than "political." An individual who violates those positive laws which go against natural law is a "political prisoner," because the arbitrary power of the political system has made the unjust rule which the individual violated. If the notion of "natural law" is rejected as not being useful in understanding the realities of power and the functioning of the legal system in society, then the liberal use of the term "political prisoner" becomes less meaningful.

Aside from the definitional argument that all imprisonment is political because it is the organized power of the state which is imprisoning the offender, imprisonment can be considered a political act in two other senses: (1) the particular forms that punishment takes and the severity of punishment accorded specific offenses is a matter of political policy and varies considerably among political systems; (2) punishment, as a deterrent to crime, is an essential tool of social control by the political system.

FORMS OF PUNISHMENT

One of the most frequent objections to the conception that all imprisonment is political is the argument that since certain acts are considered crimes in virtually all societies, punishment of these acts cannot be considered "political." This is similar to saying that the levy of taxes should not be considered a political act because all political systems levy taxes of one sort or another. The point is that the extent and types of taxation, and the social interests which it serves, vary considerably from system to system. The same is true of punishment.

Theft is a crime in every political system. Although the details of exactly what constitutes theft differ, every system of law proscribes the seizure of property which legally belongs to someone else. But the sanctions brought to bear show no such homogeneity. In medieval Europe, one of the traditional punishments for theft was the public amputation of the thief's right hand. In eighteenth-century England thieves were executed or transported to the colonies as slaves. In contemporary China, most theft is punished by placing the thief under community surveillance rather than in any penal institution.[3] In twentieth-century America, the sanctions for any given category of theft differ considerably from state to state. In Massachusetts a per-

3. See Jerome Alan Cohen, *The Criminal Process in the People's Republic of China, 1949–1963* (Cambridge: Harvard University Press, 1968), for a discussion of the patterns of punishment for theft in China today.

son convicted of first-degree burglary with no prior felony offenses serves an indeterminate sentence of 10 years to life, while in Colorado, the sentence for the same offense is a maximum of 10 years.[4]

This variability in patterns of punishment reflects deliberate political decisions. It is no more natural to put a thief in prison for 10 years than to cut off his hand, hang him, or send him to a rural commune to work. All represent political policy.

Such political decisions do not occur in a vacuum. They reflect the problems and values of the social order. Which crimes receive the harshest punishments and the particular forms these punishments take are bound up with the technology of a particular society, the nature of its social conflicts, and the interests and ideology of the social class most closely controlling political decisions.[5] In the United States, crimes that are committed by the relatively affluent, such as embezzlement or consumer fraud, are generally punished by some form of probation or even by nonjudicial administrative sanctions. Only rarely does the white-collar criminal end up in prison. The most common punishment for embezzlement, according to Lawrence Zeitlin, is simply being fired, and the most common sanction for tax evasion is a fine administered by the Internal Revenue Service.

Prisons in the United States are primarily used to punish those crimes, such as burglary, robbery, and assault, which are typically committed by the lower classes. The result is that prisons in this country are disproportionately filled with the

4. An indeterminate sentence is a prison term with a specific minimum and a specific maximum, but with no fixed term for a particular offense. The judge does not sentence the convicted felon to a particular number of years, but rather to a range of years. The prisoner will be discharged either at the expiration of the maximum or when the paroling authority grants him a parole. (See pp. 44 ff. in Chapter 3 for a fuller discussion of the indeterminate sentence.)

5. For two studies of the general relationship between social structure and forms of punishment, see George Rusche and Otto Kircheimer, *Punishment and Social Structure* (New York: Russell and Russell, 1968), and William J. Chambliss, "A Sociological Analysis of the Law of Vagrancy," *Social Problems,* 12 (1964), pp. 67–77.

poor and the uneducated (see Tables 1 and 2). Forty-one percent of the general labor force falls into white-collar employment categories (clerical and sales, managers and owners, and professional and technical workers), compared to only 14 percent of the prison population. At the other extreme, 43 percent of the prisoners are manual laborers or service workers, compared to only 17 percent of the total labor force. The same pattern is found for education: 55 percent of the prisoners have an elementary school education or less, compared to only 34 percent of the general population; 45 percent of the general population are high school graduates compared to only 18 percent of the prison population.

Prisoners overwhelmingly tend to be poor. Yet, in terms of economic loss, more crime is committed by the relatively affluent (see Table 3). This is not surprising, since the opportunities for relatively safe, lucrative illegal activity are so much greater for the wealthy than for the poor. According to the task force report entitled "Crime and Its Impact," prepared for the President's Commission on Law Enforcement and the Administration of Justice, the economic losses from various white-collar crimes such as consumer fraud, price fixing, and tax evasion are many times greater than all street crimes combined. Accurate figures on white-collar crime are, of course, extremely difficult to obtain, but the report estimates:

> The cost to the public annually of securities frauds, while impossible to quantify with any certainty, is probably in the $500 million to $1 billion range. A conservative estimate is that nearly $500 million is spent annually on worthless or extravagantly misrepresented drugs and therapeutic devices. Fraudulent and deceptive practices in the home repair and improvement field are said to result in $500 million to $1 billion losses annually; and in the automobile repair field alone, fraudulent practices have been estimated to cost $100 million annually. . . .[6]

6. *Crime and Its Impact—An Assessment,* Task Force Report for the President's Commission on Law Enforcement and the Administration of Justice, (Washington, D.C.: U.S. Govt Print. Off., 1967), pp. 103–104.

TABLE 1

COMPARISON OF OCCUPATIONAL EXPERIENCE
IN GENERAL LABOR FORCE AND PRISONERS (1960)

Occupation	Percentage of General Labor Force*	Percentage of Prisoners
Professional and technical workers	10.4	2.2
Managers and owners, including farm	16.3	4.3
Clerical and sales	14.2	7.1
Craftsmen, foremen	20.6	17.6
Operatives	21.2	25.2
Service workers, including household	6.4	11.5
Laborers (except mine), including farm laborers and foremen	10.8	31.9

*All data are for men only; since the prison population is 95 percent male, data for males were used to eliminate the effects of substantial difference between male and female occupational employment patterns.

SOURCE: President's Commission on Law Enforcement and the Administration of Justice, Task Force Report on Corrections, p. 3.

TABLE 2

COMPARISON OF EDUCATIONAL LEVELS
IN GENERAL POPULATION AND PRISONERS (1960)

Years of School Completed (by persons 25–64)		Percentage of General Population	Percentage of Prisoner Population
College	4 years or more	8.4	1.1
	1 to 3 years	8.4	4.2
High school	4 years	27.5	12.4
	1 to 3 years	20.7	27.6
Elementary	5 to 8 years	28.0	40.3
	4 years to none	6.0	14.4

SOURCE: The President's Commission on Law Enforcement and the Administration of Justice, Task Force Report on Corrections, p. 2.

Not all of the crimes that are labeled "white-collar crimes" are committed by the well-to-do. The task force report correctly points out: "Crimes such as employee theft range from pilfering by truck drivers, stock room personnel or retail sales people to embezzlement by top executives. Cheating the government can include failure to report tips or other cash receipts and major tax or government contract frauds."[7] While this is true, in the present context the important point is that nearly all of the crimes that are committed by the middle class and the rich fall into the general category of white-collar crime, and that the perpetrators of these crimes rarely get sent to prison.

Occasionally, of course, the very rich are imprisoned. In 1960, seven executives involved in the gigantic electrical equipment price-fixing case went to jail for 30 days for their crimes. However, such instances are rare. The President's Commission (1967) reports: "Since that case no anti-trust defendant has been imprisoned. In seven cases since then, involving 45 individual defendants, prison sentences were imposed, but in each case the sentence was suspended."[8] In 1970 it was reported that the federal government had been overcharged some $100 million by various defense contractors. These crimes were handled by negotiation; no one was sent to prison.

In 1969, 502 people were convicted of tax fraud amounting to just under $100 million. This, needless to say, was only a tiny fraction of the people who actually committed the crime. The President's Commission reported: "The exact financial loss to the Government caused by tax fraud is difficult to determine but undoubtedly enormous. Estimates of the amount of reportable income that goes unreported each year range from $25 to $40 billion. Some of this is inadver-

7. *Ibid.*, p. 102.
8. *Ibid.*, p. 106.

TABLE 3

THE ECONOMIC COST OF CRIME (1965)

	Annual Economic Cost in Millions of Dollars
WHITE-COLLAR CRIME	
Embezzlement	$200
Fraud	1,350
Tax fraud	100
Forgery	80
CRIMES OF THE POOR	
Robbery	27
Burglary	251
Auto theft	140
Larceny, $50 and over	190

SOURCE: Based on data in The President's Commission on Law Enforcement and the Administration of Justice, Task Force Report, *Crime and Its Impact*, pp. 44–49.

tent, but undoubtedly a sizable amount is deliberate, criminal evasion."[9]

Most people caught by the IRS for cheating on their tax returns are simply fined outside the courts, or have their cases handled through other nonjudicial channels. People caught for street crimes rarely are given such leniency. The average individual theft from the government in the 502 tax fraud convictions in 1969 was about $190,000. The average burglary in that year amounted to $321; the average auto theft, $992. Only 95 of the 502 people convicted of tax fraud were sentenced to prison, serving an average term of 9.5 months. Another 91 were sentenced to "split" probation (i.e., probation with a very short prison sentence), and most of the rest to straight probation. Of those people convicted in federal courts for burglary and auto theft, more than 60 percent were sentenced to prison, and the average time served was 28 months and 21 months respectively[10] (see Table 4).

9. *Ibid.*, p. 103.
10. Unfortunately, it was not possible to get data indicating what percentage of people convicted of burglary and auto theft in state courts are sent to prison,

TABLE 4

ALTERNATIVES USED IN SENTENCING
CONVICTED DEFENDANTS IN THE
UNITED STATES DISTRICT COURTS*
(1969)

Offense	Total Convicted Defendants	Percent Imprisoned	Percent Probation	Percent Other	Average Prison Term Served in Months (Releases in 1970)**
Income tax fraud	502	18.9	66.7	14.3	9.5
Larceny	2,283	37.0	61.2	1.9	15
Selective Service Act	900	57.6	41.8	.6	17
Auto theft	3,791	62.6	36.4	1.0	21
Burglary	254	63.4	36.6	–	28
Robbery	961	92.3	7.6	.1	52

*SOURCE: Based on data in *Federal Offenders in the United States District Courts, 1969* the Administrative Office of the U.S. Courts, Washington, D.C., p. 47.

**SOURCE: Federal Bureau of Prisons, *Statistical Report,* 1969 and 1970, p. 140.

There is no intrinsic reason why burglary and auto theft should be considered more serious offenses than tax evasion. All three crimes are nonviolent forms of theft, although burglary, in involving the illegal entry of a building, is sometimes thought of as potentially violent. Certainly auto theft cannot be consid-

but there is no reason to believe that nationally the figures for state courts would be significantly different from those of the federal district courts.

Burglary is a federal crime when it occurs in a bank, in a post office, or on federal property. Such burglary would tend to involve more money than other kinds of burglary. No government publications were found, however, which reported the dollar amount of federal burglary. Auto theft is a federal crime when it involves the transportation of the stolen vehicle across state lines. As with federal burglary, it would be expected that such auto theft would be above the average in value, but again, no figures were found.

ered more violent than tax evasion. In some societies, tax evasion would be considered the more serious since it involves
theft from the whole community rather than simply from an
individual. And certainly, in the United States, the economic
loss from tax fraud is far greater than from burglary and auto
theft. Yet burglars and auto thieves are frequently locked up
behind bars; tax evaders are generally set free. Burglars and
auto thieves are typically poor; tax evaders are typically
wealthy.[11]

One of the consequences of using imprisonment to punish
those crimes committed primarily by the poor is that there is
a disproportionate number of blacks in American prisons.[12] In
the United States in 1960, the average daily population of jails,
prisons, and juvenile institutions was approximately 400,000, or
approximately one out of every 450 Americans.[13] The rate,
however, is much higher for blacks than for whites, and it is
especially high for black men in their twenties (see Table 5).
One out of every 26 black men between the ages of twenty-five

11. There are, of course, differences between burglary and auto theft on the
one hand and tax fraud on the other. Perhaps most importantly, the victim in
burglary and auto theft is an *individual*, whereas in tax fraud it is the government. American society in many ways values the rights (especially property
rights) of the individual above the rights of the collectivity, and this is one of
the reasons why burglary and auto theft are treated more harshly than tax
evasion. The important point in the present context is that there is no intrinsic
reason why this should be the case. The fact that one kind of crime is dealt with
so much more severely than another reflects a political choice which is bound
up with the underlying social and economic structure of the society.
12. Another reason there is a disproportionate number of blacks in prison may
be that the courts discriminate against blacks in their procedures, in the predis-
positions of judges and juries to convict blacks of certain crimes, and in sentencing policies. Many black prisoners certainly feel that this is the case.
13. These figures are from the 1960 census because, as of mid-1972, the
figures for institution populations from the 1970 census were not yet available.
There is no particular reason to believe that they would be significantly different. The figure of 400,000 incarcerated individuals from the 1960 census breaks
down to 120,000 people in local jails and workhouses, 230,000 in state and
federal prisons, and 50,000 in various kinds of juvenile institutions. If probation
and parole are added, well over 1,000,000 Americans are being "corrected" by
the state on an average day.

TABLE 5

INCARCERATION RATES BY RACE, AGE, AND SEX

Number of individuals in prisons and jails in the United States on an average day in 1960, for each 100,000 individuals in the relevant population

Age	Black Men	White Men	Black Women	White Women
under 20	118	66	15	4
20–24	3698	864	199	27
25–34	3876	649	230	21
35–44	2494	404	144	16
45–64	1009	239	55	9
65+	200	53	10	3

SOURCE: These data are based on figures in the special report of the 1960 census, *Inmates of Institutions*, PC (2)–8A, 1963.

and thirty-four was either in jail or in prison on an average day in 1960, compared to one out of 163 white men in the same age group. For black men twenty to twenty-four years of age, one out of 27 were behind bars compared to one out of 116 white men. These rates, of course, vary considerably from state to state. In Alabama, for example, the rate for black men twenty to twenty-four was one out of every 41, for white men, one out of 130; in Mississippi the figures were, respectively, one out of 62 and one out of 180. In California, on the other hand, one out of 22 blacks between the ages of twenty and twenty-four was behind bars on an average day compared to one out of 83 whites, and in New York the figures were one out of 20 blacks compared to one out of 123 whites.[14]

14. It is interesting to note that the disproportion of blacks to whites is generally greatest in the northern states. In New York the rate of imprisonment for black men in their early twenties was six times that of whites, whereas in Alabama and Mississippi it was only three times.

In California in 1970 approximately 50,000 people inhabited the state prisons and the county and city jails. Another 100,000 were on probation and 12,000 on parole. No age-race data are available for the parole and probation population. If it is assumed that the age distribution is approximately the same among probationers as among the prison population, then it would be estimated that on an average day approximately one out of seven or eight black men in California between the ages of twenty and twenty-four is in prison, in jail, on parole, or on probation, compared to about one out of every thirty white men in the same age group. This is at any given moment in time. Extrapolating from these daily figures, a conservative estimate is that, *during a given year, one out of every three to four black men in his early twenties spends some time in prison, in jail, on parole, or on probation* compared to about one out of every fifteen white men in the same age group.[15]

By the time a black man in America is twenty-five years of age (perhaps even earlier) he has in all probability had some serious encounter with the criminal justice system, and there is

15. This estimate was obtained in the following way. Every year at least 300,000 different people in California spend some time in jail, in prison, on parole, or on probation. Exact figures for the annual jail population were unavailable, but a rough estimate was obtained from a report published by the California Bureau of Criminal Statistics which states: "In the administration of criminal justice, several hundred thousand persons are processed throughout the county jail system, with about 150,000 actually serving sentences." I have taken the low figure of 150,000. The annual population of the state prisons (1968) was about 30,000, and the average parole population about 8,000 (not counting parolees who also spent some time in prison during that year). The total probation population was about 115,000. All of these figures taken together make a total annual correctional system population of just over 300,000 people. This, if anything, is an underestimate. Since no age-race distribution is available for this total annual population, it was necessary to extrapolate from the distribution for the daily prison and jail population. This, of course, introduces a certain margin of error. Still, the figures do indicate the order of magnitude of the black's experience of punishment in the United States. The estimate extrapolating from the daily age-race distribution was that one out of every 3.6 black men between the ages of twenty and twenty-four pass through the system each year.

a good chance he has spent some time behind bars. For most whites, especially affluent whites, the criminal justice system is an abstraction. Except in rare instances, it does not directly impinge on their lives. For young blacks, the repressive arm of the law—arrest, probation, jail, prison—is an immediate reality.

PUNISHMENT AS DETERRENCE

Conceptions vary as to the central function of prisons in society. They are sometimes seen as serving the benevolent function of "rehabilitating" maladjusted individuals, of trying to help the criminal find a better way of life. The disproportionate number of blacks and poor people in prison is taken as an indication that blacks and poor people are simply more in need of such rehabilitation than are whites and the well-to-do. In this perspective, prisons are closer to hospitals than to instruments of political control.

Another image of prisons is that they are instruments of social vengeance, an institutionalization of the ethic "an eye for an eye, a tooth for a tooth." In this view, prisons express society's wrath at wrongdoing and expiate the wrong through punishment; but they still are not considered instruments of social control. Even if the central function of prisons is seen simply as physically isolating "dangerous men," prisons are instruments of social control in only a limited sense: the political power of the state is brought to bear to control the lives of these particular "dangerous men," the prison population; it is not being used to control the larger community on the outside.

Only when the central function of prisons is seen as *deterrence* does their operation as a political tool of social control become clear. In this conception, the fundamental function of prisons is to create a significant risk factor in the commission of crime. The basic focus of the punishment apparatus is not the specific individuals who happen to end up in prison, but the mass of people on the outside. The convicts within the walls serve as examples to the general population: "This is what will happen if you violate the law." As I will argue, prisons in any political system protect the existing social order by threatening people with severe sanctions for breaking certain laws.

Much criticism has been leveled against the deterrence theory of imprisonment. A study entitled "The Deterrent Effects of Criminal Sanctions" by the California Assembly Office of Research indicates that most people were not aware of the specific penalties for various crimes. Additionally, the majority of the subjects stated that internal controls of various sorts were more important than external controls (punishment) in preventing them from committing crimes. The general conclusion of the study was:

> One might argue that the best deterrent for crime would be to develop social systems that would strengthen internal sanctions rather than to depend solely upon stiffer penalties or more law enforcement officers. In short, it is man's view of himself as a lawful and responsible person that will deter crime, not just the legal sanctions applied by strangers in authority positions.[16]

Many criminologists feel that the fear of imprisonment has only a marginal deterrent effect because most people simply do not make rational evaluations of risks when they engage in crime. Like the problem of cancer from cigarette smoking or the danger of not wearing safety belts in cars, people can always reason away their fears by saying, "It can't happen to me." Thus, it is argued, what prevents people from committing crimes is not so much the external sanctions, the punishments, but the internal controls, the feelings of guilt, the respect for the law.

This is a very narrow conception of the ways in which internal and external sanctions can influence behavior. As discussed in Chapter 1, the ethical considerations involved in the decision

16. "The Deterrent Effects of Criminal Sanctions," prepared by the California Assembly Office of Research for the Assembly Committee on Criminal Procedure, May, 1968, p. 16.

to commit a crime are not always simple. Often contradictory ethical forces operate within the individual. In certain circumstances, the "internal controls" may contribute to, rather than prevent, criminal activity, particularly in the realm of politically motivated crime. And very importantly, as long as an individual does not need seriously to consider committing a crime, he is likely to feel that it is his own internal controls which prevent him from doing so. A home owner, for example, is likely to claim in moralistic tones that he would never break into a house because it is *wrong*. Fear of punishment, he will say, has nothing to do with it. Only when committing a crime becomes a real possibility does punishment become a relevant issue.

Still, it could be argued that even for the poor and downtrodden the fear of punishment is not an effective deterrent. The fact that each year approximately 30 percent of all young black men have a serious encounter with the criminal justice system could be interpreted as indicating an utter failure of the prison and other forms of punishment as crime deterrents. This, however, assumes that the only issue involved in deterrence is simply whether or not to commit a crime. Of even greater significance is the question of *which crimes an individual commits*. While the threat of punishment may not have much impact on the decision to break the law, there is no question that it has a great impact on *how* the individual chooses to break the law.

The most lucrative places for robbery are big city banks, yet they are robbed much less frequently than gas stations, liquor stores, and individuals. In 1969 the average bank robbery yielded more than $4,500, while the average highway robbery (i.e., the robbery of an individual on the streets) yielded about $175. Yet only one-half of one percent of all robberies were bank robberies, while 55 percent were highway robberies.[17] This is hardly because robbers feel any greater ethical proscrip-

17. *Crime in the United States—Uniform Crime Reports, 1969*, issued by J. Edgar Hoover, p. 105.

tion against robbing banks. It is simply because banks are heavily guarded and the FBI investigates bank robberies thoroughly. Consequently, an individual is much more likely to get caught, or even killed, trying to rob a bank.[18] The fact that the average robbery results in only $288 is a tribute to the effectiveness of the system of punishment as a deterrent.[19]

The effect of punishment on how a person chooses to break the law can be seen in other forms of theft. A black man is much more conspicuous in a white middle-class suburb than in the ghetto. Residents are much more likely to call the police to report "suspicious behavior" by a "prowler," and he is much more likely to be apprehended while burglarizing a home there. He knows his way around in the ghetto far better; he

18. The possibility of getting killed in the course of a crime may be as important a factor in determining which crime an individual commits as the possibility of getting caught and sent to prison. An unpublished study of police killings of civilians conducted by Paul Tagaki, a professor of criminology at the University of California, and Philip Buell, a public health statistician, indicates that between 1963 and 1968 the police killed 1,805 men and 21 women throughout the United States. Nearly half of these were black. Needless to say, many additional people were seriously wounded by the police. During this same five-year period, a total of 362 policemen were killed by civilians. Thus, for every one policeman "killed in the line of duty," the police kill five civilians.

19. The deterrent function of prisons is reflected in the economics of the prison system. In 1966 the per capita annual cost of confinement for felons in California was about $2,400. As stated in a special report by the California Assembly Office of Research: "The cost of confining the average 5,200 robbery cases, during 1966 alone was $12,740,000—more than double the estimated direct cost of all robberies reported in the state in that year. Had all these imprisoned men been in the community, they would each have had to commit 10 'average' robberies during the year in order to inflict property loss equal to the cost of their incarceration for the year. The cost of 36 or 43 months incarceration is likely, in the majority of cases, to exceed the direct costs of the robber's entire crime career" (*The California Prison, Parole and Probation System*, p. 90). If the primary focus of the prison were on the people *inside* the prison— either in terms of their rehabilitation or in terms of simply isolating them from the rest of the community—it would make little sense to spend twice the total amount stolen in robberies each year to punish robbers. On the other hand, if the central function of prison is focused on people *outside* the prison, then this expenditure is more reasonable. If the purpose of prison is to deter people from committing high-risk crimes, then it is rational to spend $12 million a year imprisoning robbers. It is at least in part because of the state's expenditures of $12 million to imprison robbers that the average robbery amounts to a mere $288.

knows people's living patterns; he knows how the police operate. Houses in the suburbs are more likely to be equipped with burglar alarms and good locks than tenements in the slums. Wealthy apartment buildings in the city are frequently guarded by private police. Thus, even though white suburbs and wealthy urban apartments are a far richer field for burglary, the risks of getting caught are greater, and consequently, most burglaries occur in poorer areas of the city. This is one of the great ironies of crime: the poor are more likely to steal from the poor than from the rich because it is easier and safer. It is also easier and safer for the rich and powerful to steal from the poor and powerless—through consumer fraud, price fixing, loan sharking, and indirectly, even through tax evasion.

A variety of data on the victims of crime exists which supports this general conclusion. In a study of the incidence of crime in various police districts in Chicago, one "very low-income Negro district" had 35 times as many serious crimes against persons (robbery included) per 100,000 residents as did a high-income white district, and 2.5 times as many property crimes (see Table 6). The President's Commission on Law Enforcement and the Administration of Justice reported that nonwhites were much more frequently the victims in all offense categories except larceny over $50 (see Table 7). This single exception is due to the fact that most larcenies are from stores, and most stores, even in the black ghetto, are owned by whites. A similar pattern was found when victimization was broken down by income (see Table 8). It is especially important to note that the reported rate of victimization by burglary for people earning less than $3,000 was nearly twice that for people earning more than $10,000, and the reported rate of victimization by robbery was five times greater.

It would be an oversimplification to attribute this greater victimization of the poor entirely to the deterrent effect of the system of punishment. It is also important that it is generally much easier and more convenient for the poor to steal from the

TABLE 6

INCIDENCE OF INDEX CRIMES PER 100,000 RESIDENTS IN FIVE CHICAGO POLICE DISTRICTS (1965)

	High-Income White District	Low-Middle Income White District	Mixed-High- and Low-Income White	Very Low-Income Black District No. 1	Very Low-Income Black District No. 2
Index crimes against persons, including robbery	80	440	338	1,615	2,820
Index crimes against property	1,038	1,750	2,080	2,508	2,630

NOTE: There are two statistical issues which need to be kept in mind in this table. First, robbery, which is a major crime in the ghetto, is included under crimes against persons rather than crimes against property. This contributes to the greater disproportion in crimes against persons compared to crimes against property. Second, crimes, especially property crimes, are reported at a *much lower* rate in the ghetto than in upper-income areas. This is due to a variety of factors, including the antipolice norms of the ghetto, the higher levels of theft insurance in the suburbs, and so on. This lower reporting rate artificially deflates the difference between the rates of property crime in the ghetto and in the high-income white district.

SOURCE: From *Report of the National Advisory Commission on Civil Disorders* (Washington, D.C.: US Govt. Print. Off., 1968), p. 134.

poor. The greater risks of attempting burglaries in the suburbs are reinforced by the greater convenience of stealing from the poor in the slums.[20]

20. Since residential segregation is itself one reason why it is riskier for a poor black to burglarize a white suburb, it is very difficult to disentangle the two and say whether segregation per se or risk is more important. What we can say is that the two factors reinforce each other and contribute substantially to the concentration of crime in poor areas.

TABLE 7

VICTIMIZATION BY RACE
(Rates per 100,000 population)

Offenses	White	Nonwhite
Forcible rape	22	82
Robbery	58	204
Aggravated assault	186	347
Burglary	822	1,306
Larceny	608	367
Auto theft	164	286
Total	1860	2,592
Respondents	27,484	4,902

SOURCE: *The Challenge of Crime in a Free Society*, (Washington, D.C.: US Govt. Print. Off., 1967), p. 39.

TABLE 8

VICTIMIZATION BY INCOME
(Rates per 100,000 population)

OFFENSES	INCOME			
	$0 to $2,999	$3,000 to $5,999	$6,000 to $9,999	Above $10,000
Forcible rape	76	49	10	17
Robbery	172	121	48	34
Aggravated assault*	229	316	144	252
Burglary	1,319	1,020	867	790
Larceny over $50*	420	619	549	925
Auto theft*	153	206	202	219

SOURCE: *The Challenge of Crime in a Free Society*, (Washington, D.C.: US Govt. Print. Off., 1967), p. 38.

*The figures for assault, larceny, and auto theft seem to contradict the generalization that the poor are more frequently the victims of crime than the more affluent. In the case of larceny and auto theft, it is easy to explain the apparent exception: most larcenies occur in stores, and most stores, even in high-crime areas of a city, are owned by the relatively affluent. Similarly, most cars that are worth stealing will be owned by the wealthier segments of the population. The most likely explanation for why assaults should be so high among individuals earning above $10,000 is that they report assaults at a much higher rate than the poor.

The deterrent effect of punishment also operates in white-collar and business crime, but in a somewhat different way. Rather than influencing the target of crime, the risk of punishment has a regulatory effect on the amount of crime an individual is likely to commit. Embezzlement and tax evasion are good examples. When an employee of a business decides to embezzle funds, he is faced with the choice of how much to embezzle. If too much is embezzled, the chances of getting caught and punished increase considerably; if too little is embezzled, it is not worth the trouble. The result is that the embezzler settles on a level of theft which seems relatively safe to him. Lawrence Zeitlin reports that: ". . . the evidence indicates that well over 75 per cent of all employees participate to some extent in merchandise shrinkage. . . . The fact remains that in retail establishments internal theft averages out to an unevenly distributed five to eight per cent of the typical employee's salary."[21] Similarly, in the case of tax evasion, the threat of punishment obviously does not deter many people from cheating on their income tax; but it does keep the level of cheating within tolerable limits. While people will illegally exaggerate their tax deductions, they rarely exaggerate them to the point where they pay no tax at all.

The system of punishment is thus a real deterrent, for crimes of the rich and for crimes of the poor. While the threat of punishment may not be very effective in preventing criminal activity per se, it is a potent force for regulating criminal activity in ways which are less threatening to the social order.

21. Lawrence Zeitlin, "A Little Larceny Can Do a Lot for Employee Morale," *Psychology Today,* June, 1971, p. 24.

CHAPTER 3

The Rehabilitative Prison Model

Among prison administrators and prison researchers it is common to divide the world of prisons into two broad categories: the archaic, vengeful, brutal, custodial prisons of the past and the modern, enlightened, rehabilitative institutions of the present. The difference between these two images of what a prison should be is reflected in the language used to describe various features of the system:

Traditional Custodial Prison	Modern Rehabilitative Prison
Prison	Correctional facility
Guard	Correctional officer
Prisoner, convict	Inmate
Solitary confinement, "the hole"	Adjustment center

In the custodial prison, the basic principles of operation are secure confinement of prisoners and punishment for their wrongdoing. Besides protection of the public, the rationale of prison practices is to make prison life so unpleasant that prisoners will, upon release, hesitate to commit new crimes. In the reformed, rehabilitative prison, the central principle

of the institution is "treatment" designed to "cure" the inmate of his criminality, to rehabilitate him from his fallen
state.

The California prison system is often considered a model of
this enlightened penology. The name of the prison administration itself—the Department of *Corrections*—proclaims its liberal, rehabilitative intent. The official self-image of the Department is that it uses its benevolent authority to constructively
change inmates from violent, antisocial criminals to good citizens. Dr. Norman Fenton, former assistant to the director of the
Department of Corrections, and founder of the Department's
group counseling program, expresses this self-image over and
over in his book *Treatment in Prison: How the Family Can
Help:*[1]

> The point of view of the institutional staff is treatment.
> Unfortunately, however, whereas persons who go to a
> physician ordinarily are quite willing to give previous his-
> tory in detail, with men in prison there are emotional fac-
> tors which handicap such faith and trust in the officials
> concerned with the treatment of the men . . . (p. 17).

> The employees of the prisons ask you to try to believe in
> their good will towards the inmates. If you can aid your
> relative in changing any attitudes of suspicion and resent-
> ment toward authority he may have, it will be a great help
> to him. . . . Actually, the hopes of the prison employees
> resemble yours for the well-being of your loved-ones while
> he is in prison and for his welfare and happiness later on
> when paroled (p. 20).

> Crime is certainly in part a mental trouble. We hope also
> that prisons are becoming more like hospitals (p. 7).

> If only there were some quick and certain cures for the
> behaviors that cause men to go to prison! But there are
> none as yet (p. 36).

1. Norman Fenton, *Treatment in Prison: How the Family Can Help* (Sacramento: California Department of Corrections Publication, 1959).

Dr. Fenton captures a great deal of the ethic of the rehabilitative prison in his support of the introduction of television into prisons:

> Some persons who dislike men who are sent to prison raise questions in regard to the introduction of television in the institutions. They say these men are in prison for punishment. Many persons on the outside cannot afford television sets—why should they be provided for prison inmates? The answer is, first, that prison is not for punishment. The loss of freedom is punishment enough. The purpose of prison is rehabilitation and re-education. It is to inculcate attitudes and interests that will make for good citizenship later. Staying at home and enjoying television when on parole is a lot better than going some places where they will waste their money and be influenced harmfully by criminal associations. The parolee can spend his money more wisely on the purchase of a television set for his family than on many other things. The prison has a responsibility for getting him interested in doing so and staying at home to enjoy his set (p. 42).

Since 1944, when the Department of Corrections was first established, this orientation toward imprisonment has been generally accepted throughout the United States. Several features of the California system are particularly important in the rehabilitative prison model: the indeterminate sentence; the pattern of rehabilitation programs within prisons; the system of evaluation of inmates; and sophisticated custody classifications.

The indeterminate sentence.[2] One of the canons of the "correctional" prison is the indeterminate sentence. In such a system, when a man is sentenced for a crime, the judge does not set a fixed sentence, but rather a sentence with a maximum and minimum term. A prisoner with an indeterminate sentence is ostensibly released when he is "rehabilitated" rather than when

2. For an excellent discussion of the history of the indeterminate sentence in California, see Sheldon Messinger, "Strategies of Control" (unpublished Ph.D. dissertation, University of California, Berkeley, 1969).

he has served some preestablished fixed term. The punishment —or rather, the "correction"—is designed to fit the criminal rather than the crime.

If the indeterminate sentence system were in fact completely indeterminate, all prison terms would have a life imprisonment maximum and a zero minimum. As it is, in California first-degree robbery and first-degree burglary both have 5 years to life sentences; second-degree robbery, 1 year to life; forgery, 6 months to 14 years; assault with a deadly weapon, 1 to 15 years; possession of marijuana, 1 to 10 years; rape, 3 years to life; and so on. Only about 7 percent of the inmates who are released from California prisons are discharged at the expiration of their maximum sentences; the rest are released on parole.

The indeterminate sentence has two basic rationales. First of all, it is argued that since the purpose of imprisonment is not punishment, but rather "rehabilitation," a person should be kept in prison until he is in fact rehabilitated. Second, it is felt that if the prisoner knew exactly when he would get out, he would just sit back and bide his time. When his release is contingent upon his "rehabilitation," there is pressure on him to participate in various treatment programs which will help to demonstrate that he is rehabilitated and thus ready to be released. The corollary to this, of course, is that if he refuses to be "rehabilitated" or is incapable of rehabilitation, he will be kept in prison indefinitely.

Many assumptions underlie the indeterminate sentence philosophy. Most fundamentally, it is assumed not only that prisoners need to be rehabilitated, but also that prisons create an environment where this is possible. Furthermore, it is assumed that the Adult Authority (the parole board) is capable of dispassionately and justly evaluating when a prisoner has been rehabilitated. These assumptions pose grave problems. As discussed in Chapter 1, the assumption that criminals are emotionally disturbed and in need of help is open to serious question. But even if they were, prisons, as we shall see, are in many ways the least likely place for a human being to make constructive changes of any sort.

There is little evidence that the procedures of the Adult Authority enable it to make reasonable judgments as to when a prisoner should be released from prison. The AA members are all political appointees, nearly all of them with strong law-enforcement backgrounds. The parole hearings are sometimes as short as five minutes. The AA board members rarely know the prisoners individually and have only a few minutes before each hearing to glance through their dossiers. By and large the AA accepts the recommendations of the prison authorities. The prisoner has no opportunity to present evidence in his behalf in order to challenge statements of fact or interpretation made by the prison, and he is never allowed counsel during the parole hearing. As a result of these procedures, many of the Adult Authority decisions are essentially arbitrary.[3]

Programs within the prison. A second canon of the correctional prison is that it should offer constructive programs for inmates and that each inmate's program should reflect his particular needs. In most prisons a fairly wide variety of programs

3. The indeterminate sentence in one form or another is used in most states throughout the country. Only in the South are fixed sentences still relatively common. But the California indeterminate sentence has a distinctive feature. In most states, once the parole board has decided to give the prisoner a parole, a firm discharge date is fixed. Thus, if after a prisoner had served three years of a one-year-to-life sentence for robbery, a parole board agreed to give him two years parole, the prisoner would be discharged from parole after having been under judicial supervision for a total of five years. If he violated his parole during that two-year period and was returned to prison, he would have to serve in prison only the time that remained in the two years. In California, however, if a parolee is sent back to prison on a technical parole violation—which could amount to as little as getting married without permission of one's parole officer —his prison term is *refixed at the maximum.* Thus, in the example above, if the parolee had served three years in prison and 23 months on parole, and was then returned to prison for a technical violation, his term would be reset at life imprisonment. As in the parole board hearings, the parolee is not allowed counsel during a parole-revocation hearing, and the Adult Authority almost inevitably accepts the decision of the parole officer. This procedure was upheld by the California Supreme Court in 1971 on the grounds that parole is an act of grace rather than a right, and thus there is no need for a defense counsel.

is formally available to prisoners. All prisons in California have educational programs at least through high school, and some offer a meager college program as well. Vocational trade programs are generally available, although for the more desirable ones the waiting list is long. A variety of "productive employment" is offered, ranging from prison industries to the prison kitchen and a clerk's job in the prison chapel. Some therapy programs are also available in each institution, including group counseling, some psychotherapy, Alcoholics Anonymous, and religious and group therapy. Some institutions have special programs not available elsewhere, and prisoners may be sent to such institutions specifically for those programs. One prison in particular, Vacaville, has extensive inpatient psychiatric programs, and prisoners felt to be in need of such treatment are generally sent there. In theory these alternatives form the basis for a constructive program that is expected to change the inmate into an acceptable member of society.

Classification and custody. It has always been difficult for proponents of liberal prison ideology to feel comfortable with the reality of custody—the deprivation of freedom. In the traditional, authoritarian prison this posed no serious problem because the basic purpose of the institution was accepted as punishment. But the liberal prison is ostensibly meant to be more like a hospital than a dungeon. Many supporters of the correctional prison feel a contradiction between its avowed goal (rehabilitating criminals to function in a "free" society) and some of its methods (the deprivation of freedom, tight regulation of the inmate's life). This contradiction is generally handled pragmatically by saying that prisoners are dangerous men and careful confinement is necessary for effective treatment. A complicated classification system is then created which attempts to assess the potential security risk of each prisoner and to assign him accordingly to a particular level of custody. Such evaluation and classification procedures attempt to give the prisoner "as much freedom as he can handle" and are thus part of the general notion of fitting the treatment to the criminal.

In California these evaluation and classification procedures are an essential part of the operation of the prison system. Immediately after a prisoner is sentenced, he is sent to the "Reception-Guidance Center" (RGC), where he undergoes an intensive evaluation period. On the basis of the RGC recommendations, the new prisoner is sent to one of eleven prisons in the state, or to one of the many forestry or conservation prison camps. If the prisoner is a first-termer and is considered a minimum-security risk, he will probably be sent to a minimum-security prison or conservation camp. If he is considered a serious security risk and has served a prior prison term, he will probably be sent to one of the medium-close-security prisons (Soledad and San Quentin), or, if he is a security risk and an older prisoner, to Folsom, technically, the state's only maximum-security prison.[4] If he is diagnosed as having serious psychiatric problems, he will probably be sent to Vacaville. Prisoners may also be assigned to different institutions on the basis of the training programs available, although such considerations are generally given much less weight than simple security questions.

These gradations from minimum- to maximum-security institutions reflect significant differences in the conditions and regulations of confinement. In a minimum-security institution, prisoners are housed in dormitory fashion. There are no gun towers around the perimeter of the prison. Prisoners may move freely in the prison without passes. They may watch television and engage in other recreation in their free time with few restrictions. In a medium-close-security or maximum-security institution, on the other hand, inmates live in tiny cells in large cell

4. The distinction between a "medium-close-security" prison and a "maximum-security" prison is really a technical one. For all practical purposes San Quentin is a "maximum-security" institution.

blocks. Barbed wire covers the tops of the walls, and gun towers guard the perimeter of the prison. Prisoners need passes to move about the institution, and leisure time is carefully controlled.

Not only are the prisons graded from minimum to maximum security, but individual prisoners are classified from minimum- to maximum-security status within each institution. Shortly after he arrives from the Reception-Guidance Center, the new prisoner appears before the prison's classification committee. The committee reads through the evaluation of the RGC and then classifies the individual according to its assessment of the security risk he poses. These classification decisions are reviewed periodically. If the prisoner has not caused any trouble and has cooperated with the rules of the prison, then his custody level will eventually go down and his privileges correspondingly increase. If he has been involved in conflicts within the prison or is seen as a "management problem" by the prison administration, then his custody level is likely to increase and his freedom of movement to be restricted.

This system of graduated classification of both prisons and prisoners has a dual function. On the one hand, it is part of the rehabilitative notion of fitting the institution and program to the inmate. On the other hand, it is an essential part of the system of control within the prison.[5] Any prisoner knows that if he "causes trouble" he might get shipped off to a tighter-security institution or he might have his own security status increased. The pattern of security gradation is a pattern of privilege gradation, and the threat of withdrawing privileges is one of the primary techniques of control within the prison. This is a central contradiction of prison life: most programs and

5. See Chapter 15, especially pp. 326 ff., for a fuller discussion of the structure of control within the prison system. See also Messinger, "Strategies of Control," for an interesting discussion of the structure of social control in the prison system.

procedures that result from the rehabilitation ideology simultaneously serve as instruments of coercion and control. What seems to the outsider or the liberal prison administrator like a positive program that encourages change and development becomes a mechanism of oppression to the prisoner.[6]

The most humane supporters of the "enlightened" correctional prison philosophy hoped that the liberal, correctional prison would avoid the brutality and dehumanization of the traditional custodial prison. In actuality, many prison administrators have little or no faith in the ideals of rehabilitation penology. While feeling that it is politically expedient to use the language of the liberal prison, they continue to run the institution along traditional custodial lines. Thomas Murton, former head of the Arkansas prison system and a strong critic of current prison practices throughout the United States, has said:

> There is no basic difference between the Arkansas prison system and the California prison system. The only difference between the primitive system and the sophisticated system is that the sophisticated system operates behind a façade of rehabilitation. The degradation of the prisoner in both systems is just the same. It doesn't make much difference to a prisoner whether he is being shot by a well-educated guard in California or a high school dropout in Arkansas. The only difference is that in the primitive system they are more honest about what they are doing. There is no hypocritical façade like in California.[7]

Euphemistic language and changes in official rationale for different practices do not necessarily reflect substantive change in

6. A full discussion of the meaning of this contradiction within the liberal, rehabilitative prison is presented in Chapter 7, "Liberal Totalitarianism in Prison."

7. Speech at a Prison Day Conference, sponsored by the Campus Committee for Prisoner Humanity and Justice, University of California, Berkeley, Feb. 26, 1971.

the practices themselves. The California "correctional officer" is still a guard; the "adjustment center" is still the hole; the "inmate" is still a prisoner; and above all, the "correctional facility" is still a prison.

PART II

San Quentin Prison: A Portrait of Contradictions

by Erik Olin Wright

From October, 1970, until June, 1971, I spent one to two days a week at San Quentin prison working as a student chaplain. During those eight months I had numerous conversations with many prison officials and a number of prison guards. Some were formal interviews, others informal conversations over lunch. In addition, I had the opportunity to observe many of the important committee meetings in the prison, including Adult Authority hearings, disciplinary hearings, segregation review hearings, classification committee meetings, and a warden's full committee hearing. I was thus in a position not only to talk to prison officials concerning their attitudes toward prison life and their views about how prisons should be run, but also to observe these same officials functioning in various capacities. The material in Chapter 5, "San Quentin Prison as Seen by the Prison Officials," is based primarily on information gathered during those eight months when I worked in the prison.

During that time, I also interviewed a total of nearly 150 prisoners. My central duty as a student chaplain consisted of interviewing prisoners about their religious backgrounds and attitudes for the Protestant chaplain, but generally there was time in these interviews to spend at least half an hour, and often more, with each prisoner discussing his experiences in prison and his feelings about various aspects of prison life. These discussions were very unstructured and tended to focus on problems that were of concern to the prisoners. In addition to the formally scheduled interviews, I met quite regularly with a number of prisoners for extended conversations. These interviews and conversations form the basis of most of Chapter 6, "San Quentin Prison as Seen by the Prisoners."

CHAPTER 4

General Features of San Quentin Prison

San Quentin is the oldest prison in California. It was founded in 1852 when a prison ship anchored off Point San Quentin with the fifty men and women who were prisoners of the new state of California. One of the first tasks given the prisoners housed aboard the ship was to build cells on the shore. By 1853 the first cellblock of San Quentin prison was completed, a cellblock which was to remain continuously in use until 1959.

Since those early days, the prison has undergone substantial change. It grew from a small prison of a few hundred inmates in the 1850s to one of the largest prisons in the world with more than 5,000 inmates at one point in the 1950s. (Since the late 1960s, the prison population at San Quentin has been steadily reduced in an effort to relieve serious overcrowding. By early 1972 the population had dropped to about 2,000.) It has changed from an institution whose expressed philosophy was one of stiff punishment and which offered prisoners no program but "hard labor" to an institution which strongly avows a variety of "constructive" programs for the reformation of the prisoner. It has changed from an institution that openly tortured prisoners for infractions of rules to an institution that denies the existence of any cruel punishment and handles problems of discipline with "disciplinary hearings" and "adjustment centers." In short, San Quentin changed, at least officially, from the traditional prison of vengeful punishment to the modern prison of enlightened correctional treatment.

The prison itself is an impressive fortress located on a promontory jutting out into the San Francisco Bay. It undoubtedly has one of the most beautiful views of any prison in the world, although the high walls of the structure make it impossible for most prisoners ever to see their surroundings. These high walls, the gun towers and barbed wire, and the castlelike appearance of the main entrance to the prison have given San Quentin the nickname "the Bastille by the Bay."

The following description is a complete copy of the official brochure, "California State Prison at San Quentin," prepared by the warden's office. It should be read both for the concrete information that it gives about the institution and for the image of the institution which it tries to create. Where the warden's description, which is indented, needs clarification additional comments are presented in brackets or as regular text.

> San Quentin is the oldest and largest of California Prisons. Established in 1852, it now houses approximately 4,000 inmates [in 1969]. A walled institution, San Quentin is considered a close-medium security facility. The average inmate is 32 years old and will serve a median of 32 months prior to parole.
>
> San Quentin is one of 13 major correctional facilities and some 34 forestry camps operated by the California Department of Corrections and housing some 27,000 inmates. Some 35% are housed in open institutions. San Quentin's particular role is to work with men who are serving long sentences, who have committed seriously violent offenses, who require special medical and psychiatric attention, or have failed to adjust in institutions of lesser custody. Each year we make many transfers of men to other institutions due to their progress in programming at this institution. Over 14,000 men are on parole from the 13 institutions. California's lethal gas execution chamber is located here.

Since 1938, there has been a total of 194 executions, including four women. Prior to 1963, an average of nine executions took place yearly. The condemned unit population is presently 85. [As a result of the 1972 Supreme Court decision on capital punishment, the condemned unit has been disbanded.]

San Quentin exists to protect society. This is accomplished in two ways: (1) by maintaining and controlling prisoners in a restricted community separated from the rest of society; (2) by programming [which] helps individual prisoners develop constructive patterns of behavior. Eventually 98% of the men will return to society and they must be prepared to make a socially approved adjustment.

Academic Education

Because men who come to prison are generally educationally deficient, raising the level of academic and vocational skills and thus their ability to earn a living is of great importance.

The academic program affords basic literacy training, formal elementary, secondary and junior college training to over 2,200 inmates. Half attend school in the evening.

The academic staff is supplied by contractual agreement with the Marin County Superintendent of Schools, and the local junior college district. Diplomas for elementary and high school work are awarded by the Marin County Superintendent of Schools. The associate of arts degree is awarded in 7 fields.

A correspondence school program provides educational opportunities for advanced students and for special groups.

The academic program works to promote changes in attitudes. The instructors are skilled in group behavior. In addition to teaching necessary skills, they train inmates in inter-personal relationships, proper acceptance of job, work, completion of goals and to operate cooperatively under supervision.

Vocational

The vocational program provides formal trade training to about 350 inmates in 17 trades or crafts applicable to the institutional operations and release employment. The vocational trade training classes are:

1. Auto Mechanic	10. Plumbing
2. Body and Fender Repair	11. Practical Nursing
3. Baking	12. Composition
4. Bookbinding	13. Sheet Metal
5. Dental Technology	14. Shoe Repair
6. Landscape Gardening	15. Office Machine Repair
7. Machinist	16. Offset Photo Process
8. Meatcutting	and Letterpress
9. Painting	

Eligibility for this training is determined from the evaluation of inmates by the Reception-Guidance Center, length of training period, and inmate motivation. A special prevocational diagnostic shop tests skills and interests.

The instructors are civil service employees. Their basic qualifications include seven years journeyman experience, 60 college units in directed study, and a valid vocational teaching credential.

There are long waiting lists for many of these vocational programs, since of all the activities in the prison these offer the greatest promise of providing improved work opportunities when the prisoner is released. The auto mechanic vocational program in particular is in great demand, and few prisoners who want to take it actually get to do so. Approximately 10 percent of the inmates are involved in vocational programs.

Trade Advisory Committee

Each vocational trade is guided by a trade advisory committee, composed of citizen volunteers representing both management and labor. They advise in establishing criteria for the selection of the inmate students and professional instructors. They aid in defining training standards, establishing completion criteria and assistance in job placement. They are concerned with both vocational competence and the development of constructive social attitudes.

The trade advisory committee provides the administration with competent assistance in maintaining a financially sound, practical training program in line with current trade practices.

Group Counseling

Group counseling involves inmates who meet in small groups on a weekly basis and discuss their problems with institutional personnel and one another. The aim is to so develop sufficient confidence and group cohesiveness that the men can express feelings that are important to themselves. In the process, they examine the way they have solved problems in the past and check new methods and solutions that are socially accepted and yet satisfying to themselves.

This is an idealized view of group counseling. Most inmates are suspicious of the group counseling leaders, and frequently of other inmates. Often there is great reluctance to go beyond a superficial level in discussion, and there is little data to indicate that group counseling has made any significant difference to most inmates.

Industries Program

An extensive industrial program reduces inmate idleness and also prepares men vocationally by on-the-job training skills and in good work habits. Related training classes enhance the man's employability.

Over 700 men are assigned jobs in San Quentin's industries. Trade advisory committees provide guidance here in the same manner as in the vocational program.

The furniture factory is the largest industry, producing office and school furniture. The detergent plant, clothing factory, and dry cleaning plants are other major industries. The cotton textile mill has been closed and will be replaced by a mattress factory and a large laundry.

Industrial products are sold to tax supported agencies only. The sales revenues pay for all costs of supervision and production so that this valuable program operates without cost to the taxpayer.

The inmates working in the industries program are usually paid approximately five cents an hour. The maximum is around thirty cents an hour, but practically no prisoners ever earn more than fifteen cents an hour. In certain jobs, such as in the laundry, most of the inmates are paid nothing at all.

In a report prepared by the Assembly Office of Research entitled "Report on the Economic Status and Rehabilitative Value of California Correctional Industries," several general conclusions directly contradict the view of the industries program presented by the warden at San Quentin:

> 1. The extent of rehabilitative process in correctional industries is limited by the nature of work itself. The inmate can only work at blue-collar or menial occupations. Even the most motivated inmate cannot, while in prison, engage in any work that would increase his opportunity to enter highly paid occupations upon release.
> 2. The Department objective of reducing idleness is obviously achieved by correctional industry, but in a manner that is no more successful than other institutional "busy work" programs.
> 3. The Department objective of teaching work habits, attitudes and skills that would be of value after release is not achieved. Inmates appear to be poorly motivated and the skills taught are often antiquated. . . .[1]

While the industrial activities are of dubious value to the inmate, certain of the industrial programs are of considerable value to the employees at the prison. Guards and prison officials have their clothing cleaned at the San Quentin cleaners and their automobiles repaired in the prison garage at nominal rates.

Medical Facilities

San Quentin's 150 bed hospital is fully accredited. It receives surgical and other serious cases from all institutions of the Department. The deep therapy X-ray unit is outstanding. The services of many well qualified consultants and specialists in the San Francisco Bay Area are available.

---

1. "Report on the Economic Status and Rehabilitative Value of California Correctional Industries," Assembly Office of Research, California State Legislature, Feb., 1969, pp. 21–22.

The psychiatric section of the
primarily on an out-patient basis. Th
trists, two clinical psychologists, an
workers spend a large portion o
weekly group psychotherapy s
mates.

A majority of the Departm
cared for in San Quentin's
methods, including surge

Religion

The spiritual needs
San Quentin's two f
full-time Catholic (
lain with assistan
the surroundin
been develope
of represent
the Bay Ar
Chaplains
School c
the ch
coun
and

F

The only fo
not be racially
to riot" within
materials is left
tration. The seve
the general politi
prison.

Classification

Placement in
made through ac
resentatives from
serve on the comm
vidual basis.

In practice many clas
classification committee.
by the lieutenant in char
oners themselves throug
prisoner society. Since the
desirable activities, the cru
waiting list (a decision mad
but who gets into the activi
gram director often makes su
sonal likes and dislikes, or pur
the clerical work in the prison i
them to control the informatio

64
who re
larly m

Li

Re
priso
mate
A larg
are dis
sory ser
magazin

efuses to work and is given an "unassigned" status simi-
ay be denied recreational privileges.

brary

eading is an important leisure-time activity for men in
n. The San Quentin library has 35,000 books, approxi-
y evenly distributed between fiction and non-fiction.
e number of magazines, newspapers, and pamphlets
tributed. The Librarian maintains a readers' advi-
vice. Men can subscribe to daily newspapers and
es.

rmal restriction on reading material is that it can-
inflammatory and that it cannot "tend to incite
the prison. Of course, the designation of such
entirely to the discretion of the prison adminis-
rity of these restrictions depends very much on
al climate and the level of tensions within the

Procedures

most of the aforementioned activities is
tion by the classification committee. Rep-
all areas of activities in the institution
ittee and consider each case on an indi-

sification decisions are not made by the
They are made more or less arbitrarily
ge of program assignments or by pris-
the network of connections in the
re are waiting lists for most of the
cial decision is not who gets on the
e by the classification committee),
ty from the waiting list. The pro-
ch decisions on the basis of per-
ely arbitrarily. Or, since most of
s done by prisoners, it is easy for
n that appears on a program

director's desk, to make "mistakes" in typing up lists, and in other ways to make it possible for a particular prisoner to get a position before his turn.[2]

In addition to placing prisoners in different activities (or on waiting lists), the classification committee determines the security level of the prisoner. This is of considerable importance, since the prisoner's privileges are closely tied to his security status. At San Quentin there are fine distinctions between different levels of privilege. At one extreme are the prisoners with minimum-security status living in the West Block, the "super-honor" block. These prisoners can have radios in their cells (some even have stereos), and TV's in the cellblock which they can watch until 10:00 P.M. They can leave their cells more or less at will. The tiers are watched by a committee elected by the prisoners rather than by guards so that prisoners are not likely to be disciplined for minor infractions. To get into the West Block it is necessary to have 18 months of "clean time" (i.e., time in prison without a disciplinary infraction). Just below the West Block is the North Block, which requires only 9 months of clean time. Conditions are similar to the West Block, but the block is patrolled by guards rather than an inmate committee. In these two honor blocks live about one-third of the total inmate population. Most other inmates live in the East and South blocks, the regular units of the prison. There they are much more tightly controlled, have less freedom of movement, and are not allowed personal radios in their cells. Overall, life is much less comfortable than in the honor blocks.

In addition to privileges related directly to the housing units, there are privileges concerning jobs, recreation, education, and as of spring, 1971, conjugal visits with wives. The jobs with the highest responsibility and status, and often with the most pay

2. These observations were reported by several counselors and other administrators at San Quentin in personal conversations.

(which, it should be noted, is still minimal), are generally given to prisoners in the honor blocks, especially the West Block. In order to participate in recreation programs an inmate needs a privilege card, which he will not be issued if he has a maximum-security status and which he will lose if he commits an infraction. Similarly, he must have a low-security level to participate in the evening classes of the San Quentin educational program, and a minimum-security level (as well as being legally married) to participate in the conjugal visiting program.

The official brochure continues:

> A staff of Correctional Counselors conduct interviews. Prior to an inmate's appearance before the Adult Authority (Parole Board), a progress report is prepared. This report describes institutional adjustment and inmate's attitude from the time of leaving the Reception-Guidance Center until his appearance before the Adult Authority. Social agencies such as the Salvation Army, Volunteers of America, Jewish Committee for Personal Service, and many others, send representatives to the institution for case-work services.

Writing reports on prisoners is the main activity of counselors, rather than "counseling" per se. It is on the basis of these reports that parole decisions are made, and thus in principle the counselors have considerable power over the lives of the inmates. Yet, since there are so few counselors in San Quentin (about one for every 250 to 300 prisoners), the counselor almost never knows a prisoner directly. The men who have direct contact with the prisoners—the guards, the supervisors, the teachers—are the people who have the most control over the lives of the prisoners: it is they who write the reports on the prisoners which the counselors use to write their reports to the Adult Authority. And of all the reports written by people in direct contact with the prisoners, the reports of the guards (particularly the disciplinary reports of the guards) are the most decisive in influencing parole. Thus the men who have the greatest physical control of the prisoners, the men with guns who lock the cells, also have the greatest practical power over the eventual freedom of the prisoners.

An orientation program for newly arrived men includes a tour of the institution, visits to the major industries and vocational areas, and talks by department heads and key institutional officials.

A pre-parole class is conducted for men who are about to leave the institution. In sessions with Correctional Counselors, anticipated parole problems are discussed. Representatives from the parole field, labor organization, employment offices and recreation department are brought in for appropriate talks. Parolees who are adjusting successfully are brought back to the institution to discuss the transition problems with men who are about to leave on parole.

Each of the large housing units (cell blocks) have become locally managed units, with its own counselors and its own counseling programing. This has brought the classification committee and program administrators into closer contact with the inmates, with a resulting increase in effective communication along socially constructive directions.

The unit system was abandoned, primarily because of budget cuts, in early 1971. However, even while the institution was decentralized into smaller housing units, there was nothing that could reasonably be called "effective communication along socially constructive directions." The prisoners' mistrust toward prison staff makes effective communication difficult under the best of circumstances. In San Quentin, where there are so few counselors, it is simply impossible for them to have any "close contact" with the prisoners.

NTCU and STRU

The Narcotic Treatment Control Unit is a community living program designed to treat parole addicts who have returned to the use of drugs. When it is determined that a parolee has used narcotics, he is immediately returned to San Quentin where he is placed in the NTCU for a period not to exceed 90 days. While he is in the unit the parolee is involved in group therapy, individual interviews and a work program. A *Short Term Return Unit* (STRU) provides a similar program for non-addict parolees whose adjustment to society shows signs of deterioration.

Typical Day at San Quentin

What is a day like to an inmate in San Quentin?

On a week day, Monday through Friday, activities begin with the wake-bell at 6:30 A.M. The inmate arises, dresses, and tidies up the cell. The cell doors are unlocked at 7:00 A.M. and the inmates go to breakfast. At 8:00 A.M. they proceed to various work assignments throughout the prison or to the Educational Department if they are attending academic or vocational classes.

Inmates assemble in the main yard at 12:00 noon and line up to pass into the mess halls for the mid-day meal, returning at 1:00 P.M. to their assignments. At 4:00 P.M. the inmates go back to their quarters in the cell block for the regular count procedure. The evening meal is served at 5:00 P.M. and immediately following they return to their cells. Those who are eligible for evening activities beginning at 6:00 P.M. are unlocked accordingly to proceed to night educational classes, handicraft shop or the gymnasium. In the cell blocks, television programs may be observed. Inmates who are educationally qualified may participate in cell study courses via extension services offered by educational facilities.

Evening activities end at 10:30 P.M., with lights out. However, inmates may listen to the radio (earphones) in their cells until midnight.

On Saturdays, Sundays and Holidays, breakfast is served one hour later and inmates return to their cells in the evening for the regular count at approximately one hour earlier. Church Services are available to inmates on Sundays. Athletic events are scheduled with outside competition on weekends and movies are shown. Inmates who are eligible may attend the weekend movie during the evening on Saturday or Sunday, plus an additional incentive movie on Tuesday or Wednesday nights, each week.

There are many group activities for inmate participation

such as the Toastmasters' Gavel Club, Inmate Advisory Council, members of which are selected by the inmates themselves to be representative of common wants, needs, and problems, etc.

This "typical day" is not typical for many inmates at San Quentin. Approximately 10 percent of the inmates in the prison are in isolation and are kept locked in their cells roughly 23 hours a day. Another 15 percent are unassigned or in close custody and therefore spend most of their time in their cells, although they leave their cells for meals and certain activities. Only about half of the inmates in the institution are eligible for night movement; the rest have to stay in their cells after dinner.

Other Activities

Inmates may participate in Alcoholics Anonymous, a discussion group called "General Semantics", a public speaking group, music and drama groups, and other special interest groups sponsored by employees who give of their own time to such activities. He may participate in the handicraft program—selling leather, wood and metal crafts. The products are exhibited at two hobby stores open to the public. Inmates can purchase cigarettes, personal grooming aids, stationary supplies, and candy at the inmate canteen. Proceeds from the canteen sales and a percentage of each hobby sale goes into the Inmate Welfare Fund, which pays for movies, television sets, library books, and other recreational equipment.

Voluntary organizations such as SATE, EMPLEO, and the Indian Culture Group address themselves to the particular problems of minority groups.

Mail and Visiting

Men may write and receive visits from approved relatives and friends. Over 3,000 visitors come to San Quentin each month to see their friends and relatives.

All mail is censored, both incoming and outgoing, except for mail to public officials. Unacceptable letters are returned to the inmate to be rewritten. For about one year (spring 1970, to spring 1971) letters from prisoners to lawyers were allowed to be mailed without being read or censored, but the policy was reversed because the director of the Department of Corrections felt prisoners were sending "contraband" to their lawyers (i.e., written materials not related to their cases, such as letters to be forwarded to someone else). As of 1972, it is not possible for an inmate to write a confidential letter to his lawyer. This obviously creates serious problems, especially if the prisoner is involved in a suit against the prison itself.

Preparation for Release to the Community

A work furlough program permits men within 90 days of parole to work at a regular job in any of the nearby communities; returning to the institution every night. This program helps men to make the transition from prison life to living in the community. Money earned goes for family support to provide a sound financial state on parole.

Furloughs up to 72 hours may be granted within 90 days of parole so the men may seek employment and make other arrangements for their return to the community.

Trends for the Future

Although adult felony arrests and convictions are increasing in California, fewer offenders are being sentenced to prison. In 1969 the Department of Corrections received only 13.5% of the adult felons legally eligible for prison. [Less than 10% in 1971.] This is a decline from the 28% received in 1960. Most of those, (65% in 1969) not sent to prison were placed on county probation. Thus, the current trend is toward treatment of as many offenders in the community as possible. This means that those that are sent to prison will be increasingly difficult people to manage, and most will have been failures in some community level program. Department planning and research are aimed at developing more effective programs for institutional and parole management in light of these trends.

Several significant features of prison life were not included in the warden's description of San Quentin:

Cells

The cells at San Quentin measure 4 feet wide, about 10 feet deep, and 7 feet high. They usually contain a bunk bed, writing table and chair, perhaps a shelf, and a toilet. They are not wide enough for a man to stretch his arms fully apart. Until mid-1971, most of these cells contained two people. A prisoner spends a minimum of about 9 hours a day in his cell. If he does not have the "privilege" of leaving his cell after the evening meal, he spends at least 13 hours a day there. If he is unassigned to any activity (because he refuses to work or because he is considered too much of a security risk to be allowed to work), he may spend 20 to 22 hours a day in his cell. And if he is being punished in isolation or is being held in "protective custody" (because of threats on his life) or is in "administrative segregation" (i.e., segregation resulting from an administrative decision rather than a disciplinary hearing), he may spend as much as 23½ hours a day in his cell, 4 feet wide and 10 feet deep.

Disciplinary Procedures

In the official handout on San Quentin, no mention is made of disciplinary procedures. There are several gradations of punishment for various infractions of prison rules: loss of privileges, isolation, isolation and segregation, and the adjustment center. *Loss of privileges* means that the prisoner will be unable to leave his cell for evening and weekend activities, to use the canteen or library, and so on. *Isolation,* or as it is more commonly called by prisoners, the "hole," means that the prisoner is placed in a special cellblock (B Section) where he is confined 23½ hours a day. The cells are damp, dirty, and furnished simply with a fold-down bed with a mattress, a toilet, and nothing else. Until 1971, an inmate could be placed in the hole for up to 29 days; since then this has been reduced to 10 days, although he can be indefinitely placed in "segregation" or the "adjustment center." *Segregation* means that a prisoner is kept in an isolation cell, although he may be allowed to leave his cell for meals. Finally, the *adjustment center* is the area where chronic troublemakers (as the prison defines them) are placed for long-term confinement. The cells are locked 23½ hours each day; prisoners leave their cells only for a half-hour of exercise daily.

Almost all disciplinary action is initiated by the guards. When they see an infraction, they have several choices. They can let the infraction go by; they can give the prisoner involved a verbal reprimand; they can take away the prisoner's privilege card; or they can send the prisoner to B Section (i.e., isolation). If they choose one of the last two options, the prisoner must appear before the disciplinary committee, consisting of several counselors and a lieutenant in charge of the block. The committee meets once a week, so a prisoner may spend six days in the hole before his case is formally heard.[3]

For most infractions—preparation of home brew, stealing cookies from the kitchen, insolence to an officer—the punishment will be 5 to 10 days in isolation and loss of privileges for 30 to 60 days. But the prisoner can be sentenced to a period of isolation and then a period (perhaps indeterminate) of segregation from the general population. He can have his security level raised and his activities restricted for an extended period. If he is considered a serious threat to prison order, he can be sent to the adjustment center, where he will be kept completely out of contact with the general population of the prison.

For prisoners sentenced to segregation or to the adjustment center, hearings are periodically held to determine whether they should be allowed to return to the mainline population. All prisoners sentenced to punishment have the formal right to

3. For a detailed discussion of a number of disciplinary hearings at San Quentin, see Chapter 5, pp. 83 ff. The prisoners' view of these hearings is presented in Chapter 6, pp. 125 ff.

appeal the decision as far as the warden. However, few prisoners ever go through this procedure, either because they feel it is pointless or because they are not informed of it. A disciplinary action is virtually never reversed.

San Quentin Prison as Seen by the Prison Officials

CONCEPTION OF THE ROLE OF THE PRISON

In the view of most prison officials, the two basic functions of prisons are custody and rehabilitation. To a certain extent these two functions are seen by many officials as reinforcing each other, as being mutually interdependent. In October, 1970, I attended an orientation day for new employees at San Quentin. During his introductory remarks, the director of in-service training at San Quentin stated, "We are here to teach conformity." The rules of proper conduct, the discipline, the enforced conformity of dress and haircuts—all are part of this effort to "teach conformity" to the prisoners. It is hoped, he said, that some of these habits will continue on the outside and that the prisoner will learn to conform to the rules of society. This general orientation was expressed many times to me by various officials at San Quentin. From this perspective, the procedures of custody become simultaneously the means for rehabilitation.[1]

1. Gresham Sykes, in his book *The Society of Captives* (Princeton, N.J.: Princeton University Press, 1958), makes this same general point: ". . . the Warden [of the New Jersey State Prison] has hammered out a philosophy of custody in which the prevention of deviant behavior among inmates while in

Central to this view that custody and rehabilitation are compatible goals is the conception of the ideal prison guard. On the orientation day, new employees were shown a film on what makes a good guard. In the film, the early careers of three archetypal guards were portrayed. The first guard was an authoritarian militarist who insisted on rigid discipline and the necessity of obeying the rules to the letter. The second guard was an easygoing liberal who wanted to be pals with the prisoners. The third was a square-jawed, straightforward type who treated the prisoners firmly but fairly. The first guard, the militarist, drove his prisoners to the point of rebellion and was plagued with constant troubles. The second guard, the lax type, got conned into carrying out illegal letters and bringing in contraband for the prisoners. The third, the firm-but-fair ideal, managed to establish a trusting relationship with his prisoners. They respected him and tried to emulate his honesty.

This "firm-but-fair" image of the ideal guard is presented in the official orientation booklet for new employees at San Quentin. In it is a page entitled: "Some Rules to Guide You as New Employees":

1. Always imply that you expect the correct attitude. Don't take it for granted that you are going to have trouble in enforcing a rule.

2. Keep a proper sense of proportion. Don't make a tremendous issue over some minor infraction, and then let a larger situation get out of hand because you fear to tackle it.

3. Do not fail to show respect for the inmate as a personality and as a reasonable human being; allow him to express himself.

4. Do not refuse reasonable requests, but when you have

prison is the most potent device for preparing the prisoner to follow the dictates of society when he is released. Education, recreation, counselling and other measures designed to lessen the oppressiveness of prison life assume a relatively minor position compared to a system of control which attempts to make the prisoner learn compliance to duly constituted authority" (pp. 35–36).

to do so, explain why it is necessary and express your regret.

5. Never show the slightest uncertainty as to the course of your action. *You must be a leader in the strongest sense of the word; must know and show your authority. Never show that you have been angered personally. To be most effective, discipline must be sure and impersonal.*

6. NEVER THREATEN DISCIPLINE YOU DO NOT INTEND TO ENFORCE. And be sure that the discipline you threaten will be enforceable and upheld by your superiors.

7. Endeavor not to punish an entire group, but when it is necessary, explain why. If any loophole can be left for the clearly innocent, leave it.

8. When behavior is commendable, express your appreciation. Inmates are just as grateful for praise as you and I, and it seems that precious little comes their way. The praise you bestow today, may make tomorrow's discipline unnecessary.

9. When you have threatened discipline and find it necessary to invoke the aid of your superior officer in enforcing it, give him all the facts and reasons. Don't grumble, "Aw, they never back me up. How can I get anything done?" *Your superior officer has as much, perhaps more at stake, as you in maintaining discipline, but don't expect him to be a mind reader.*[2]

A number of prison officials I interviewed expressed the feeling that when the custodial officials live up to these rules, the dual goals of custody and rehabilitation can be harmonious. The firm-but-fair guard can act as the agent, in this view, of both custody and rehabilitation: he can simultaneously maintain order within the prison and "teach conformity" to the wayward prison population.

Some prison officials, however, see the goals of custody and rehabilitation as operating against each other. Prison counselors who tend to be more committed to the rehabilitation ideal than

2. Italics in the original.

most prison officials especially feel the tension between these goals. However, if a choice between the two goals has to be made, even the counselors almost invariably give priority to custody. The warden's official orientation booklet of rules states this unambiguously in the first rule under the heading "General Custodial Orders for Personnel": "Remember, CUSTODY is always first in order of importance."

Raymond K. Procunier, the director of the Department of Corrections and an advocate of the liberal prison, has said that his primary job is "to control the behavior of men deemed criminal by society," and that rehabilitating them is only a secondary purpose.[3] As with state mental hospitals, the essential task of the penal institution is to take men out of circulation in the larger society in order to "protect society."

Although there is general unanimity that rehabilitation is a lower priority than custody, there is considerable disagreement as to the real possibilities of rehabilitation and the emphasis it should be given within the prison. Most counselors, teachers, chaplains, and other noncustodial employees of the prison tend to feel that rehabilitation is a meaningful goal of the prison. By and large, they embrace correctional ideology. They tend to feel that rehabilitation would succeed if only more funds were available for rehabilitation programs, and if only the custodial mentality of the guards and some of the prison administrators was changed. Many guards and custodial administrators, on the other hand, feel that rehabilitation is futile and that the only responsibility of the prison should be to maintain internal order through strong custody. They are suspicious of new "treatment" programs and see many of them as making their custodial jobs more difficult. One lieutenant at San Quentin reported that many of the guards strongly opposed the work furlough program. They see this innovation as resulting in an

3. Interview in the *Christian Science Monitor*, Nov. 7, 1970.

increased flow of contraband within the prison, rather than as helping the prisoners in any way.

Two studies of employee attitudes in the Department of Corrections indicate these different orientations toward the rehabilitation goals of the prison. In a survey conducted in 1960, Joseph W. Eaton found that of all the categories of personnel in the prison system, the only one in which a majority of the employees were *not* in favor of experimentation with treatment programs was correctional officers: 54 percent were opposed to experimentation. In contrast, only 5 percent of the "policymakers," 14 percent of the chaplains, and 23 percent of the educators were opposed to treatment programs (there was no category in his study explicitly covering "counselors").[4] A study conducted by Gene C. Kassebaum, David A. Ward, and Daniel M. Wilner in 1961 found similar results. In response to the question: "Which in your opinion would contribute *most* toward reducing incidents and problems among inmates?" 63 percent of the correctional officers and 72 percent of the correctional sergeants responded "firm discipline and hard work" or "swift and sure punishment." On the other hand, 60 percent of the counselors and 71 percent of the academic teachers responded that "group and individual treatment programs" would contribute most.[5]

Two factors may explain these differences in attitudes between custodial and noncustodial officials. First of all, guards are under pressures in the prison system very different from those of noncustodial employees. They are directly responsible for the control of prisoners, and they bear the brunt of criticism when that control breaks down. Second, it would seem likely that the sort of person who chooses to become a guard differs

4. Joseph W. Eaton, *Stone Walls Not a Prison Make* (Springfield, Ill.: Charles C. Thomas, 1962), p. 115.

5. Gene C. Kassebaum, David A. Ward, and Daniel M. Wilner, *Group Treatment by Correctional Personnel*, cited in Sheldon Messinger, "Strategies of Control" (unpublished Ph.D. dissertation, University of California, Berkeley, 1969), p. 241.

from one who becomes a counselor, a chaplain, or a teacher, and that this is reflected in attitudes toward the role of the prison. It would be expected that guards would tend to be more authoritarian than noncustodial employees, that they would have a stronger internal need to dominate and control other people, and that in many cases they became guards in the first place at least in part to fulfill those needs.[6]

The staff at San Quentin is not a monolith, in short. There are clear disagreements among the prison officials over some of the objectives of imprisonment. Some administrators have fully embraced the liberal penal philosophy that justifies imprisonment as a means of reforming the criminal. Others see the task of the prison in terms of punishment. Most prison officials fall somewhere in between. They feel that most of the men in prison "deserve" to be in prison or "had it coming" (i.e., punishment per se is justified), but at the same time they feel the prison should try to change the criminal, to make him less likely to commit crimes in the future. But whatever their differences in opinion, virtually all the prison officials I interviewed at San Quentin shared a general conception that the prison served a necessary and desirable social role. Eaton's study of attitudes in the Department of Corrections summarizes this underlying consensus well:

> Differences in outlook between the more reform and the more punishment oriented correction officials were a matter of degree rather than of mutually exclusive convictions. Proponents of both penal philosophies were agreed upon the ultimate objective of correctional work: the attainment of maximum social control over deviance. No society can survive if the laws and morals can be violated without constraints.[7]

While prison administrators may differ in their notions of the best techniques for accomplishing "the attainment of max-

---

6. This is more of a hypothesis than an observation, and it may reflect my prejudices as much as the concrete reality of the prison.
7. Eaton, *Stone Walls*, p. 134.

imum social control over deviance" and in their perceptions of
how well that goal is accomplished at San Quentin, there is
almost complete acceptance of the goal itself.

ATTITUDES TOWARD
THE ACTUAL FUNCTIONING
OF THE SYSTEM

A counselor for several years at San Quentin summed up his
feelings about the role of counselors when he told me: "It is
pure tokenism. The Department of Corrections has never
placed any confidence in their counseling staff. They only have
counselors in order to say publicly that they have 'rehabilitation.' " He stressed that with one counselor for 250 prisoners it
was impossible for the counselors to do anything but act as a
liaison between the prisoner and the prison administration and
parole board. Whatever rehabilitation occurred in the prison,
he said, "occurred more by accident than by design."

One administrative official at San Quentin, with whom I had
many conversations, frequently expressed strong criticisms of
the rehabilitation programs in the prison. He felt that the emphasis on activities such as psychotherapy and group counseling
was, in general, a waste of time. The only meaningful kind of
rehabilitation, in his eyes, would come through the development of effective conditioning techniques. He saw criminal
behavior as a collection of bad behavioral patterns essentially
equivalent to bad habits. The solution to the problem of criminality was to reprogram the habits of the criminal in socially
desirable ways. He was not sure how this could be accomplished, but he felt the present programs were misdirected.

Two associate wardens in the prison expressed considerable
cynicism about the effectiveness of the prison system as it was,
and about the possibilities of significant change. Both men told
me that new men typically come into the Department of Corrections with aspirations to "change the world," but their ideal-

ism is soon "shattered by the realities of prison life." They begin to realize that the best that they can hope for is to have an occasional positive impact on individual inmates. In an article in the *Christian Science Monitor* (Nov. 7, 1970), San Quentin associate warden Park said, "I challenge you to come up with an alternative to this . . . I'm not saying that conditions here are necessarily ideal, but they aren't barbaric either. What we are trying to do is operate on a level that is acceptable." Another associate warden, when asked how he would change conditions in San Quentin if he could do anything he wanted, without any financial constraints, told me:

> There is really very little of importance that could be done. This may shock you, but if I had the resources, I would not put them into San Quentin, but rather into the counties, into the local level. That is where the resources are desperately needed and that is where most prisoners should be kept. The role of the Department of Corrections should be only to handle hardened criminals, people who cannot be handled at the local level. Only destructive prisoners should be handled by the state, because the counties cannot handle these prisoners. I don't care how much money you put into San Quentin, there is a rapid rate of diminishing returns of more education, more psychologists and so forth with these kinds of prisoners.

Most prison administrators feel that San Quentin is doing its job reasonably well, and that that job is by necessity basically a custodial one.[8]

8. There are a few prison employees who feel that the prison is doing a terribly inadequate job. Most notably at San Quentin, this view was held by the Reverend Byron Eschelman, the head of the Protestant chapel from 1951 to 1971. In numerous conversations Chaplain Eschelman expressed the view that the prison is a microcosm of the outside society with all of the alienation and oppression of the outside society magnified. He regarded the absolute priority of custody as disastrous for helping prisoners to make meaningful changes, and he felt that the prison was "a monstrosity" and a "hypocritical institution." "The Prison," said Eschelman, "is nothing but a super ghetto stuffed with people who come from ghettos, the people who have been voiceless and impotent across the years, the recipients of persecution and abuse, the scapegoats of our culture" (interview in the *San Francisco Chronicle*, Nov. 29, 1970).

Eaton's study of attitudes in the Department of Corrections presents some interesting findings which reflect the level of complacency and acceptance of the status quo among prison employees. The subjects in his study were asked whether they agreed or disagreed with the following statement: "We can make some improvement in the department, but by and large, conditions in all institutions I know about are as good as they can be, considering the type of prisoners that have to be kept there."[9] To agree with this statement means that the respondent accepts the status quo in the Department of Corrections. To disagree with it would indicate a very mild level of criticism of the Department (you need only believe that things are not "as good as they can be"). Only 40 percent of the employees disagreed with statement (39 percent agreed with it, and 21 percent couldn't decide; in the present context, not being able to decide itself reflects a high level of complacency). The range of responses among different employee categories was considerable: 80 percent of the Department's research staff were critical of the department; 61 percent of the policymakers; but only 39 percent of the correctional officers and 27 percent of the clerks.

All prison administrators interviewed at San Quentin agreed on one important issue: whatever problems there might be in the prison, they should be handled by prison authorities, not by outsiders. Prison officials see themselves as the best qualified to deal with these problems, and they insist that "interference" from the courts and the legislature only makes things worse. These people, one administrator told me, "are simply do-gooders. They don't have any idea of the real problems of running a prison. They don't understand the kind of people that we have to deal with. They believe everything the inmates have to say and always assume that we are the ones who are in the wrong. Whenever they meddle in the internal functioning of the prisons, they only make our problems more difficult."

9. Eaton, *Stone Walls*, p. 113.

Several San Quentin officials expressed particular animosity toward academic researchers who, they felt, could criticize the prison system from their armchairs without having to assume any responsibility for events in prison: "They can say that our custody is too harsh, but they never have to face the problems of life and death in prison. We have a responsibility to protect the lives of the inmates and the staff, and we do what is necessary for that."

DISCIPLINARY PROCEDURES

The priorities of the prison system are clearly reflected in the disciplinary procedures within the prison. The disciplinary hearings which I attended in November, 1970, were held on the ground floor of B Section, the isolation section of the prison. The hearings took place in a small room next to the showers; windows in the room looked out at the cells. At the hearing were two counselors, one correctional lieutenant, and one guard. They sat on one side of a table which took up nearly half the room; the prisoner sat on the other side, facing the disciplinary committee. As a visitor, I sat in a corner of the room. The sound of jackhammers repeatedly intruded into the hearings, making it difficult to hear. (There had been a riot in B Section several months before during which many of the cells had been severely damaged, and they were still in the process of being repaired.)

Each prisoner who appeared before the committee was escorted by a guard from his isolation cell to the hearing room. When he entered the room he was told by the chairman of the committee to sit down and then was read the formal charge of which he was accused. The chairman then asked the prisoner what he had to say for himself. There followed a brief interrogation by each of the committee members, after which the prisoner was told to leave the room and wait outside. The committee then discussed the case for two or three minutes and reached a decision about what punishment should be given the prisoner. In none of the cases which I witnessed was there any discussion of the possible innocence of the accused prisoner; all that was discussed was the appropriate harshness of the punishment. The prisoner was then called back into the room and told the verdict. There usually followed a brief admonition by the chairman that the prisoner should mend his ways if he wanted to stay out of the hole in the future, and the prisoner was sent back to his cell.

During an average committee session 10 to 15 cases are heard. On the day I attended the disciplinary hearings at San Quentin, 15 cases were heard:

1. Several inmates were accused of having made home brew in their cells. Most of these were Chicano prisoners. The head counselor in charge of the hearing scolded them for their misbehavior and stressed that the prison could not tolerate home brew, since prisoners often became violent when they became drunk. Each of the inmates was convicted of the infraction and sentenced to 10 to 15 days in isolation and 30 to 60 days suspension of privileges.

2. One prisoner was accused of stealing six cookies from the mess line. He had previously had a disciplinary infraction for stealing a banana. One of the counselors said several times to me while the accused was in the room: "Mr. Wright, you have before you an ambulatory example of sheer stupidity." There was considerable sarcastic joking among the members of the committee and with the prisoner, who also appeared to treat the affair as a joke. He was given five days in the hole.

3. One young Chicano prisoner was convicted of "possession of militant literature." The inmate had been found with a list of militant-revolutionary newspapers in his possession (not with any of the newspapers themselves). At the top of the list were the words: "These papers will help in the revolutionary war, antipropaganda struggle against the fucking pigs." Officially, it

was for this sentence at the top of the list, and not for the list itself, that the inmate was punished.

During the hearing, the head counselor said to the prisoner: "You can have any political beliefs that you want as long as you keep them in your head. There is nothing that we can do about that. But if you put them down on paper, or have in your possession a paper with those beliefs, then it is no longer just a question of your beliefs. We take that as proof of active involvement. It is our belief that this is detrimental to the institution. We can't have revolutionary activity in prisons, so we cannot leave you in the general population." In the discussion about the case when the prisoner left the room, it was noted that his last "beef" (infraction) had been during the prison strike of August, 1970, when he had been a "leader" in the troubles. By this was meant that he had been seen in the yard talking to a small group of prisoners, encouraging them to join the strike. Furthermore, he was currently participating in a hunger strike in the isolation section of the prison, and this was taken as a strong indication of his subversive intentions. The committee decided that isolation was not sufficient and that he should also be put in segregation for an indeterminate period of time.

When the prisoner returned to the room the head counselor said to him: "We have decided to put you in isolation for ten days and revoke your privilege card for thirty days and then put you in segregation. The choice is up to you now what will happen to you. Only you will make your time here difficult. Only you can decide which way you will go." The inmate responded, quite upset and embittered by the situation: "You'll see which way I go. You'll definitely see which way I go." This response was noted in his record.

4. One prisoner was convicted of "insubordination." The situation, which no one disputed, was that he had been returning something to a friend on the tier below his cell just before lockup. The correctional officer on duty thought that he was

loitering and asked him for his I.D. card. The accused prisoner said that he had left it in his cell, at which point the guard asked him for his privilege card as a means of identification. The inmate responded, "Why?" being reluctant to part with his privilege card, for fear of having to go through a long procedure in order to get it back. The guard took this as insubordination, as a "threatening attitude," and brought him to isolation. The disciplinary committee sentenced the prisoner to 10 days in isolation and loss of privileges for 30 days.

This prisoner had already served 10 years in prison. The previous year, when he went before the Adult Authority, he was told that he would probably receive a parole date the following year if he had a completely clean record for at least 12 months. The prisoner had had no infractions for 15 months and was going up before the Adult Authority in a few weeks. The disciplinary committee, when discussing his case, was completely aware that their decision would probably mean that the Adult Authority would deny this man a parole date, but they decided to convict him anyway. The head counselor told the prisoner several times during the hearing: "That was pretty stupid of you to throw away a clean record on such a petty beef. It would have been so easy for you to have just given him the privilege card."

In discussing this case with me later, one of the counselors admitted that it was unfortunately true that the committee had not merely sentenced the prisoner to 10 days in isolation, but probably to at least one more year in prison. The counselor justified the action on grounds that the committee really did not have any choice in the matter because they had to consider the effect of their decision on the authority and control of the guards. This means that unless there is positive evidence that no breach of the rules had actually occurred (i.e., unless there is clear indication that the guard made a mistake), the decision of the guard will always be upheld. The prisoners had to know, it was stressed, that the power of the guards would be backed up by the administration, for otherwise "the authority of the guards would not be respected."

5. Two prisoners in the adjustment center were accused of selling narcotics. The committee informed them that it had received reports that they had been selling narcotics, although it explicitly admitted that it had no real substantive evidence whatsoever. The committee, nevertheless, had the power to make an "administrative" decision. Such a decision is based on the principle that the institution cannot risk letting a guilty person into the general population, even if this means some innocent people will end up in solitary confinement. The accused prisoners were thus asked: "Can you give us any solid reasons why we shouldn't think you have been selling narcotics?" All they could say was, "I just wasn't selling any, that's all." The prisoners were confronted with the necessity of proving their innocence, which they could not do. The committee decided they should be administratively confined to the adjustment center for several months.

Segregation review hearings followed much the same pattern as disciplinary hearings. A prisoner can be placed in segregation for a variety of reasons—for punishment, for "protective custody" (i.e., if his life is in danger), or as an "administrative" classification (i.e., the prison doesn't bring formal disciplinary charges against the prisoner, but feels that he is a security risk and so keeps him segregated from the mainline population). Once in segregation status, his case is formally reviewed every 90 days by a committee similar to the disciplinary committee. A decision is reached whether to keep the prisoner in segregation for another 90 days, to transfer him to another institution, or to return him to mainline in San Quentin. The following is a brief account of the segregation review hearings I observed one day in February, 1971:

1. A young Chicano prisoner, very depressed, had been transferred to San Quentin from Tracy, where he had allegedly been

involved in a prison disturbance in which he had assaulted an officer. He had spent 29 days in the hole before his transfer and had been placed in segregation upon his arrival in San Quentin. He asked for a transfer to southern California so that "I could be closer to my people; they can never come this far to visit me," but the committee told him that this would be impossible. They said that perhaps after another 90 days in segregation they could make some arrangement for him.

2. A highly effeminate homosexual, whom the committee referred to as "she" and as a "queen," was in segregation because, according to the committee, "she" was constantly involved in "love triangles" and "enjoyed trying to get other prisoners to fight over her." The prisoner was very unhappy in segregation, but was told that the committee could not take the risk of putting him back in the mainline and that he would have to stay in segregation at least another 90 days.

3. A young, bitter, and very depressed black prisoner had served five years on a six-month to ten-year sentence for assault of a police officer. His disciplinary record was not particularly bad, but the committee said that he was a "known troublemaker." He had been transferred from Tracy to Susanville after refusing to go to work at Tracy. At Susanville he had apparently become involved in a short strike and was immediately transferred to San Quentin. The parole board said on his last appearance that he would not be given a parole until he showed "some progress in personal adjustment." At San Quentin, he had been locked up in segregation since being charged with possession of a knife in August, 1970 (i.e., seven months at the time of the review). An officer, who the prisoner said disliked him, reported seeing the prisoner give the knife to another prisoner in the mess hall. The prisoner still adamantly denied having anything to do with the knife, but the committee felt that they had to accept the word of the guard, and thus kept the inmate in segregation. At San Quentin possession of a knife receives a mandatory sentence of one year in segregation, so

this prisoner still had five months in the hole before being eligible to return to the mainline population.

4. Two brothers in the same cell were also charged with possession of a knife. One of the brothers had accumulated debts and was being threatened by other prisoners, so he obtained a knife to protect himself. The knife was discovered, and both brothers were given the mandatory one-year segregation. The brother who did not actually have the knife was put in segregation for not having reported the knife or asked for a cell transfer. It was felt that since he was a cellmate of his brother he must have known about the knife, and thus he shared the responsibility for its "possession." During the segregation review hearing, one of the counselors repeatedly said to the prisoner, in a righteous tone of voice, "We are not doing this to you: it is you who put yourself in this situation, and only you can get yourself out now."

5. Several prisoners were in segregation for "protective custody" (PC)—for owing gambling or drug debts, for resisting sexual advances, for being informers, and so forth. In each case it was felt that it was necessary to keep them locked up in the 4-by-10-foot segregation cells in order to protect their lives. Generally, in such cases, prison officials try to arrange a transfer for the prisoner to an institution where he will be in less danger, but sometimes this is not possible. In two cases the prisoners strongly denied that their lives were in danger and accused the segregation review committee of using PC as an excuse for locking them up.

In addition to short-term disciplinary placement of prisoners in isolation and longer-term placement in segregation or the adjustment center, transfers from one prison to another often serve as disciplinary measures. Prisoners who are considered troublemakers in a lower-security prison are frequently transferred to San Quentin as a disciplinary sanction. Transfers can disrupt the programs in which the inmate is involved and, in certain cases, seriously reduce his chances for a parole. Yet for such transfers there is not even the pretense of a hearing.

During the initial classification committee meeting which I observed in April, 1971, three prisoners appeared who had been transferred to San Quentin from Tracy for allegedly participating in a strike there.[10] The first was a young black prisoner who was accused of being "an active participant" in the strike, and of "encouraging other inmates to participate in it." He denied this to the classification committee, saying that he had participated in the strike only because everyone else had and that he had in no way been a leader. The committee noted that his work record was excellent and that he had not had any disciplinary infractions (he had not been given a formal disciplinary infraction for his alleged participation in the strike), and they decided that the Tracy officials had probably exaggerated his involvement. They thus ignored the recommendation from Tracy that he be put in segregation, classified him medium custody, and placed him in the mainline population.

The second case was also a young black prisoner who was transferred to San Quentin on the accusation that he was a leader of the strike and an "effeminate homosexual." He vehemently denied both, especially the homosexuality. He said that there was an officer at Tracy who had a grudge against him and had made up the charges. The committee again made the judgment that the inmate's story was probably at least partially true, and thus they did not put him in segregation.

The third prisoner transferred to San Quentin was a Chicano inmate, again accused of being a leader in the strike. The committee looked at his disciplinary record and saw that he had been in a number of incidents before; thus, they accepted the recommendation of the Tracy officials and had him placed in

10. The initial classification committee is responsible for making classification decisions for inmates (i.e., custody level and activity placement) who have just arrived at San Quentin, either directly from the Reception-Guidance Center or after having been transferred to San Quentin from another institution.

segregation rather than in the mainline like the other two prisoners.

When I discussed these cases with the committee chairman, he freely acknowledged that it was common practice for officials to exaggerate accusations in order to make punitive transfers appear reasonable to the receiving institution and to the Department authorities in Sacramento. "Often," he said, "if the information on an inmate's participation in some incident is just hearsay, the officer may still say in his report that the inmate was a leader. The officer certainly would not say that his information was not certain. This is common practice at all prisons, even San Quentin." That is why the San Quentin officials did not take the transfer explanations of the Tracy officials seriously. "When there is a strike," one committee member told me, "a lot of guys get caught up in it and get shipped out. Most of them were not active in the strike and they won't cause any trouble here at San Quentin, so we don't need to put them into segregation. So when we are told that they were 'leaders' in the strike, we don't take it very seriously unless there is other evidence that they are troublemakers." The problem is that even though the classification committee takes these transfer explanations with considerable skepticism, they become part of the prisoner's official record and they may have a strong effect on the Adult Authority when they consider the prisoner for parole. One administrator at San Quentin told me: "If an individual was transferred from one institution to another officially because of involvement in a strike, he would not be given very serious consideration for a parole by the board that year." This, the administrator admitted, was "most unfortunate, but unavoidable. Transfers are important for maintaining institutional order."

These disciplinary and segregation review cases and transfer procedures reflect the central priority of the prison system: the maintenance of the internal order of the prison. If the exigencies of order clash with justice, order must prevail. Many counselors feel ambivalent about this situation. They *believe* in justice, but they feel that in the context of a prison, order and control must be given absolute priority over all other values or else, as one counselor put it, "the prison will deteriorate into absolute anarchy." They fear acutely the consequences of laxness and the possibility of undermining the ability of the guards to control the prisoners.

ATTITUDES TOWARD PRISONERS

One theme was repeated over and over during orientation day for employees at San Quentin: "As free men you should be friendly with the inmates, but never friends." We were told to keep a "professional distance" from the prisoners at all times. This attitude toward relationships with prisoners is formalized in the "Basic Rules and Regulations" set out in the new employees' orientation booklet:

> 8. Relationship with inmates: Maintain a friendly but business-like relationship with the inmates placed under your supervision. Do not discuss your personal affairs or the affairs of your fellow employees. Accepting favors or gifts from inmates is forbidden. Remember that bribe attempts do not just suddenly happen. They are the result of a gradual process of becoming overfamiliar, accepting favors or small gifts and gradually working yourself into a position where you must suffer the loss of your job for past violations of institutional rules or accede to their demands.

The warden of San Quentin presented a bleak scenario of the employee who becomes friends with inmates:

> You become friends with an inmate; he asks you to do a little innocent favor for him: "Would you mail a birthday card to my daughter? If I mail it through the prison mail service it will arrive two days after her birthday." So you look at the card and sure enough, it is just a birthday card. So, you take the card out of the prison, an act which is

strictly prohibited [and liable to 6 months in prison]. The
prisoner then uses this offense to blackmail you into carrying out illegal letters and bringing in contraband. You are
trapped, and before long another good man goes down the
drain.

Approximately two officers a month are dismissed for such
infractions of the rules. In September, 1970, according to the
warden, one officer was so blackmailed into bringing a gun in
for some prisoners. All of these problems, it was stated time and
time again, stemmed from the fatal error of becoming too close
with the inmates. The captain in charge of custody in the prison
expressed it this way:

> Many of the prisoners will be very nice to you, will try
> to make you feel that you are the greatest. They will tell
> you that you are not like the other guards; you are really
> a good guy. But they are only trying to exploit you, to
> manipulate you and get something from you. These men
> have exploited people all of their lives, and they will try to
> exploit you as well. There are some people who will always
> try to exploit others.

All of these warnings are intended to accomplish one thing: to
make the new employee extremely suspicious and mistrustful
of the prisoners.

In explaining the behavior of prisoners, officials almost exclusively point to characteristics within the prisoner. Practically no
importance is given to the situation in which that prisoner lives.
This is true both for the behavior that leads the prisoner to end
up in prison and for his behavior within prison. Thus, if prisoners tend to be manipulative, it is not because the system pressures them to be manipulative, but because "these men have
exploited people all of their lives." No prison official with whom
I discussed these issues ever placed any significant responsibility for inmate behavior on the prison itself.

Undoubtedly, there are certain prisoners who are pathologically manipulative and exploitative. But for most prisoners

there is no indication that this is the case. If many prisoners attempt to manipulate prison officials for their own ends, it is in large part because they face a structure which has absolute power over them. They are defined by the system as totally unfree, powerless, dependent. Manipulation, like other aspects of prisoner behavior, is for many prisoners a way of coping with this situation. The only freedom, power, and autonomy that the prisoner has he must create through some kind of manipulative maneuvers.

The view that the causes of prisoners' behavior lie almost exclusively with the prisoners rather than in their situation is also reflected in the frequently stated admonition: "Only you will make your time here difficult. Only you will decide which way you will go." In the initial classification committee meeting which I attended, nearly every prisoner was told something like the above. One inmate in particular, who had had difficulties at other prisons, was told: "You should get yourself together and follow the Adult Authority's recommendations if you ever want to get out of here. It is your life; you can do what you want with it. It seems to me that you plan to stay here forever." By placing the responsibility for his behavior completely on the shoulders of the prisoner, the prison officials wash their hands (and ease their consciences) of the consequences of the prison environment on inmate behavior.

Another common tendency among prison officials is to constantly denigrate prisoners. The director of one of the vocational programs expressed this sentiment clearly: "Most prisoners are failures. They failed in school, they failed on jobs, they failed in marriage, and they failed as criminals. They can't even succeed as criminals because they got caught. They are failures in life and they mess up whatever they do." "The prisoners," said the warden on orientation day, "are not generally wicked. They are simply impulsive and juvenile, and they simply cannot control their impulses. Prison is good for them because the prison authorities help them to control their impulses." Many other prison officials expressed similar feelings.

One way to denigrate adults is to treat them as children. One associate warden referred to the prisoners as "impulsive children who have never learned to act in a civilized manner." The whole pattern of prison life supports this notion. Only children would have their lives so closely regulated. What is more, under extreme stress and frustration, people often regress and act like children. Thus the original diagnosis becomes fulfilled and the warden can honestly say prisoners are "simply immature and juvenile." When prison officials express such feelings, they are saying in effect: If they, the prisoners, are failures and immature, then we, their guardians, must be successful and mature. This makes it much easier for officials to justify their absolute power and the priority they place on custody and order in their treatment of prisoners.[11]

ATTITUDES TOWARD RADICAL POLITICS AMONG PRISONERS

In the past several years radical political ideology has increased significantly among prisoners.[12] In general, the prison has reacted to this growth by trying, often unsuccessfully, to repress expressions of radical politics. In discussing the case of a young Chicano inmate placed in segregation for possession of militant literature (see pp. 84–85), one of the head counselors at San Quentin said:

> You know, this is not like the outside. You can't allow prisoners to do things which might lead to a riot. If prisoners were allowed to read and discuss politics and to organize without restrictions it would only end up with people

11. Numerous studies of life in "total institutions" emphasize the ways in which the role of the inmate defines him as an inferior, worthless being in the eyes of the custodians. The best general discussion of this process is Erving Goffman's *Asylums* (New York: Anchor Books, 1961). For a more specific discussion of these issues in prison, see Sykes, *The Society of Captives*.

12. See Chapter 12 for a thorough discussion of the development of radical politics within American prisons.

getting killed. We can't let prisoners do anything which might encourage a disturbance in the prison, and that is exactly what these revolutionary writings do. If you were the warden, what would you do? Would you risk letting prisoners become revolutionaries? What would you do? We don't have the choice.

In early 1971 members of a number of inmate organizations began openly to express radical ideas. On a San Francisco educational television station, prisoners belonging to SATE (Self-Advancement Through Education, a black self-help group) made statements highly critical of the prison. Shortly thereafter, most of the leadership of the organization was transferred to Folsom prison and the warden issued the following statement:

CALIFORNIA STATE PRISON
SAN QUENTIN

Date: March 22,1971

To: ASSOCIATE WARDEN, ADMINISTRATION
ASSOCIATE WARDEN, CUSTODY
ASSOCIATE WARDEN, CLASSIFICATION & TREATMENT
From: WARDEN L. S. NELSON Subject: Inmate Activity Programs

We are reading in the public press, and hearing via television and radio, that the best breeding and/or recruiting ground for neo-revolutionaries is in the prison system.

I am being told that our new educational systems must encompass preparing the men for community activity, whatever that means, upon release.

I am witnessing the deterioration of our ethnic organizations, which were once dedicated to the educational improvement of our men inside San Quentin, to para-military organizations with revolutionary overtones. It appears to me that by pursuing this path, the organizations are destined to undo all the good they may have done, and may result in harm, in the form of added time coming to all men confined within our walls. For if the prisons of California become known as "Schools for Violent Revolution," the Adult Authority would be remiss in their duty to not keep the inmates longer.

I do not believe that as the administrator of this institution it is proper for me to utilize State facilities or State monies for the purpose of providing facilities or time for the propagation of revolutionary acts or material. In fact, I believe it to be the exact opposite of my duty.

I have been told that if I deny organizations the right to use para-military methods of operation, they will go underground. This is an alternative that they may choose. The alternative they might better choose is to revert to the purposes established in their constitutions, and to adhere strictly to them. None of the organizations were set up as "political" organizations. Their motivation of minorities to enter our education programs is commendable, but their purpose is not in itself to educate, nor are they an educational entity within the prison; if they were, they would be required to operate within our structured educational department.

I intend to draw the line at revolutionary education. I do so with the full knowledge that criticism will be heaped on my head, but I believe I have a deeper and more abiding responsibility to the State of California than I do to the small handful of individuals who are dedicated to the overthrow of our present system of government.

No one can shake the hand of a man who has his fist clenched over his head!

[Signed] L. S. Nelson
Warden

LSN:h
Copy to:
Director R. K. Procunier
Supervisor of Education
Marin County Superintendent of Schools
Coordinator of Inmate Activities
Representatives of EMPLEO, INDIAN CULTURAL GROUP, SATE

When asked if prisoners are ever denied parole because of their political beliefs, most prison officials said that this almost never happens. One or two officials admitted that a prisoner with known radical ideas is less likely to get a parole date than a prisoner who has not expressed such ideas, but they felt that this was justified, since a prisoner who expressed radical ideas in prison did not "respect authority" and was likely to have difficulties "adjusting" on the outside.

In February, 1971, I observed one day's sitting of the Adult Authority at San Quentin. One of the prisoners who appeared before them was a young black who had openly proclaimed that he was a member of the Black Panther party. He had spent three years at San Quentin for second-degree burglary, and during that time had had only a few minor disciplinary infractions for such things as "abusive language to an officer" or "refusing to obey an order." When he sat down before the Adult Authority, the first question he was asked was: "Tell me, why are you a Panther? What do you see in them?" He replied: "All black people in America are really Panthers because all black people in America are oppressed." There followed a long discussion about the meaning of "oppression" and the legitimacy of the Panthers' response to that oppression. One of the Adult Authority members admitted that "there has been a certain amount of injustice against Negroes over the years, but things have gotten much better recently, and I just don't see how you can say that you are oppressed. This is a democracy, and if you have grievances, there are nonviolent ways that you can solve them." The prisoner replied, "It may be a democracy for you, but it isn't for blacks, and particularly it isn't for me. George Washington broke the laws of King George because he thought that they were oppressive. And he broke them violently. We are just doing the same thing. This country is more oppressive against us than England ever was against George Washington. Washington just didn't want to pay a tax on tea; we want to live like human beings." The discussion continued, and one of the Adult Authority members asked the prisoner, "Well, even if there are still some injustices against Negroes, do you think that

it is justified to steal like you did?" The prisoner replied, "Everyone here steals. Everyone. This country is built on stealing. A
shop owner steals when he raises his prices so that the people
in the ghetto can't afford to buy enough to eat. That is stealing
as much as burglary." After about twenty minutes of heated
political discourse (*nothing* else was discussed), the hearing
ended. The prisoner was denied a parole.

Later in the day, in another parole hearing, an inmate appeared who had been actively involved with the Minutemen
before he was sent to prison five years before. He was asked by
one of the Adult Authority members: "Are you still a *Weatherman?*" "Weatherman?" replied the inmate. "There weren't
any Weathermen when I was on the outside. You mean 'Mi-
nuteman.'" The AA member replied: "Weatherman, Minute-
man—they're all the same thing anyway."[13] Later in the interview, the prisoner was asked, "What do you now feel about
Minutemen, Weathermen, Nazis, Panthers, and those kinds of
groups?" The inmate tactfully replied, "Well, like you said, they
are really all the same. They may have different rhetoric, but
there is no real difference in their organizations. They are all on
ego trips." The prisoner was recommended for a parole.

As in nearly all totalitarian systems, alternative ideas about
power (i.e., political ideology) are severely censored in prison.
In order to maintain absolute control over the lives of prisoners,
prison officials feel that they cannot tolerate the open questioning of the legitimacy of their authority. Severe sanctions are
brought against individuals who try.

13. The Minutemen are an extreme right-wing group that has stockpiled
weapons, explosives, and ammunition ostensibly to protect America from Communism. The Weathermen, on the other hand, are an extreme left-wing group
that has advocated urban guerrilla warfare and revolutionary sabotage. While
both groups thus condone illegal acts of violence, the ideologies of the two are
almost polar opposites. To think of Weathermen, Minutemen, Panthers, and
Nazis as all being more or less the same reflects either extreme ignorance about
these groups or total naïveté about the meaning of ideology.

THE SAN QUENTIN PRISON STRIKE
OF AUGUST, 1970, AS SEEN BY
THE PRISON ADMINISTRATION

Many of the attitudes discussed above are clearly illustrated in the reaction of the prison administration to the San Quentin prison strike of August, 1970. The strike grew out of the fact that the Marin County Superior Court was planning to hold court sessions within the walls of San Quentin prison in connection with the case of the Soledad Brothers. Prisoners feared that prison officials would be able to manipulate court sessions much more easily if they were held within prison. Approximately 800 inmates staged a sit-down in the yard to protest this action. A prisoners' manifesto of demands was written and submitted by Warren Wells, a Black Panther, to various prison officials. The manifesto contained 14 demands:

1. That all political prisoners be freed.
2. That the Soledad Three be freed.
3. That a black warden be hired.
4. That a black associate warden of custody be hired.
5. That a black associate warden of care and treatment be hired.
6. That a Mexican warden be hired.
7. That a Mexican associate warden of custody be hired.
8. That a Mexican associate warden of care and treatment be hired.[14]
9. That nonwhite prisoners have proportional representation in all administrative, industrial, and vocational positions in the prison.
10. That B Section and A Section be closed until they are made to conform to sanitary and health standards.

14. At present there is only one warden, one associate warden for custody, and one for care and treatment. The implication in demands 3–8 is that three individuals—one white, one black, and one Mexican—would replace the one individual presently holding the post. There is no implication, as the warden insisted, that the demand was for a black warden in lieu of a white warden.

11. That men in B Section, A Section, and the adjustment center be given one full hour of exercise a day and be given the rights that other prisoners have.
12. That all men presently condemned to death be given political asylum abroad.
13. That all forms of capital punishment and mass genocide on the people by the brutal hands of the American bureaucracies immediately cease by order of the Free World Solidarity Revolutionary Army for the People.
14. That all prisoners being tried by the Superior Court within the walls of San Quentin be tried by their peers.

The demands were presented to the warden and other officials. The warden tried, over the public address system, to get the strikers to disperse, but they refused unless he promised to negotiate. This, the warden told me, he would not do "because you do not promise to negotiate with prisoners in a state of insurrection." The warden then read the demands over the loudspeaker, trying to discredit them, but still the crowd did not disperse.[15] They were then ordered to disperse, and when they refused, a heavy barrage of tear gas was released on them. No one was seriously hurt in the affair. A number of prisoners were transferred to Folsom prison, and a number of others were sent to the adjustment center or to isolation.

The universal reaction of all prison officials with whom I have discussed the demands was that they were "asinine" and "ridiculous and childish" (to use the expressions of two associate wardens). No one took them as serious statements of sincerely felt grievances. They all stressed that virtually none of the demands lay within the jurisdiction of the prison administration (with the exception of 9 and 11) and that it was "absurd" for the prisoners to make such demands. Most of the officials maintained that the strike was organized from the outside by the Panthers or the Communist party. One associate warden said

15. As is discussed in Chapter 6, many prisoners reported that the warden read only demands 1–8 over the loudspeaker, thus making the manifesto appear to be simply a racial platform for nonwhite prisoners.

that the strikers were living under serious delusions about the possibility of changing things and about the support they had on the outside: "They saw some Panthers and hippies demonstrating on the outside of the prison and fell into the trap that the public supported them. This was a childish illusion. The public doesn't give a damn about prisoners." He went on to say that these demands and the apparent militancy of some of the prisoners was no more than "political labels being put on just plain orneriness."

The captain in charge of custodial officers informed me that "the sit-down was really led by about a dozen or so inmates who coerced the others into joining the strike." He added that the demands were "outrageous." "Ninety-eight percent of the prisoners," he said, "were on our side; it was only two percent that kept everything messed up all the time. For people who haven't been so wonderful in life, these inmates are real critical of the officers."

None of the officials I talked to saw the demands as reflecting the deep alienation and sense of injustice experienced by prisoners within the prison. They saw the demands for a black and Chicano warden as "ridiculous," showing how racist the Panthers were, not as an attempt to make the power structure of the prison more responsive to the needs of nonwhite prisoners.[16] They did not see the demands for a change in the conditions of punishment within the prison as reflecting the real barbarity of the treatment of prisoners and the real injustice which it symbolizes to them, but rather as an unrealistic attempt to make life easier in prison. Above all, the prison officials did not take the demands as reflecting a responsible affirmation of mature human values to be taken seriously, but rather as "childish illusions."

16. There is no reason to believe that in fact the presence of a black warden at San Quentin would significantly make the prison power structure more responsive to the black prisoners.

CHAPTER 6

San Quentin Prison as Seen by the Prisoners

THE SAN QUENTIN PRISON STRIKE OF AUGUST, 1970, AS SEEN BY THE PRISONERS

Warren Wells, a black dude, was the head of the strike. He was a pretty good guy. There were no threats or intimidation; the majority of the prisoners in the prison supported the strike, even if they didn't sit down in the yard. Everyone was together. Some of the demands were ridiculous, but most of them were good. The officials tried to make a racial thing out of it. The warden only read out the black demands. Before that, even the Angels and the Nazis were with the Panthers on the strike. Only one of the instigators of the strike was black; but the rest were white. After the strike was broken up with tear gas, the guards kept saying to the white guys, "Whitey got ducked," and "What do you want with a fucking black warden?" That has created a lot of bitterness. [Account of a white inmate in his late twenties, November 1970.]

The view of the San Quentin strike expressed by most of the prisoners with whom I discussed it is totally different from that of the prison administration. What is impressive is that the accounts of white and black prisoners are generally the same, and very few prisoners have expressed any opposition to the strike. There is general agreement among the prisoners interviewed that most of the prisoner population supported the strike, even if they thought some of the demands were unrealistic or inappropriate. The fact that 800 inmates, or about 25 percent of the total population, actually sat down in the yard does not reflect the full extent of the support for the strike. Many prisoners were unable to join in because they were locked up in isolation, in the adjustment center, or in "close confinement" (segregation). Many others who supported the strike refrained from participating because they had parole dates or had hopes of getting a date the next time they went before the board. Participation in the strike was seen by most prisoners as a sure way of having a parole date canceled.

The prisoner's view of the strike is very different from that of the captain of the custodial officers, who said that only a dozen or so inmates really supported the strike, the rest being intimidated, or that of one associate warden, who viewed the strike as limited to a hard core of militants being used by political forces outside of the prison. As one white prisoner put it: "Everything always gets started by a few. But things always peter out unless they gain support among a large number of prisoners. A small group of prisoners simply cannot intimidate the majority of prisoners. I'm not saying that there was no pressure at all, but there weren't any real threats that I know of. In the strike Warren Wells organized things calling for 'Blue Power' [i.e., Prisoner Power—prisoners in California wear blue clothing]. It was not at all antiwhite or pro-Panther." The fact is that one-quarter of the prisoners joined the strike actively, and probably most of the remaining prisoners were sympathetic to the action.

Prisoners and officials also differ in their interpretation of the warden's role in the events. One associate warden reported that the warden read the demands over the loudspeaker and tried to convince the prisoners to disperse. The account of most of the prisoners interviewed was quite different:

Everyone supported the strike, at least until the warden spoke over the loudspeaker. The warden said over the prison radio and the loud speaker, "You guys must go to work or you will be locked up." The warden told the strikers that they were striking for a black warden and said, "You don't really want a black warden, do you?" The strike was really against holding a court within the prison and not for a black warden, but the warden wanted to make a racial thing out of it. The strike leaders had run off a manifesto illegally in the print shop and distributed it to the cells, so we knew what the real demands were and everyone supported most of them. [Account of a white prisoner, age twenty-five.]

While it is true that some of the prisoners interviewed felt that a few of the demands were "ridiculous," particularly the demands for the release of political prisoners and the end of capital punishment, none of the prisoners thought that these were the core of the demands. Also, only one of the prisoners I spoke to felt that the strike was organized by outsiders and that the prisoners had been used for ulterior ends. Most felt that the demands were entirely sincere, and most shared the grievances expressed in the demands. (Although most of the white prisoners did not particularly support the demands for non-white prison officials, only a few whites were strongly against those demands.) They all took the strike seriously; not merely as using "political labels for plain orneriness."

The seriousness of many of the prisoners in the strike is reflected in the preamble to the manifesto that was distributed to the prisoners the night before the strike took place:

Brother Convicts, the seed has been planted to Strike, to Strike for what? Isn't it so grandly expressed, in words & Deeds, every second of the minute by our keepers. First, it's the Officers in charge, angels to the gods, who believe they can do no wrong; then there's the god who says, "I know I'm doing wrong, but until the People tell me different, I can't change anything." Men, you Convicts, you Human-beings, the People are telling this corrupted part of

our society: "No more, stop the taking of human rights."
What more proof do you want that the People, our People,
want Justice! Cops are getting killed everyday, etc., Revolution, Protesting for us.

Right now things are definitely not normal, but here in
S.Q. we have the angels & the god with the West-Block &
North-Block minority to back them up against us. Sure,
they'll threaten us with taking of Board Dates, Etc., Etc.,
Etc., and segregation, further degradation of Human Right
& Human Dignity. Here, take my privilege card, take the
West-Block & North-Block, take everything that's used to
institutionalize me, giving Convicts extra years in prison
because the "Goodship Lollipop is running smoothly." Yes,
they'll probably break the strike but the seed has been
planted again and it'll grow, for many Convicts are realiz-
ing that the cause is Right, that the taking of Human rights
& Slavery were abolished many, many years ago. If you
can't see the light, stay in the darkness where you'll not be
seen or heard. Black, White, Brown Convicts, Blue Power,
the saying is, "We shall overcome," by peacefully being
slaves no longer & peaceful is until it's not Suicide and
there's no other way. . . .

HELP US HIT THEM WHERE IT HURTS, IN THEIR
POCKET. . . .

RACISM IN PRISON LIFE

One of the crucial issues highlighted by the prisoners' accounts of the San Quentin strike is racism within the prison
system. The prison administration readily asserts that racism
exists among the prisoners. They will even admit, if pressed,
that there are a few guards who might be racist. As one associate
warden put it, "No matter how hard we try, an occasional racist
guard slips through." But the administration denies that racism
is in any way an implicit part of prison policy or that it is a
general phenomenon among the prison staff.

As far as the prisoners are concerned, black, brown, and
white, racism is a pervasive fact of prison life. Many of the
prisoners interviewed felt that racism is systematically encour-

aged by the prison officials. A number of prisoners reported that the unity of the strike was broken basically through racist tactics by the prison administration. As one young black prisoner reported: "Warren Wells here was the first man in the history of San Quentin to unite whites and blacks. The prison didn't know how to handle that. All they could do was to try to make the strike into a racial thing. Nelson [warden of San Quentin] said to everyone that whites should follow whites, not blacks, and he said that the strike was for a black warden. It was only then that the unity began to break down."

Furthermore, many white prisoners (including several from the South) reported that in the aftermath of the strike it was common for white guards to needle the white prisoners for having been taken advantage of by the blacks. Typical remarks by the guards (as reported by the prisoners) included: "Whitey got ducked," "The niggers sure ran a game on you," "You whites really got suckered by them niggers." "This has made for a lot of bitterness and tension since the strike," one white prisoner stated about six weeks after the strike. "The guards do this because racism is the best way to control the inmates."

Racism, then, is seen by at least some prisoners as a strategy used by the prison administration to keep the prisoners divided, to prevent the emergence of prisoner unity. This view was expressed not just by black prisoners, but by white and Chicano prisoners as well:

> Most of the whites here don't want racial conflict. There is only a small minority that really push the racial hatred, the Nazis and the Angels [Hell's Angels]. Whenever there is a fight, the administration of the prison says that it is "black against white"; they don't say that it was only the Nazis who were fighting. They make it a racial thing between all the whites and all the blacks to scare people and to keep us divided. [Account of a black prisoner in his early thirties.]

> Whenever we get together, the administration brings up

race to divide us. The blacks have been very progressive pushing for changes, but some times they make very frivolous demands, like for a black warden, and the administration plays on this to divide the prisoners. A black warden would be just like a white warden, just as beholden to the power in Sacramento as any white warden. [Account of a white prisoner in his forties.]

Strikes can have a positive effect if you are together. But the bulls don't give us any time for organizing. They condone small groups that split us up, like the Nazis, but not any larger groups that include different races. Divide and conquer is the way that they run this place. [Account of a Chicano prisoner in his mid-twenties.]

While not all prisoners accept the view that racism is part of a conscious strategy to prevent unity among the prisoners, most of the prisoners interviewed stated that racism by the prison staff was commonplace. The prisoners at San Quentin reported a wide range of actions which they considered racist. On one level there was petty harassment:

Harassment on hair length is really a big thing now. It comes down every day. There are movies on the weekends. The guards let white guys go in if their hair is longer than the regulation, but if a brother's hair is too long, he is not let in. His I.D. card is taken and he has to get his hair cut. It is a constant petty harassment. It used to be against the Muslims because they shaved their heads and that wasn't allowed. Now it is against us for having naturals. [Account of a black prisoner in his early twenties; this observation was confirmed on two separate occasions by white prisoners.]

There is a real harassment of the black inmates by the guards. After the strike there was one black prisoner who was caught with four or five knives on him. After that there were constant shakedowns in the yard. The blacks were really shook down hard, but the whites were only superficially searched. Everyone was aware of this, that the blacks were being treated harsher. [Account of a white prisoner in his late twenties.]

There are always several lines of men lined up to go into the block. The lines are always more or less segregated. The guards always let the white lines go in before the blacks and Chicanos. The same is true for movies. The whites almost always go in first. When sheets and things are handed out, the black inmates often get the worst. I got a dirty sheet once that was torn in two. [Account of a black prisoner in his mid-twenties.]

Undoubtedly in some of these accounts there is a certain amount of selective perception by the prisoner concerned. If an individual expects to be discriminated against and then randomly is given a dirty torn sheet, he may perceive the situation as proof of racism by the guards. However, since the reports of such incidents were so frequent, and since they were reported by white prisoners as well as black prisoners, it seems likely that this kind of petty racial harassment is common within the prison.

Racism in the prison, according to many prisoners, is not limited to these instances of petty harassment. A number of black and white prisoners reported that blacks are often treated more severely than whites for the same infraction of the rules:

Two months ago a white guy working in the blue room [where prison clothing is handed out] was found with a balloon of stuff [a balloon filled with heroin]. He was just suspended for two days and then was back on the job without any punishment. A brother was found with a kit without any stuff. He was fired from his job and sent to the hole. Things always come down heavier on the brothers . . . another thing is inflammatory literature. They only bust the brothers for that, never the Nazis. The Panthers hold lessons where they teach the Panther view on things. If you get caught with a lesson, you get busted. [Account of a black prisoner.]

The black prisoners are definitely hit harder than the white prisoners for the same offense. A guard will give a white prisoner a warning for something but will send a

black prisoner to the hole for the same offense. It happens
all the time. [Account of a white prisoner.]

The most serious accusation of racism made by prisoners at
San Quentin is that prison officials deliberately encourage racial
violence:

> The guards here stir up prisoners. There hasn't been a
> serious race riot here now for over a year and things were
> going pretty smoothly, but the guards started spreading
> rumors that the cells were going to be integrated just to
> make things tense. No one wants that. The whites do not
> want to live with the blacks, and the blacks don't want to
> live with whites. The guards come up to a white prisoner
> in his cell and say, "How would you like a black cell part-
> ner?" That gets the white prisoner up tight and increases
> the tensions in the prison. [Account of a white prisoner.]

> There was a fight between a black and white inmate.
> The black guy won the fight, even though the white guy
> put up a good fight. The guards said to the white inmates
> afterward, "Man, that black dude really dusted the white
> dude. I thought you white dudes could fight better than
> that." The guards said that because they hoped to start
> another fight. [Account of a Chicano prisoner.]

> Several months ago I overheard a white guard tell a
> white prisoner that the blacks in the East Block were arm-
> ing themselves to stick some white dude and that the
> whites should stick together to protect themselves. Late
> that day the same guard came up to me and took me aside
> and told me that the whites in the East Block were going
> to stick a black dude and that we should be careful. The
> rumors spread, and by that evening everyone was scared.
> When we left our cells the next morning the black and the
> white prisoners were ready to jump on each other if any-
> one made a wrong move, but somehow nothing happened
> that time. [Account of a black prisoner.]

Not only do prisoners feel that guards deliberately foment racial
conflict, but some prisoners report that guards actually help to
arm different groups of prisoners for the ensuing racial fights.

In the spring of 1971 there were some 20 stabbings at San Quentin, several of which resulted in death. One incident in the course of those stabbings was reported by several black and white prisoners:

> A few weeks ago a guard shook down this white prisoner and said that he was clean. A second guard came up and felt that the first guard had not done a thorough shake-down. So he shook down the prisoner also and found seven knives on him. The first guard was suspended for three days because of that. They tried to keep it quiet, but we all knew about it. I think personally that this can only mean that the guard who got suspended was trying to get those knives smuggled into the prison. [Account of a black prisoner who had been in San Quentin for nine years.]

> At San Quentin racism is so strong because the officials encourage it. They arm the whites. There is no question about that. One sergeant was suspended for a few days because he searched a white and let him pass, but the guy was searched again and was discovered to have three or four knives on him. There is no way that the sergeant could just not have detected those knives. Usually when a guard does this sort of thing, he gets away with it. At any rate, this sergeant is back on the yard again. [Account of a black prisoner.]

> I didn't see it myself, but I hear that there was a guard who got caught letting a guy in with some knives. A friend of mine saw it, and I think it is probably true. [Account of a white prisoner.]

Several black prisoners made the observation that in some of the stabbings, especially of black prisoners, "street knives" were used (i.e., knives purchased in stores rather than knives made by prisoners within the prison itself):

> The day I arrived at San Quentin a white dude got stabbed and then a whole series of stabbings followed. They went on and on. Some of the guys had Kresge knives, and you know that they didn't go over the walls to get them. [Account of a black prisoner.]

> In the recent stabbings, the brothers were stuck with street knives. They were given to the Nazis by the guards. That is the only way they could get a street knife. It couldn't come in through visits because they search you too carefully. [Account of a black prisoner.]

The strongest statement about guard complicity in stabbings came from a white prisoner who openly sided with the Nazi party in the prison and who felt that the guards were justified in giving weapons to certain white prisoners. He felt that most of the trouble in the prison was caused by the "niggers" and that it was necessary to "stick them occasionally to keep them in line":

> One of the niggers who stabbed a white was called Big Jim. We knew that he had done the stabbing. The day after he stabbed this white guy he went out to court on an appeal that he had filed before. A sergeant came up to one of the bike riders [Hell's Angels] and said to him: "We know that Big Jim did one of the stabbings. We would rather have him carried off to the hospital than have to try to make a real case against him in court for the stabbings. I'll see that nothing happens to you for doing this. I'll make it worth your trouble." The bike riders will be waiting for Big Jim when he gets back from court. I know the guy the sergeant talked to well. Everyone knows that he has been involved in sticking the spooks [blacks]. I know for a fact that he recently stabbed a nigger and killed him. If it weren't for guys like this, I think that the blacks would cause even more trouble than they do.

While it is probably only a small minority of prison officials who go this far, the unwillingness of the administration to take strong action against overt racism by guards and the racism implicit in many prison practices create an atmosphere conducive to staff involvement in racial violence.

A number of facts give considerable credibility to the prisoners' view of racism within prison. First of all, the vast majority of guards and officials at San Quentin are white. Even with the

best of intentions, a white prison establishment is likely to feel
less empathy with black prisoners than with white prisoners, to
be more suspicious of their actions, and to react more harshly
to their infractions of prison rules. Second, there is a disproportionate representation of blacks and Chicanos in the hole at San
Quentin. One counselor in the prison estimated that more than
70 percent of the prisoners in the hole were nonwhite compared to only 50 percent of the general San Quentin population.[1] Third, the perception that the prison officials are more
lenient with whites was expressed not only by black prisoners,
but by many white prisoners as well. Some white prisoners, of
course, strongly denied that there was any discrimination
against blacks. And one white prisoner even insisted that blacks
were treated more leniently than whites "because the prison is
afraid of blacks." Nevertheless, a majority of the white prisoners
interviewed expressed the feeling that blacks had a harder time
in prison than whites.

One final source of data strongly supports the prisoners' perception of racism within the prison. If racism were a significant
feature of prison life, it would be expected that black prisoners
would frequently serve longer prison terms before parole than
white prisoners convicted of the same offense. This is in fact the
case. Data are available for 3,692 white prisoners and 1,634
black prisoners paroled for the first time from the California
Department of Corrections in 1967 and 1968. This is about 85
percent of all black and white prisoners paroled for the first
time in those two years. In 1967 the median time served before
parole by white prisoners for all offenses was 26 months; for
black prisoners, it was 34 months.[2] In 1968 the figures were 32
and 36 months respectively. The figures are even more striking

1. This is only an estimate. Since no racial data are kept on disciplinary action,
it is not possible to make a more precise estimate.
2. Data for time served before parole is presented in terms of the "median"
time served, i.e., the time served by the "middle" prisoner in a list of prisoners
arranged from least to most time served.

TABLE 9
OFFENSE, ETHNIC GROUP, AND TIME SERVED
FOR Male FELONS PAROLED FOR THE FIRST TIME

Offense*	Median Time Served in months**			Number of Prisoners		
	White	Black	Chicano	White	Black	Chicano
1967						
All Offenses	26	34	33	2,332	997	619
Manslaughter	41	43	–	31	21	8
Robbery 1st	45	48	44.5	239	142	32
Robbery 2nd	36	36	39	102	83	19
Assault	36	36	35	63	56	29
Burglary 1st	36	41	–	56	24	9
Burglary 2nd	24	23	22	531	171	116
Grand Theft	23	24	23.5	117	54	32
Auto Theft	19	24	21	172	48	25
Forgery & checks	19	19	17	404	73	35
Rape	31	39.5	–	33	22	12
Opiates	38	48	44	49	47	134
Marijuana	26	36	36	135	120	77
1968						
All Offenses	32	36	36	2,066	908	543
Murder 2nd	76	64	–	29	19	5
Manslaughter	42	40	–	23	22	8
Robbery 1st	45	44	45	289	158	39
Robbery 2nd	36	36	36	122	73	15
Assault	34	36	31	67	54	34
Burglary 1st	39	48	–	49	19	13
Burglary 2nd	26	28	30	399	145	91
Grand Theft	24	29	33	93	37	16
Auto Theft	24	30	21	106	31	21
Forgery & checks	24	24	24	316	48	35
Rape	46	48	–	28	20	9
Opiates	43	42	48	67	38	114
Marijuana	30	36	36	118	109	77

* Only those offenses for which comparative data on black and white prisoners exist are given.

** No medians are given when there are less than 15 cases.

Source: *California Prisoners, 1968* (Sacramento; Department of Corrections), pp. 85–86.

for specific offenses (see Table 9). In 1967, for example, the median time served by whites for rape was 31 months; for blacks, 39.5 months. For marijuana offenses, the figures were 26 months and 36 months respectively. Taking the two years together, there are 25 offense categories for which data on the median time served of both black and white prisoners are available. Of these 25 offense categories, blacks served a longer median than whites in 15 cases, whites served longer terms than blacks in 5, and they served the same median sentence in 5 (see Table 10). Put in terms of individuals, 55 percent of the black prisoners paroled in 1967 and 1968, and 47 percent of the white prisoners, were in offense categories in which blacks served longer median terms than whites. However, only 28 percent of the white prisoners and 21 percent of the black prisoners were in offense categories in which whites served longer median terms than blacks. Furthermore, in those offenses in which blacks served longer median terms than whites, the black median was an average of 5 months longer than the white median, whereas in those few offenses in which whites served longer than blacks, the white median was an average of only 1.3 months longer than the black median.[3] The perception by black prisoners that they are held in prison longer than white prisoners convicted of the same offense is thus confirmed by the statistics published by the Department of Corrections.

These differences in time served cannot be explained away simply by saying that black prisoners tend to have longer prior records than white prisoners or that black prisoners cause more trouble in prison than white prisoners. While it may be true that

3. The averages of 5 months and 1.3 months represent numerical averages of the median time served by different race-offense groups. All of these data come from the official Department of Corrections publication, *California Prisoners*, for 1968.

TABLE 10

COMPARISON OF THE MEDIAN TIME SERVED FOR
BLACK AND WHITE PRISONERS
(1967–1968)

Offense Categories	Percent of each race in offense categories		Average of difference in medians
	WHITES	BLACKS	
OFFENSE CATEGORIES IN WHICH THE MEDIAN TIME SERVED BY BLACKS IS *LONGER* THAN FOR WHITES (1967: manslaughter, robbery 1st, burglary 1st, grand theft, auto theft, rape, opiates, marijuana; 1968: burglary 1st, burglary 2nd, grand theft, auto theft, rape, marijuana)	47.0%	54.6%	5 months
OFFENSE CATEGORIES IN WHICH THE MEDIAN TIME SERVED BY BLACKS IS *SHORTER* THAN FOR WHITES (1967: burglary 2nd; 1968: murder 2nd, manslaughter, robbery 1st, opiates)	25.4%	24.9%	1.3 months
OFFENSE CATEGORIES IN WHICH THE MEDIAN TIME SERVED FOR BLACKS IS THE *SAME AS* FOR WHITES (1967: robbery 2nd, assault, forgery; 1968: robbery 2nd, forgery)	27.6%	20.5%	—
	100%	100%	

SOURCE: Based on data in *California Prisoners, 1968* (Sacramento: Department of Corrections), pp. 85–86.

the average black man on the street is likely to have had more encounters with the law than the average white man, it is not true that the average black prisoner has a longer record than the average white prisoner. If anything, there is a slight tendency for black prisoners to have shorter records than white prisoners (see Table 11).

Similarly, while it may be true that blacks are convicted of more rule infractions than whites, there is no indication that they actually commit a greater number of infractions. Yet, even if they did, since the figures for time served before parole consist of *median* time served, it would be necessary that more than half of the blacks commit more infractions than more than half of the whites for this to explain their longer median time. Although some black prisoners may be "chronic troublemakers," there are no data whatsoever to indicate that this is true for anything approaching 50 percent of the black prison population.

A study of women prisoners in California, conducted by the Department of Corrections research division, also supports these general observations.[4] The study compares the median number of months served before first parole for black and white women prisoners, controlling for offense type, prior commitments, and narcotics history. The results indicate that there is a clear racial bias in the setting of prison terms for women (Table 12). Of the thirteen comparisons between black and white women prisoners in Table 12, black women served longer median terms than white women in 12 cases. In one instance the median time served by black women was a full year longer than for white women (narcotics offense with some narcotics history).

4. Unpublished study by Norman Holt. (Internal CDC memorandum dated June 17, 1971.)

TABLE 11

PRIOR PRISON RECORDS OF BLACK AND WHITE PRISONERS ADMITTED TO CALIFORNIA PRISONS IN 1970, by OFFENSE

OFFENSE	Percent of Prisoners with Prior Prison Records		Number of Prisoners	
	WHITE	BLACK	WHITE	BLACK
Murder, 1st	36.8	33.3	79	54
Murder, 2nd	19.2	13.5	68	54
Manslaughter	23.4	29.8	76	67
Assault	27.5	34.0	149	153
Robbery, 1st	43.3	31.9	344	290
Robbery, 2nd	39.9	36.7	158	136
Burglary, 1st	42.4	46.9	66	32
Burglary, 2nd	53.3	50.2	483	177
Larceny	50.6	50.8	164	65
Auto theft	43.7	34.6	126	55
Forgery	57.3	51.3	325	80
Receiving stolen property	52.8	39.7	91	31
Rape	25.8	22.5	62	62
Other sex offenses	32.1	20.0	112	20
Opiates	47.5	60.0	139	115
Marijuana	23.0	43.9	198	29
Dangerous drugs	24.4	32.4	201	34

Source: Computed from data supplied by the Bureau of Criminal Statistics, Sacramento, California.

The fact that black prisoners spend a longer time in prison before receiving a parole lends considerable support to the accusations of racism by prison officials made by both black and white prisoners at San Quentin. Racism is neither a rare phenomenon, as the prison authorities would like the public to

TABLE 12

TIME SERVED BY WOMEN PRISONERS IN CALIFORNIA

Median Time Served in Months by Women Prisoners in California before First Parole, by Race, Narcotics History, and Offense (1967–1968)

OFFENSE	No Narcotics History			Some Narcotics History		
	WHITE	BLACK	OTHER	WHITE	BLACK	OTHER
Manslaughter, robbery, assault	22	20	22.5	21.5	25.5	18
Forgery and checks	13	13.5	12	16	18.5	12
Narcotics	15	23.5	37	26	38	31.5
Burglary, theft and other	14	18	12.5	15	18	12.5

Median Time Served in Months by Women Prisoners in California before First Parole, by Race, Narcotics History, and Prior Commitments (1967–1968)

PRIOR COMMITMENTS	No Narcotics History			Some Narcotics History		
	WHITE	BLACK	OTHER	WHITE	BLACK	OTHER
No priors	15	18	21	(no/low priors combined below)		
Low priors	14	18	17	18.5	27	17
High priors	16	17	13.5	19	24	22

SOURCE: Department of Corrections Memordum, June 17, 1971, "Results of Study of Race and Time Served at C.I.W."

believe, nor simply a holdover from a previous era. It is a pervasive fact of prison life and an important element in the prison's efforts to control the lives of the prisoners.

RACISM AMONG PRISONERS

It would be an oversimplification to attribute all the racism within the prison to the Machiavellian designs of the prison establishment. Racism among prisoners would be a problem even if it were not actively encouraged by guards:

> On the streets I never was a racist. I was never down on the blacks. But here I have been forced to be a racist. I was told the first rule was that "you never talk with a black off the job." If you talked with a black you would be isolated by the rest of the whites and then attacked. The institution wants it that way because it makes it easier to control prisoners and it makes a strike almost impossible. But some of the prisoners don't need much encouragement from the institution. They made it perfectly clear to me when I got here that "if you associate with a nigger, we'll kill you." [Young white prisoner.]

> If there is a white sissy who hangs out with blacks, he gets it from the whites. The same goes for blacks. If they see a brother hanging around with whites they call him an Uncle Tom. [Black prisoner.]

The strongest racist sentiments of any prisoner interviewed came from a white prisoner (quoted previously concerning guards' complicity in racial violence) who strongly supported the prison Nazi party:

> Most of the blacks at San Quentin are mentally defective, lazy and vicious. I know that you disagree with me, but all you have to do is open your eyes and you will see. All that they want to do is play a game on whitey, live off of our backs. When I first got here ten years ago there was a real Nazi party with a real political outlook. If the spooks started anything, the Nazis went out and took care of things. They would stab a few spooks and get things under control so no real troubles would develop. If we had a strong party now, the blacks wouldn't start things so much. It really is the blacks or the Mexicans who start nearly all

of the trouble here. I know that for a fact. There was less race trouble ten years ago because of the Nazis. Since then they declined, and the race troubles have been steadily mounting.

Such virulent racism cannot be explained simply by the institutionalized racism of the prison. Many prisoners bring these attitudes with them and find prison a fruitful environment in which to act out their hostilities. But such flagrant, bitter racism is not characteristic of most of the prisoners I met at San Quentin. By and large, racism is the path of least resistance. It represents a response to the pressures and cues from the institution and the already existing racist relationships among the prisoners.

Recently, with the growth of a more sophisticated political awareness among some prisoners, there have been signs that racism may be breaking down and that interracial solidarity may be emerging, however feebly. The San Quentin strike of August, 1970, embodied an incipient form of this interracial unity, even though the strike ultimately collapsed amid racial conflict. The call for "Blue Power" was a statement of the class solidarity of prisoners across racial lines, and many men felt that for a short while Warren Wells managed to create some sense of solidarity. The strike at Folsom prison three months later (see Chapter 12) demonstrated even more impressively this new prisoner unity: for 19 days virtually all prisoners supported a strike and insisted upon its antiracist character.

A number of prisoners I spoke with at San Quentin expressed hope for the development of unity within the prison across racial lines. One Chicano prisoner who had already spent five and a half years in San Quentin said:

> Naturally, when you are put here and you've never lived with blacks before, you don't like them. But in the past couple of years people have begun to realize that you have to work together. . . . Soledad has been a good lesson here. They are not having race riots there anymore. People are

fighting the pigs, not each other. Soledad is getting a lot of publicity for that. Some crazy people here are saying we have to get a pig so that we can get some of this publicity. But most people are learning that we have to work together. Little by little we are getting things together, but the guards are always trying to break things up. If we get things together, we can get something, we can get what we want. If all of us refused to work, they would have to hire people to cook for us. They have to feed us something. I feel that if we had real unity we could win. It is going to take a while. People are used to hating, and that takes a while to get over. But we will, we will.

A white inmate expressed the same view:

I think that the racism between prisoners is getting a bit better. All the different races were together on the last strike, at least for a while. Still, the last killing in the prison was over race. A white homosexual who hanged out with the hams [blacks] was killed after selling knives to the hams. But I think that the different races will get along better in the future.

Most of the black prisoners interviewed were somewhat more skeptical about the emergence of any real unity among prisoners of different races, but several expressed some hope. One young black who strongly identified with the black militants in the prison said:

White prisoners are so naïve. They are easily used by the prison officials. The black prisoners are really much more aware of what goes on here. I guess they learned it on the streets. Most of the white prisoners don't want racial fights, but they don't understand the political forces in the prison. That is what makes it so difficult for us to get together. Perhaps as their political consciousness changes it will be easier.

For the moment at least, even if there are signs that racism among prisoners may be giving way to greater unity, racism is still one of the dominant features of human relationships within prison. The causes for this racism are essentially the same as the causes on the outside. Many prisoners bring racist attitudes with them into the prison. Once inside the walls, prisoners experience enormous frustration and insecurity in their own lives, and many whites displace the hatred and anger generated by the social situation onto blacks and Chicanos as the most available scapegoats. They feel impotent to attack their real enemies, so they attack the blacks instead.

But this is only a partial explanation for racism among prisoners. Such attitudes are positively encouraged by guards through rewards for racist behavior. If a white prisoner is openly antiracist he is immediately considered a radical by the prison and is likely to be harassed by the guards as well as by other white prisoners. Since the approval and support of the guards is important for gaining one's freedom, racism has positive survival value for the individual white prisoner. It is only as white prisoners resist these pressures and develop a sense of their common interests with prisoners of all races that racism among the prisoners will significantly decrease. Until then, racism will remain an effective tool of social control within the prison.

PATTERNS OF SOCIAL CONTROL AT SAN QUENTIN [5]

Racism is only one of the strategies of social control within the prison. Three other strategies were seen by many prisoners as

5. For a different treatment of the problem of social control within the prison, see Richard Cloward, "Social Control in Prison," in *Theoretical Studies of the Social Organization of the Prison* (Social Science Research Council, 1960). Cloward argues that the central mechanism of social control centers on the prison's regulation of inmate access to the scarce goals of wealth, power, and status within the prison. A prisoner elite emerges which, in Cloward's analysis, has a strong stake in the status quo and which therefore acts to control the rest of the prisoner population. "The inmate elite," Cloward argues, "constitutes the single most important source of social control in the prison." While there is some truth in Cloward's analysis, I think that he greatly underestimates the direct effectiveness of coercion and the threat of coercion as control mechanisms within prison.

being particularly important: (1) the system of privileges and status stratification within the prison; (2) the disciplinary procedures; (3) the operation of the indeterminate sentence and of the Adult Authority.

Most of the prisoners interviewed saw the privilege system as a method of control employed by the prison authorities. Only two prisoners expressed any gratitude whatsoever for a privilege "given" to them by the prison or felt that the prison was justified in withholding privileges from prisoners. One white prisoner described the system this way:

> The West Block is the honor-honor block. They are given the most important jobs in the custody office with the highest pay. They also get the most privileges: there are no guards, they have real playing cards, they can have their own radios, their doors are always unlocked, and so on. A committee of inmates supervises the block so that they keep the place in order. They give people warnings so that they don't get write-ups as easily as in the rest of the prison. The administration likes all of this. It makes the public think that things aren't so bad: if you are a good prisoner you get to have all of these privileges. But really all it is is a control tool. The people in the West Block are unwilling to risk their privileges. That separates them from the rest of the population. . . . The prison can always count on the West Block prisoners to break a strike. People are always afraid of losing their little privileges, the crumbs they give us. That is what breaks up unity in the prison. They threaten to take away the crumbs. But if we were really together, they couldn't do it.

A black prisoner put it more bluntly:

> Fear is a big thing here. The Man is so down on the militants that he has people scared. He gives them some nice things to pacify them and they say, "Man, I don't want to lose this." I am in the South Block. A dude in the honor block thinks that he has something to lose. But he is still in prison, so he is really fooling himself. Now they are starting

a conjugal visiting program. That is going to be just another way they will try to pacify us, to divide us. They will use it as another privilege which people will be afraid of losing. We have to say fuck all these privileges. We have got to get together.

The preamble to the San Quentin strike (see p. 105) reflects the bitterness of the politically conscious prisoner regarding the system of privileges in the prison: ". . . here in S.Q. we have the angels & the god with the West-Block and North-Block minority, to back them up against us. . . . Here, take my privilege card, take the West-Block & North-Block, take everything that is used to institutionalize me. . . ." While not every prisoner interviewed had this hostile a view of the honor blocks and the privilege system, nearly all prisoners felt privilege stratification was oppressive.

The prison administrators at San Quentin feel that disciplinary procedures are reasonably fair. Most of the prisoners interviewed had a very different view. One white prisoner in his middle forties, who had spent considerable time in California prisons, expressed the general view of prisoners:

> The disciplinary hearings here are a farce, a real kangaroo court. They decide that you are guilty and then hold a hearing so that the public thinks that they are fair. A guard can dislike you because you don't laugh at his jokes and trump up some charge against you. He can say that you refused to obey an order or something, or that you have a "bad attitude." And so you'll get thrown into the hole for a week or so. If you deny the charge, who are they going to believe? A prisoner or a guard? You can't cross-examine your accuser, you can't call witnesses. It is your word against his, and you suffer because he doesn't like you. That happens all the time.

A number of prisoners related personal accounts of what they considered to be arbitrary disciplinary actions against them:

On the Wednesday before my parole date I overslept for approximately 15 minutes during the noon lunch break and was given a CDC 115 [the official write-up for a disciplinary infraction] for sleeping during work hours. That same day there was another inmate who was caught trying to smuggle a letter out of the ranch and he was just warned. But then, he was a white inmate. They didn't do anything to him. I asked the guard to consider the fact that I had a parole date for the following Monday and that I hadn't had a write-up for 18 months and that I had been down for almost four years. But he wouldn't listen. He felt that he had to show his authority and so he wrote me up. The 115 read: "Inmate _____ has received a disciplinary for being asleep when he should have been on his job and I am sending him in for this."

I appeared before the disciplinary committee the following day, Thursday, at 8:30 A.M. with the associate warden for custody. The hearing lasted about five minutes. The associate warden told me that he was going to cancel my parole date and refer me back to the parole board. The committee also gave me 30 days loss of privileges and five days in the hole which they suspended. That means that I am not going to get out next Monday. The associate warden told me that he would recommend to the board that they give me a new date, but who knows what they'll do. They are making me stay in this place for at least a month just because I overslept for 15 minutes. In Susanville where I had been, they would have never have been that strict. [Account of a young black prisoner; the story was told to me the day after the disciplinary hearing in question.]

I attend night classes and therefore need to have my cell opened for night movement. That has become a real hassle every night. I moved from cell 504 to cell 505 because I wanted to be on the bottom bunk. But the guards' schedule still says to open cell 504 for night movement and not cell 505. I tell them that I moved from one to another, but they won't listen. I have gotten two write-ups so far for not going to classes, but it was because I was locked up. The guards have told me that if I keep arguing with them every night they will send me to the hole for disrespect of an officer. But if I miss another night of classes, I will get sent to the hole for missing three in a row. They just won't listen. [Account of a white prisoner, late twenties.]

I got locked up on March 31 for agitating. I had nothing to do with any agitating. Everyone knows that. I have been really a loner and haven't got involved in any of the strikes. But some of the guards, especially one lieutenant, dislike me, and that is why I got locked up. They were just waiting for an excuse. I was told it was because I was an agitator and that I had a bad attitude, but I haven't gotten a 115 for anything and there wasn't a hearing or anything. This is wrecking my whole program in school, but there is nothing I can do about it. [Account of a black prisoner, early twenties.]

Incidents such as these were reported by so many prisoners, and I personally witnessed enough examples of arbitrary discipline during disciplinary hearings, that these accounts can be assumed to be reasonably accurate. Most important in the present context, however, is that these accounts reflect the prisoners' general perception of disciplinary procedures which are seen as arbitrary, vindictive, and unjust. What to the prison officials is a necessary and legitimate act to maintain order becomes to the prisoner an oppressive act of brute force.

While the privilege stratification system and the disciplinary procedures are the most important day-to-day instruments of social control within the prison, the indeterminate sentence is the most important long-term mechanism. Most prisoners appear before the Adult Authority once a year, except in cases in which the prisoner's minimum sentence is long. These appearances are experienced with great tension by most prisoners; their freedom hangs in the balance. One prisoner described the Adult Authority: "The people on the board are God and they know it. They have you in their hands. They control your salvation, your heaven and your hell. Once a year you stand before

that God and they decide whether or not you stay in hell for
another. And that God is unpredictable. That is the way it is. I
just don't know how to get around it. You never really know
what they want."

The Adult Authority hearings I attended were held in a large
room just inside the main gate of the prison. Two members of
the AA and one San Quentin counselor, whose job it was to
record the proceedings of the hearings, sat behind a long table
in the center of the room. During each hearing, one AA member would interrogate the prisoner while the other member
would read the dossier of the next prisoner to appear before the
board. Most of the hearings I attended lasted about ten minutes,
although one of them went on for nearly half an hour. During
the hearing, each prisoner was asked about a wide variety of
issues: his goals, his original offense, his attitudes toward the
prison, his disciplinary record. Of these, the disciplinary record
was generally looked at first, given the most weight, and often
discussed at the greatest length. The prisoners are very much
aware of this emphasis. One black prisoner told me: "It is hard
to know what the board expects of you. How hard you work on
your job or in school doesn't seem to matter very much. One
disciplinary infraction can wipe out a whole year's good work
reports. They see a recent 115 in your jacket and they think that
this means you are still a criminal and that you need more time
to mend your ways."

Many prisoners see their relationship to the Adult Authority
as a deadly serious game in which the AA is trying to keep them
locked up and they are trying to convince its members that they
are "rehabilitated." The trick is to figure out exactly what you
need to do to prove this to them:

> Most prisoners at San Quentin spend a lot of time trying
> to figure out what they have to do to get out of here. Very
> few people try to change themselves or seriously look at
> themselves while they are here. They try to outwit the
> Adult Authority, to make them think that they are making

progress and have reformed. [Account of a white prisoner in his thirties.]

When I first got here I knew that I would serve at least five or six years. I was a three-time loser and had a five-to-life sentence, so I figured that the best I could hope for was five years. So what I did was deliberately get a lot of write-ups during my first two years. I probably spent half of my time in the hole, always for petty things. I'd swipe some extra food from the lunch line or report late for work. So I built up a terrible disciplinary record. Then in my third year here I got only a couple of beefs. And since then I have had a clean record. I figure the Adult Authority will look at this and think that I am "improving," that I have learned my lesson. I go to the board next month with four and a half years down and two years without a 115, so maybe I'll get a date. [A white prisoner.]

Frequently, prisoners feel that whatever they do they will be damned by the board:

I was sent to prison for possession of marijuana. So far I have done two and a half years. The last time I went to the board they asked me if I believed in legalizing marijuana. Now how am I supposed to answer that? If I say "no" they will just assume that I am lying; if I say "yes," they will think that I intend to continue to break the law when I get out and that I am not rehabilitated. I told them that I thought the penalties were too severe but that I didn't know whether it should be legalized or not. They denied me a year. [A white prisoner.]

For three years I was the model prisoner. I had perfect work reports. I graduated from high school and was taking college courses. I didn't have any disciplinary infractions except for one or two very minor things. I stayed away from the militants. I went regularly to therapy programs— group therapy, Alcoholics Anonymous, and even a Yokefellow group. So when I went to the board after three years I felt positive I would get a date. The Adult Authority shot me down a year. They said that they didn't feel I was sincere. They said that I was just con-wise and was playing a game with them. Now I don't know what to do. If I get any write-ups or stop going to therapy, they will take this as proving that I was faking it before. But if I don't do anything new, they will just say the same thing next year. [A black prisoner.]

One theme pervaded most of the Adult Authority hearings I attended: the members of the board were looking for indications that the prisoner felt remorse for his crime. When one prisoner responded to the question, "Do you regret that you committed the burglary?" by saying, "I didn't do it," the head of the hearing told him: "We are not a court that is going to retry your case. We must assume that you are guilty of the crime. You are only hurting yourself by denying it." After the prisoner left the room, one of the members of the board remarked: "This man obviously doesn't feel the slightest remorse for what he did. He is hostile and bitter towards the prison. It seems to me that he needs more time to think things over."

Prisoners perceive this attitude on the part of the Adult Authority. One prisoner observed: "The Adult Authority doesn't care how many positive things you have done in prison. They don't care if you graduate from high school or learn a trade. What they want is for you to feel guilty for your crime. They want prisoners who are conformists, whose spirits have been broken. What they can't take is a man with pride." George Jackson, in his book *Soledad Brother,* expressed the same feelings to his lawyer:

> An individual leaves his individuality and any pride he may have behind these walls. . . . No one walks into the board room with his head up. This just isn't done! Guys lie to each other, but if a man gets a parole from this prison, Fay, it means that he crawled into that room. . . . No black will leave this place if he has any violence in his past until they see that thing in his eyes. And you can't fake it, resignation—defeat, it must be stamped clearly across the face.[6]

6. George Jackson, *Soledad Brother* (New York: Bantam Books, 1970) p. 161.

If a prisoner wants a parole—and virtually all prisoners desperately want to leave prison—he must at some time make his peace with the Adult Authority. He has to decide to play the game according to the rules laid down by the prison, to show the "proper respect" for prison authority, to conform to the demands of prison rules regardless of how arbitrary they may be or how arbitrarily they may be enforced. If he does these things well enough—convincingly enough—he will be rewarded with privileges within the prison and, ultimately, with a parole date from the Adult Authority. If he refuses to accept that role, to conform to those demands, then he will lose those privileges, probably spend a great deal of time in isolation, and be denied a parole year after year.[7]

REHABILITATION

The hallmark of the "enlightened" liberal prison is its rehabilitation programs. Nearly all the prisoners interviewed felt that the rehabilitation programs at San Quentin were almost worthless. One prisoner used exactly the same words as had a counselor to describe the rehabilitation programs in the prison: "Rehabilitation is a farce." A Black Muslim prisoner put it even more strongly: "There is no rehabilitation at San Quentin, just mass slave labor. The only reason for prison is social revenge. When Reagan asks for money for prisons, it is not to make things better, but to lock up more men to make more money for the state through slave labor."

Another prisoner, describing the college program at the prison, stated: "This college thing is a real hoax. It is bullshit that

7. In late 1971 the Adult Authority instituted a new policy granting nearly every prisoner a "contingency parole date." In some cases these are granted as far as three or four years in the future. However, the prison can lift the parole date at any given time if the prisoner commits a disciplinary infraction. In effect, the Adult Authority has given the prison authorities even more direct control over the granting of paroles to inmates, and has thus made the indeterminate sentence an even more effective instrument of social control.

they tell the public. They don't tell the public that the program is so crowded that you can only take one course at a time. The only thing I can take this summer is Health Education because everything else is filled up. The industries program is also a hoax because most of the skills are way outdated. It is nothing, nothing whatsoever."[8] "How," one prisoner asked, "can the prison hope to rehabilitate people by hitting them over the head? How can we benefit from an educational program when we are told not to think?"

These criticisms by prisoners of the rehabilitation programs do not mean that they gain nothing at all from them. Many prisoners do in fact get high school diplomas, some prisoners learn a trade they continue to use on the outside, and a few prisoners undoubtedly benefit from the therapy programs. The overwhelming majority of prisoners I spoke with, however, feel that the rehabilitation programs are of little value and that the overall setting of the prison negates the value of even the better programs.

Yet, even if the impact of prison does not come through any of the formal rehabilitative programs, it can sometimes be positive in terms of the individual's development. George Jackson put it this way: "[Prison] brings out the best in brothers—or it destroys them entirely. But none are unaffected. None who leaves here is normal. If I leave here alive, I'll leave nothing behind. They'll never count me among the broken men."[9]

A number of prisoners expressed the feeling that before they went to prison they had never had time to stop and look at themselves, to evaluate their lives and the world around them:

> I guess I have gotten something out of prison. Prison has given me a chance to pause and reflect. Outside I didn't have time. I was always on the run. In here I have time to

8. As has already been pointed out in Chapter 4, this observation on the lack of value of the industries program was strongly confirmed by a study made by the California Assembly Office of Research.
9. *Soledad Brother*, p. 32.

think. That's something at least. [Account of a white prisoner, early twenties.]

The only positive time here is when you are lying alone
on your bunk, reminiscing and thinking about yourself and
what is happening to you. When your head is on your
pillow is the only constructive time here. That is the only
time you can really be sincere with yourself. All the rest of
the time you have to play games. A man has a lot of thinking time in a penitentiary, and if there is anything good
that comes out of this, it is because of that. But you don't
have to be treated this miserably to think. [Account of a
black prisoner, early thirties.]

Nearly every prisoner asks himself in some way: "Why is this
happening to me?" The prison has a ready-made answer, which
some prisoners accept: "This is happening to you because you
are sick, because you are weak, impulsive, unable to act responsibly. We are here to help you." Many—perhaps most—prisoners reject this simple answer. Some chalk up imprisonment to
bad luck: "I am here because I got caught. I had a bad break."
Some answer the question by becoming deeply depressed in
prison, by withdrawing into fantasies and shutting out, as best
they can, the painful reality about them. Others never really
answer the question at all and take each day in prison as it
comes without trying to comprehend the meaning of the experience. An increasing number of prisoners, however, are answering this question in political terms. At San Quentin, this is
particularly true of black prisoners, but a surprising number of
whites and Chicanos as well are seeing their imprisonment as
the result of an unjust and oppressive society.

This view was clearly expressed by Eldridge Cleaver in 1965
and by George Jackson in 1970:

One thing that the judges, policemen and administrators
of prisons seem never to have understood, and for which
they certainly do not make allowances, is that Negro convicts, basically, rather than see themselves as criminals and
perpetrators of misdeeds, look upon themselves as prison-

ers of war. . . . Rather than owing and paying a debt to society Negro prisoners feel that they are being abused, that their imprisonment is simply another form of the oppression which they have known all their lives. Negro inmates feel that they are being robbed, that it is "society" that owes them, that should be paying them, a debt.[10]

Very few men imprisoned for economic crimes or even crimes of passion against the oppressor feel that they are really guilty. Most of today's black convicts have come to understand that they are the most abused victims of an unrighteous order.[11]

For many prisoners the experience of prison is one of utter defeat and despair, and they leave prison, in Jackson's words, "more damaged physically and mentally than when they entered." But for some, the time they spent in prison was crucial in the development of their self-awareness as members of an oppressed class. Some of these—like George Jackson, Eldridge Cleaver, Malcolm X—emerge from the experience of prison strengthened, with a new sense of purpose and dignity. They have been "rehabilitated" in a radical sense; it is unlikely that they would have become the men they did without the experience of prison.

MILITANTS AT SAN QUENTIN

It is very difficult to judge how prevalent radicalism is among prisoners in San Quentin. Relatively few openly declare that they are radicals. At San Quentin, in 1971, some 30 black prisoners publically proclaimed that they were Black Panthers. That is a small proportion of the black prison population, and the prison administration took this number as an indication that very few prisoners are militant. However, a far larger proportion of the prison population is sympathetic to the militant,

10. Eldridge Cleaver, *Soul on Ice* (New York: McGraw-Hill, 1968), p. 58.
11. *Soledad Brother*, p. 30.

radical position than are willing to openly express their views. The militant prisoners would like to think that they have the large majority of the prisoners behind them. While that may be wishful thinking, the least that can be said is that, contrary to the official line, more than a small minority of prisoners are sympathetic to the prison radicals.

The prisoners I interviewed at San Quentin broke down into four general categories in their attitudes toward militants: (1) some prisoners strongly supported the radical outlook of prison militants and their willingness to actively oppose the prison system from within; (2) some prisoners supported the general ideals of the radicals and the radical critique of the prison, but felt that it was foolish for a prisoner to attack the prison; (3) some prisoners were opposed to the ideals of the radicals; and (4) a few prisoners had no opinions at all about radicalism inside or outside the prison.[12]

The most militant inmates did not generally have any illusions about the possibilities of radically changing the prisons simply by staging a revolution within the walls. But they did feel strongly that revolutionary organization and action within the prison had a place in a broader revolutionary struggle. One black prisoner, who openly said that he was a Panther and was later transferred to Folsom prison, expressed his feelings this way:

> Attacking militant blacks here in prison and outside is just another way of putting fear in other blacks. That is their divide-and-conquer mentality. We call it "mental genocide." The great majority of the brothers on the yard are for us. The prison persecutes us because they know that the brothers respond to fear more than the desire to help

12. While I feel that most of the prisoners with whom I talked were fairly open in expressing their attitudes, many were undoubtedly somewhat suspicious of me. A prisoner would be taking a risk to openly endorse revolutionary activities, even to a volunteer student chaplain. Some of the prisoners who expressed criticism of militancy may have in fact been more sympathetic to prison radicals than they were willing to tell me.

their people. But we will continue to struggle because we know that we are right. But it won't be easy: they have all the guns. But we are willing to die for our cause and the pigs are not, and that gives us an advantage. When we come here, we don't expect to get out. We know that. We are just tired of always getting fucked over, so we are going to fight. Once you decide that, it doesn't matter so much whether you fight here or on the streets. If you fight on the streets, you'll end up back here anyway. We can't wait on the courts any more. If the shit does start, we will blow the top off. There will be a blood bath. If I got to be sacrificed to get action for my people, we'll do it.

Another young black inmate wrote an essay expressing the same feelings:

Being put in prison and having the pigs get on your case (and your head) you soon realize that if you stand up you are dead and if you tom you are a living dead man, so it is up to you to get yourself together and play the game, but with the idea that as you are playing you change the rules as the game progresses, and every chance that you get you change the game, and if you get caught then that's just tough shit, you knew what the hell would happen if you fight the system! That's why it's so important to never let your mind be locked up with your body; if you have a mind that is free then you are free—they have my body locked up, but my mind is free. The system will hold men for an eternity and let the toms and the shoe shuffler hit the bricks with this idea in mind that he is harmless and a damn fool, but the pig feels that if men with the ability to think for themselves were given the freedom that is rightfully ours, that we would take him and all like him straight to hell, because we have proven that we don't give a damn for the system. . . . I have a cause and if given an opportunity I will DIE, if that is what it takes to get FREEDOM for my Brothers and Sisters. Like I was afraid to come to this [San Quentin], but I have learned not to be afraid. The hell with death!, that is if it is for a cause. To die without reason or without taking care of business is no way for a man to die; he really died and went to hell for nothing. . . .

A white prisoner who had been transferred to San Quentin following the Susanville strike expressed similar views, but in a somewhat moderated form:

> On the outside I was very close friends with a lot of Hell's Angels. I wasn't actually a member, but I ran around with a lot of them. When I was in Susanville, I began to realize that you had to get political or else you would get screwed over. That is what I told my friends who were Angels, but a lot of them couldn't care less about politics. That is also why I participated in the Susanville strike. I got shipped out because of that. . . . I've been poor always. That is all there is in prison—poor people. I am beginning to realize that there is not a war on poverty in this country; there is a war on poor people. There is not much fanfare about it, but it is true. Poor people have to start fighting back. That is why they have prisons, and I guess that makes us all prisoners of war. People aren't buying this so much any more. We know we have to get together and fight back. . . . I had a parole date before the strike. After the strike I was asked why I got involved, since I had a parole date already set. I told them that I got involved because it was necessary. I wasn't threatened or anything. I chose to get involved. Sometimes you have to make personal sacrifices. It was absolutely necessary. I doubt if it will change anything up there, but I still had to be a part of the strike.

Relatively few prisoners I spoke with shared this militant a view. Many prisoners were willing to use radical rhetoric in criticizing the prison, but only a few were willing to openly support militant action within the prison and to say that they would participate or had already participated in such action. The most frequent attitude toward radicalism within the prison was that radical ideas made a lot of sense but it was pointless to be a militant in prison:

> You can be a militant here, but you really only hurt yourself. You can't change the system from the inside. The changes can only come from the outside. Once you know the way things function here, you only hurt yourself by

fighting things. Like, I have this little mustache here. If an officer comes up to me and tells me to take it off, I could say to him: "Fuck you, you are just a pig trying to control my life," and so on. I would be right, but what would happen? I would get a write-up and end up in the hole. So instead, I smile and am polite and say that I just forgot and that I will do it the next time I am in my cell. Then I forget again. You have to act that way here. [A black prisoner, mid-thirties.]

This place is a breeding place of revolutionaries. That is true, that is really true. Right now the blacks are predominant in this, but they are not really ready for it—they are going to try to kick off the revolution before people on the outside are ready for it, and so they will all get snuffed out. That doesn't make any sense. You can't change things in prison by fighting back; they can just lock you up and forget about you. [A white prisoner, early forties.]

My main interest is to get back to my wife and daughter. She is three now. If I stay here five years, she will be going on nine. I will miss the best part of her childhood. Some guys say to the board that they are revolutionaries. What good does that do? Sometimes you just have to lie, that's all. What difference does it make if you are a revolutionary and in here? You know the story of the oak and the weed: in the storm the oak is blown over, but the weed just bends. I just have to be a weed while I am here. I dig embracing the struggle, but there is nothing to embrace in here. [A black prisoner, early twenties.]

Most prisoners try very hard to do what is necessary to get out of prison, and they see militancy as hurting their chances for a parole. One black prisoner stressed this point:

When I first came here, I only knew two or three other people. They told me about various organizations in the prison. They said that you cannot afford to be a loner because if you are you'll get stuck. They told me that you needed a group to defend you. That is when I learned about the Panthers, the Nazis, and the other organizations on the yard. I dig a lot of what the Panthers talk about, but I always try to avoid those kinds of groups because I always try to think how the people who count will look at it. Here that means the Adult Authority. If they know you are with the militants, they'll just let you sit here.

In spite of this hesitancy on the part of most prisoners to become involved in radical politics within the prison, there are situations in which the militants can mobilize considerable support for their demands. In the San Quentin strike of August, 1970, some 800 prisoners sat down in the prison yard. Not all of those prisoners knew what the strike was about; some joined in because a friend was involved. But the fact that 25 percent of the prison population was willing to sit down certainly indicates that the militants are not an isolated group with no support from the general prison population.

Some prisoners, of course, are extremely hostile to the whole radical position. One white prisoner, who identified with the prison Nazis, expressed particular venom at the black militants (see p. 120 for his comments on blacks in general):

> The black militants use a lot of high-sounding rhetoric, but they really have only one aim, to kill off all of the whites in this country. They attack the country so that people will lose faith in it and thus it will be easier for them to take over. The blacks live off of the backs of the whites in this country, and yet they attack it as oppressing them. That is just a lot of horse shit.

Most prisoners who were critical of radical ideology did not express themselves in such racist terms. The most common rejection of radicalism was that it was a form of self-deception, a way of blaming others for one's own faults:

> So many people here at San Quentin refuse to see themselves as responsible. They blame the police, the courts, the prison for their condition, but they won't face themselves and see that they are really to blame. There is tre-

mendous bitterness here, especially among the radicals, it
seems. They feel bitter at the prison because they deny
their own guilt. I'm not bitter. I did wrong. I broke the law.
I did about as low a thing as you could do. But I'm not
bitter, because I needed the punishment. I have had the
chance to look into myself and grow as a result. [A white
prisoner, mid-thirties.]

A man goes to prison because God punishes him for his
sins. Every man in here is a sinner, every one. Some prisoners say that prison is wrong or that society is to blame for
them being here. They blame everything they can except
themselves. God would not send a man here unless he had
sinned. [A black prisoner, early forties.]

Finally, there were a few prisoners who either had no opinions
about radicals whatsoever or were unwilling to discuss them.
When asked what his feelings were about prisoners who called
themselves revolutionaries, one white prisoner replied: "I don't
know nothing about that. I keep to myself and I don't want any
trouble." Such views were rare.

Whatever the actual strength of the radicals in the prison, one
thing seems clear: their support is growing, their sophistication
is increasing, and they are likely to be more active and "troublesome" as time goes on. On this last point both prisoners and
prison staff seem to agree. Where they differ is in their notions
of the causes of this unrest and the implications it has for prison
policies. The prisoners see the causes lying in the fundamental
injustice and oppressiveness of the criminal justice system and
the society at large. From the militant prisoners' perspective,
the implication for policy is that the prison and the society must
fundamentally change their priorities or else there will be, in
the words of one black prisoner, "a blood bath." The prison
officials, on the other hand, generally see the causes lying in the
impulsiveness and irresponsibility of prisoners and in agitation
from the outside. The implication for policy, in their eyes, is that
prison discipline has to be tightened.

THE MODUS VIVENDI
BETWEEN GUARDS AND PRISONERS

The militants in prison may be growing in number and importance, but they are still a minority, even if they have many silent sympathizers. Most prisoners, most of the time, cooperate, at least passively, with prison officials. They may feel much resentment and bitterness, and it may take constant reminders of the force at the disposal of the prison to keep them in line, but most prisoners try to do their time with a minimum of conflict with the prison establishment and a minimum of friction with other prisoners.

An important element in the modus vivendi of the prison system centers on the relationship of the prison population to the guards. The power of the prison is embodied in the guards. They are the agents who lock and unlock the cells, who fire the guns and tear gas, who write the disciplinary infractions, and who, in the end, have the greatest direct influence on the lives of prisoners. It is thus of crucial importance to the functioning of the prison what kind of unofficial relationships emerge between guards and prisoners.

Both guards and prisoners have the power to make each other's lives intolerable. If guards fully enforced prison rules, stamped out all illegal activity of prisoners, and cut off the supply of illegal goods within the prison (drugs, alcohol, grilled cheese sandwiches), prison life would become much harder to cope with for many prisoners. On the other hand, if prisoners resisted all of the orders of the guards, if they sabotaged the running of the prison, they would make the guards' job much more strenuous than it already is. As the captain of the custodial officials remarked: "We could not possibly control this place unless the large majority of inmates were on our side. If the inmates wanted to, they could take this place over in five minutes." It is in response to this shared desire to avoid unrestrained mutual harassment that the modus vivendi between guards and prisoners has evolved.[13]

An important element of this mutual accommodation is the complicity of guards in various underground prisoner activities. Several prisoners described this unofficial (often illegal) cooperation of guards and prisoners:

> People make wine here to make money. You have to live somehow in here. Some bulls see you doing it and leave you alone; they forget about it because they understand. They say, "It's OK; just don't front me off with it." When that kind of bull comes on, we treat him nice. But some are bad. They really fuck over the inmates, write them up for petty things all the time, take their I.D.'s. So we give them trouble in return. They don't understand the pressures on us and so they harass us all the time. With a good guard, nobody gets hassled at all. But with a dog, there is real tension all of the time. If there weren't a few guards who always looked the other way, this place would blow up. [A Chicano prisoner, mid-twenties.]

> For a year I worked in the gym. There were two guards there who were runners. They brought all sorts of stuff into the prison. One did it because he was a good guy; the other did it for money. He was eventually caught and busted for it. . . . When guys make pruno [prison-made wine] sometimes there is connivance by the cops. The other day I saw a cop with some inmates drinking pruno. It is pretty rare that it goes that far. Usually when they find the stuff they

13. Gresham Sykes, in *The Society of Captives* (Princeton, N.J.: Princeton University Press, 1958), presents a good discussion of the mutual accommodation patterns between guards and inmates. He concludes by saying, "The custodians . . . are under strong pressure to compromise with their captives, for it is a paradox that they can insure their dominance only by allowing it to be corrupted. Only by tolerating violations of 'minor' rules and regulations can the guard secure compliance in the 'major' areas of the custodial regime" (p. 58). Although Sykes sees that such accommodation is necessary for the stability of the power structure within the prison, he never explicitly states that the compromises themselves are predicated upon the essential totalitarianism of that power structure.

just dump it out and don't make a commotion about it. They bust people just often enough to show who runs things here, but not so often as to stop the stuff getting made. [A white prisoner with more than 10 years in San Quentin.]

Guards must cooperate with some prisoners making pruno because it is so easy to tell that it is being made. There are a lot of infractions of the rules which they just ignore. If they sent everyone to the hole for every infraction, there wouldn't be anyone left on mainline. When you get busted it is because they want to bust you. [A black prisoner, mid-twenties.]

The prison administration does not deny that such complicity by guards in illegal activities goes on. But the administration tends to regard this complicity as the result of prisoners' blackmailing guards and as a weakness in the functioning of the prison, rather than as part of the necessary accommodations of guards and inmates. One black prisoner explained the system of mutual accommodation in this way:

Guards can make life miserable for prisoners, and prisoners can make life miserable for guards. They both know this. Most people want things to go more or less smoothly, so each side makes concessions to the other. If a guard does a favor for me, then life will go easier for him; if I am discreet and don't cause him trouble, then life will be easier for me. That's how it works.

In most cases when guards take mail out for inmates it is a free act, a favor. It is not blackmail. Carrying letters out is their way of absolving themselves of guilt over what happens here. That is especially true of some of the black guards. They know what goes on here and they don't like it. They stay on because they feel that they can do something to help the brothers in prison. Some black guards are really pigs. One in particular is a superpig—worse than almost any of the most racist white guards. Some of the white guards also recognize what really goes on here and try to deal reasonably with you. Most guards don't want a lot of hassle, and that means that they are willing to make concessions to at least some prisoners. Only a few treat you really decently, however. Most of them still treat us like inferiors, like animals.

The result of this pattern of mutual accommodation is that, although prisoners who openly oppose the system are dealt with very harshly, inmates who make the appropriate concessions to the prison establishment are often tacitly allowed to engage in many semilegal or illegal activities. One young white prisoner told me:

> The prisoners really run this place except for custody. You can get anything you want as long as you pay for it. You can even get into the North Block, the honor block, if you have a friend who is a clerk in the right office or if you bribe the clerk who handles the paperwork for the block. The clerk will either operate around the officer in charge of the block, or through him. At any rate, for a few cartons of cigarettes you can get into the honor block.

A black prisoner with six years San Quentin residence explained:

> Everything in the prison is a big racket. Cigarettes are the money in prison. Everything is bought and sold with cigarettes. Some guys make grilled cheese sandwiches on the tiers and if you want one you have to buy it with cigarettes. You can even get someone killed if you want for a few cigarettes.

Just as most prisoners passively cooperate with the operation of the prison power structure, most guards generally passively cooperate with the operation of the inmate power structure. The problem is that this modus vivendi is not very stable. On the guard's side, there are always some guards who are extremely strict and who will give any prisoner a write-up for any infraction, and other guards who may be lenient with a few prisoners, but who are very harsh with others. If certain guards do not respect the tacit accommodation between prisoners and guards, it is more difficult for other guards to function according to the mutual concessions.

On the prisoner's side, the modus vivendi breaks down because the prison underground itself generates considerable violence. Many of the stabbings within the prison are the result of unpaid debts for drugs or gambling losses. Competition for power between different Mafioso-type groups sometimes erupts in violence. Even if the guards were willing to tolerate a certain amount of violence among prisoners, the prison administration, for political reasons, cannot, and whenever violence erupts, the administration comes down very hard on the prisoner population.

More fundamentally, the mutual accommodation between prisoners and guards is unstable because many prisoners know it is sham. It is "mutual" only in a very limited sense: the guards tacitly agree not to make life for the prisoners totally miserable if the prisoners agree not to cause the guards too much trouble. But the prisoners are still prisoners, and the "freedom" created by the modus vivendi in the prison is, to most prisoners, totally empty. An increasing number of prisoners see the "mutual" accommodation as another technique of pacifying the prison population, of manipulating the prisoner's condition so that he accepts it and won't fight back. They see the modus vivendi— like racism, privileges, disciplinary procedures, and the indeterminate sentence—as a device to keep prisoners from resisting their own oppression. With that realization, the modus vivendi within the prison becomes increasingly precarious.

THE MEANING OF PRISON IN THE LIVES OF PRISONERS

The essential reality of prison for virtually all prisoners is the absence of freedom. This means many different things: you cannot have sexual intercourse with a woman; you cannot eat what you want; you cannot wear what you want; and above all, you cannot go where you want. The loss of freedom means that you are divested of responsibility for your life—everything is done for you, all decisions of importance are outside your control. You are utterly powerless, subject to the arbitrary will of others. The loss of freedom in prison means regimentation: eating at a certain time, getting up at a certain time, locking up at a certain time. The prisoner is constantly reminded of his total lack of freedom, and the awareness of his subjugation becomes a central motif in his life:

> Freedom is the only meaningful thing to a human. Without freedom things lose meaning. The whole system in prison is designed to degenerate a human being, to break him as a man. They take away all of his freedom, his freedom to express himself and his feelings. How can you be human if you can't express yourself? The indeterminate sentence gives the authorities tremendous control over a man's freedom: you are at their mercy and are really impotent to do anything about it. [A black prisoner, early thirties.]

> The worst thing here is the way your life is regulated, always regulated, day in and day out. They tell you what to do almost every moment of the day. You become a robot just following instructions. They do this, they say, so that you can learn to be free on the outside. [A white prisoner, early twenties.]

Prisoners view their deprivation in very different ways. Some regard it as a personal cataclysm. They see their entrance into prison as marking a total rupture in their lives; prison and the "outside" are seen as two totally different worlds:

> Life here becomes a dichotomy, a dichotomy between the inside and the outside. The outside is "real life"; the inside is unreal. But after a while this place gradually becomes reality and the outside becomes unreal. And eventually you get lost. . . . I'm a twenty-seven-year-old

man, I'm tired; I'm righteous tired. I've been in here seven
and a half years now, and I'm just tired to the bone of it.
[A black prisoner.]

When you come in here, your life stops for you. This is
not life; it is a void in life. But life continues on the outside,
and the longer you are in here, the bigger is the change on
the outside. When you get out you feel like you have to live
twice as much to make up for the time lost in here. But
there is no way that you can make up for this daily death.
No way. [A white prisoner, early forties, who has spent a
total of 15 years in prison.]

Other prisoners feel that the difference between prison and
the "free" world is one of degree, not of quality. They see the
oppressiveness of prison and the powerlessness of the inmates
as a magnification of similar conditions in the society at large:

Prison isn't any big experience. A lot of guys here think
that it is and make themselves miserable in here. But if you
have lived in the jungle on the outside, you know that this
is just a different part of the jungle. The same things is
happening on the streets as in here. The same things happen in classrooms as happen in prison. The only difference
is that in the so-called free world it is more undercover.
There is more illusion. It is like polishing an old shoe: you
can put polish on a broken-down pair of shoes and make
them shine, but it is still the same old pair of shoes. The
outside has lots of shine, but it is really the same old pair
of worthless shoes as prison.

In the free world there is so much trickeration that your
mind becomes really confused. You begin to think you are
free. They tell you that you are free so often that most
people begin to think that it must be true. Everything
moves so fast that you can't think straight. It is like being
on a merry-go-round where you think you are going somewhere, but you really keep coming back to the same spot.
The merry-go-round may be really fancy, it may have lots
of glitter and cost a fortune, but you still come back to the
same spot. It never really goes anywhere. On the outside
the merry-go-round goes so fast that you get dizzy and

can't see anything. In here it slows down and things become clearer. You know, most people really don't have any more freedom or power on the outside than here. They just think they do because they can have a fuck or a steak when they want to. But that isn't freedom. [A black prisoner, early twenties, in San Quentin for "kidnapping with intent to commit robbery" with a sentence of life without possibility of parole.]

Prison is a microcosm of the whole society. There is racism outside and there is racism inside. In both cases it keeps the people divided. There are special privileges on the outside and special privileges on the inside. They both serve to make people think that they have something to lose by fighting the system. The courts on the outside may be fair if you are rich, but for most people they are about the same as the disciplinary hearings in here. Workers on the outside have no more say in how their factories are run than the slaves in the prison. So what's the big difference? Still, I'd rather be on the outside. [A white prisoner, early thirties.]

At different times during his imprisonment, a prisoner moves from one to the other of these general perspectives. A number of prisoners expressed the feeling that when they first came to prison they experienced the loss of freedom as a gigantic break with their past, but that gradually they began to realize that much of what went on in prison was present on the outside as well. Still, the majority of prisoners see their personal predicament as categorically worse than life on the outside, and most want desperately to get out.

Time and again prisoners expressed the feeling that the loss of freedom itself would not be so terrible if they were treated decently by prison officials:

Some people say that we are treated like animals here. But what farmer would ever keep an animal locked up in a dirty box four feet wide? We are treated worse than animals. Animals have the SPCA to protect them; who gives a damn about prisoners? [A white prisoner, early twenties.]

I think that there is a need for punishment in society, but not this, not years and years behind bars. And not being treated like dirt. A man is still a man, whatever he done to get locked up. This place is righteously unjust. After a while, it doesn't matter what you did; this is unjust. [A black prisoner, early thirties.]

Many prisoners felt that one of the worst things about prison life was the constant tension, the atmosphere of fear and intimidation that pervades the institution. Physical conditions at San Quentin contribute a great deal to this tension. George Jackson wrote in several letters from San Quentin:

I suffer a constant bombardment of nonsense from all sides. There is no rest from it even at night. Twenty-four hours a day my senses must endure the shock of this attack from the lunatic fringe. So I insert my ear plugs and bury myself in my thoughts and work. . . . (October 17, 1967)

This is Saturday: there is so much noise on the tier that even my ear plugs are useless. Grown men are acting like high school girls. The guards have some kind of sports on the radio. Everyone is happy, emotion-filled cries of joy come from every cell. They are trying to forget their problems or pretend that they have none. . . . (December 23, 1967)

It's 5:40 A.M. All the noisemakers are asleep; they've worn themselves out through the night making merry, laughing, singing, pretending. . . . They are afraid, confused and confounded by a world they know that they did not make, that they feel they cannot change, so they make these loud noises so they won't hear what their mind is trying to tell them. . . . Confinement in this small area all day causes a build up of tension. The unavoidable consequence is stupidity, a return to childish behavior, overreaction. (January 1, 1968)[14]

Or, in the words of one black prisoner: "San Quentin is just a madhouse. This place would just drive you crazy if you let it."

14. *Soledad Brother*, pp. 110, 118–119.

You can never really be alone in prison; you can never escape the noise, the commotion, the guns, the walls, the dirt. You are constantly surrounded by the physical reality that defines your wretchedness.

The physical conditions of San Quentin, however, are only one cause of stress within the prison. Considerable tension stems from the inmate society itself:

> At San Quentin there is a terribly hostile atmosphere. You have to adapt yourself. Everyone puts up a front that they are strong. If you are weak, people know that you won't fight back and you will be used. You will be forced into homosexual relations and be forced to buy dope. When you first arrive you are tested. We call that "getting your face." The first month I was here I had to physically defend myself. I didn't want to fight—I wanted to just do my number, but I had to fight in order to show that I couldn't be pushed around, and once I had shown that, I was left pretty much alone. There is a really strong protection racket here: if you let yourself be pushed around and don't defend yourself, you can get forced to pay for your own protection. [Account of white prisoner in early twenties.]

In March and April of 1971 more than twenty stabbings occurred in the prison, three of which resulted in deaths. Some of those stabbings were probably over drug debts, but more of them appear to have been racial retaliations in which the victim was more or less randomly selected. Many prisoners during this period felt that it was unsafe to be out on the tiers alone. As one white prisoner put it: "There is more tension here than anywhere else I have ever been. You never know when you are going to be hit. The only time you can relax is when you are in your cell and the door is locked." Eldridge Cleaver made the same observation five years earlier: "Once inside my cell I feel safe: I don't have to watch the other convicts any more or the guards in the gun towers."[15]

15. *Soul on Ice*, p. 42.

Part of this aggression of prisoner against prisoner is undoubtedly the result of the kinds of men who are sent to San Quentin. Many prisoners come from backgrounds in which there is a premium on toughness and willingness to respond violently to certain situations. But a great deal of the aggression is directly and indirectly the result of prison conditions. As has already been discussed, a considerable amount of violence stems from racism within the prison, which is often tacitly (and sometimes overtly) encouraged by prison staff. Even more fundamentally, when men are caged, when their legitimate aspirations and desires are constantly frustrated, it can be expected that they will respond aggressively. Since it is extremely dangerous for prisoners to vent aggression directly against the prison establishment, they often displace it against each other. While most acts of violence between prisoners have some specific precipitating incident—an unpaid debt, a racial insult, an ostensible doublecross of some sort—the overriding cause of violence is the high level of frustration and tension created by the prison.

CHAPTER 7

Liberal
Totalitarianism in Prison

Contemporary prisons in the United States can be described as *liberal totalitarian* institutions. The apparent paradox in this expression reflects the contradictions that pervade the life of prisons. They are institutions which, at least formally, have adopted the liberal goal of rehabilitation, while maintaining totalitarian control over the lives of prisoners. Moreover, they have adopted a variety of liberal programs (the indeterminate sentence, therapy programs) which in practice often serve to further the totalitarian goal of changing prisoners into strict conformists to authority. Many of the contradictions between the prisoners' and the officials' views of prison life discussed in Chapters 5 and 6 have their roots in the fact that prisons are simultaneously liberal and totalitarian institutions.

TOTALITARIAN MEANS AND LIBERAL ENDS

No one denies that many aspects of prison life are totalitarian. Prisoners have virtually no formal power within the prison system, and what privileges they have are given to them at the administrative discretion of the officials. The lives of inmates, in all prisons, are subject to detailed regulation and close surveillance.[1]

If in "honor blocks" or in certain minimum-security institutions these regulations appear less restrictive and the surveillance looser, it is not because the prison has yielded control over the prisoners' lives. Rather, the prisoners have tacitly agreed to conform to the demands of the prison regime without resistance. Sheldon Messinger makes this point well:

> Much was made by the administrators—particularly the custodial staff—of the opportunities extended to inmates as they moved from non-honor to honor status. But it must be seen that this was *not* a move from a subordinated position into one in which initiative might be exercised. Rather it was, at best, a move from a position in which subordination was insured by rigid regimentation and continuous surveillance to one in which these immediate controls were somewhat relaxed, the inmate having "proved" his willingness to maintain a subordinate posture on his own. He could be "trusted"—as far as any inmate could be trusted—not to take advantage of the relative lack of regimentation and supervision to change the structure of the environment in which he was expected to live. Should he breach this "trust" the full weight of officialdom would be brought to bear upon him.[2]

In spite of the rhetoric of liberal prison administrators, the correctional prison differs little from the punitive-custodial

1. Gresham Sykes, in his study *The Society of Captives* (Princeton, N.J.: Princeton University Press, 1958), described maximum-security institutions in much these terms: ". . . the maximum security prison represents a social system in which an attempt is made to create and maintain total or almost total social control. The detailed regulations extending into every area of the individual's life, the constant surveillance, the concentration of power into the hands of a ruling few, the wide gulf between the rulers and the ruled—all are elements of what we would usually call a totalitarian regime." (p. xiv.)
2. Sheldon Messinger, "Strategies of Control" (unpublished doctoral dissertation, University of California, 1969), pp. 203–204.

prison with respect to the totalitarianism of the internal power structure.

The way in which prisons have changed is in the goals those power relationships are supposed to serve. In the traditional, custodial prison, the totalitarianism of the prison structure was taken for granted. If any justification was given, it was in terms of the need for harsh punishment. In the "correctional" prison, the totalitarianism of the structure ostensibly serves to create a setting where rehabilitation can occur. The formal goal of the prison is no longer to exact retribution, but to transform the "antisocial criminal" into a "responsible, law-abiding citizen." Prison officials argue that a prerequisite for accomplishing this goal is order and security within the prison. The totalitarianism of the prison regime is seen as a necessary means to that end.

Prisoners have a quite different view of the purpose of the totalitarian structures of the prison. They see them as simply serving the goal of control per se. Most prisoners consider the rehabilitation ideology a hypocritical façade. The more politicized prisoners frequently see it as a political tactic by their captors to mislead the general public about the nature of prison. Very few prisoners feel that the totalitarian aspects of prison life facilitate rehabilitation in any meaningful way.

Attitudes toward disciplinary procedures illustrate well the difference in views between the prisoners and the officials toward prison totalitarianism. The prison officials see the disciplinary procedures as reasonable and necessary means of maintaining order within the prison, of preventing violence, even of protecting inmates. The prisoners see disciplinary procedures as arbitrary and oppressive instruments which maintain prison order by intimidating the imprisoned. The prison administration feels that in the disciplinary hearings the demands of custody and internal order must be given priority over justice, and so they feel that the sacrifice of fairness and due process is legitimate. To the prisoners, whatever legitimacy the disciplinary hearings might have had is destroyed by the arbitrary nature of the procedures. From the perspective of the prison administrators, the hearings represent a reasonable exercise of duly constituted authority which makes possible the rehabilitative goals of the prison. From the perspective of the prisoners, the hearings represent the display of arbitrary force by the prison establishment in order to oppress and control the prison population.[3]

Whichever of these views of prison totalitarianism is correct, one thing is very clear: this totalitarianism contributes substantially to the sense of frustration and despair which pervades the prison population. It matters little to prisoners whether they are forced to conform to arbitrary rules in the name of rehabilitation or in the name of custody and retribution. This is not to deny that some prison officials sincerely believe in the rehabilitative goals of the prison; but those goals make precious little difference to the reality of prison life for most prisoners.

LIBERAL MEANS AND TOTALITARIAN ENDS

Prisons not only use totalitarian means in order to further liberal rehabilitative goals, but they also employ "liberal" means for what can only be considered totalitarian goals. Many of the programs which can be considered the most liberal—the honor blocks, the conjugal visiting program, the gradation of prisons from minimum to maximum security—simultaneously serve as potent weapons of control within the prison. In the old custodial prisons, control depended almost entirely on terror and total regimentation. In the most extreme cases, prisoners were prohibited from speaking to other prisoners and spent nearly all their time in solitary confinement. In the new,

3. To say that prisoners regard the disciplinary *procedures* as oppressive and arbitrary does not mean that prisoners are generally against the existence of rules within the prison. Most prisoners feel that control is necessary within the prison, perhaps even quite strict control. But what they feel is totally unjustified is the kangaroo-court proceedings which masquerade as "hearings" for infractions.

liberal prisons, the system of control has become much more sophisticated. The prisoner is confronted with a system of progressively harsher punishments for resistance to the prison regime, and progressively greater privileges for compliance. While these techniques are not always used to their fullest advantage, they do provide prison officials with a wide range of responses to the problems of control. And, by and large, they have been used effectively.[4]

Probably the best example of the use of liberal programs for totalitarian ends is the indeterminate sentence. The essential logic of the indeterminate sentence is that prisoners should be released from prison as soon as they are rehabilitated. If a robber is rehabilitated fully after one year in prison, it is argued, there is no reason to keep him imprisoned. And similarly, if after ten years he is still unregenerate, he should be kept behind bars. However, in practice, the threat of being denied a parole hangs constantly over the heads of all prisoners. They know that a bad disciplinary record will almost certainly mean extra years in prison, and this is one of the most potent pressures on prisoners to conform to the demands of the prison regime.[5]

To the prisoner, then, not only are the liberal goals of the prison seen as a sham, but the liberal programs are seen as largely serving totalitarian ends. The result is that the central

4. For a fuller discussion of the system of internal control, see Chapter 15 below, especially pp. 326 ff.

5. Messinger, in "Strategies of Control," argues that there has frequently been considerable conflict between the prison officials and the Adult Authority which has reduced the effectiveness of the indeterminate sentence as an instrument of control within the prison. The Adult Authority is less preoccupied with the exigencies of internal prison control and more with the probability of the prisoner's committing a new offense. If the members of the AA feel that a prisoner is likely to commit a new offense, they will hesitate to release him even if his in-prison disciplinary record is good. This reduces (but by no means eliminates) the ability of prison officials to use the offer of a parole as an inducement for compliance to their demands. It also contributes to the extreme sense of futility that many prisoners feel. Since the prison officials and the Adult Authority often operate on different criteria, a prisoner can be left with a sense that nothing he does will help him get out of prison.

experience of prison for most prisoners is *control.* Obedience and conformity become, in practice, the core values of the prison system; and the liberal rehabilitation programs become devices for furthering those values. This does not mean that many of these programs are not intrinsically desirable. Parole, conjugal visits, and recreation, at least in principle, are certainly worthwhile and humane. But in the context of the prison regime, they are also instruments of totalitarian control.

THE TOTALITARIANISM OF PRISON LIBERALISM

Beyond the relationship of means to ends there is an even more basic sense in which prisons can be described as "liberal totalitarian" institutions: the very liberalism of the rehabilitative goal in prison is fundamentally totalitarian. The central rehabilitative goal of the liberal prison, simply stated, is to change criminals into law-abiding citizens. The system tries to "cure"an underlying *disrespect for authority* among prisoners. This notion is part of the official ideology of the rehabilitative prison:

> Disturbed attitudes towards authority and inability to accept responsibility represent two areas in which prison inmates need the most help. It is believed that their inability to mature in their attitudes towards authority and responsibility are the sources of failure on parole. . . .
> Persons with strong hatred toward authority are in many cases influenced thereby to rebel against the laws of society. . . . Some men enter prison with great hatred and suspicion of the staff—yet actually they have never previously had contact with a single employee of the prison. Obviously, these feelings are a handicap to the efforts of institutional officials to achieve a treatment environment in the prison.[6]

6. Norman Fenton, *Treatment in Prison: How the Family Can Help* (Sacramento: California Department of Corrections Publication, 1959), pp. 20, 59.

The ideal liberal rehabilitative prison finds ways of taking the angry, defiant, disrespectful criminal and transforming him, as Dr. Norman Fenton has said, through "quick and easy cures" into the responsible, obedient, respectful worker.[7]

It is in this emphasis on the prisoner's relationship to authority that the liberal goal of rehabilitation becomes in essence totalitarian. Respect for authority is a central value in both liberal and totalitarian political perspectives, although adherents differ in their conception of the sources of legitimacy for that authority. In a liberal system, authority is legitimate if it is accepted democratically by the people subjected to that authority. In classical liberal theory, an implicit contractual relationship exists between the individual and the authority, and it is this contract which gives the authority legitimacy. In a totalitarian system, on the other hand, the legitimacy of authority is not based on any theoretical contract. Rather, it rests on the absolute control of power by the authority and on an ideology which proclaims that this control serves the interests of some category of people. In the case of Nazi Germany, for example, this category was ethnic: the absolute control of power was in the hands of the Nazi party, which proclaimed that it was exercising that power in the interests of the German people. Regardless of the significant differences between liberal and totalitarian political perspectives as to what constitutes legitimate authority, both stress the importance of respecting that authority and rigorously obeying the laws emanating from it.[8]

7. A discussion of why "respect for authority" is the central goal of the rehabilitative prison appears below in Chapter 15, pp. 323 ff.

8. There are other conceptions of the sources of legitimacy for authority. In a theocracy, the legitimacy of authority is based on religion. In certain personal dictatorships, it may be based on the charisma of the leader. In a radical democratic system, legitimacy is based on the active participation of the people in the exercise of power, in their real and immediate control of decision making. This is different from the liberal notion, in which legitimacy is based on the contract between the people and the state, and the people let their representatives make decisions for them. And in an anarchistic perspective, no state authority at all is legitimate.

Prisons are peculiar institutions with regard to this notion of respect for authority. The authority prison administrators wield is to them liberal and democratic. Their powers are delegated to them by elected legislatures, and they see the legitimacy of their own authority in terms of the implicit contract of a liberal political system. To most prisoners, on the other hand, the authority of the prison system has no liberal democratic legitimacy. Few prisoners feel any sense of contractual relationship between themselves and the prison authorities. The fact that a felon is disenfranchised in most of the United States emphasizes that the authority of the prison, *with respect to the prisoner,* is not a liberal, democratic one. Different prisoners view the power base for the totalitarian authority of the prison in different terms. Some prisoners see it as being the "capitalist class." Many black prisoners see it as being "white America." Most inmates simply see the power base for the prison's authority as being the "outside" or "free" society.[9]

Since from the prisoner's point of view the authority embodied in the prison is totalitarian, the rehabilitative goal of changing prisoners into people who unquestioningly obey that authority is also totalitarian. Through a variety of techniques, ranging from psychotherapy to long-term confinement in the adjustment center, the prison tries to transform prisoners from

9. It could be argued that although the prison represents totalitarian authority to the prisoners once they are imprisoned, it was a liberal, democratic authority with respect to them when they were on the outside. This is an argument of classical liberal theory; the prisoner is viewed as a free man who willfully broke his contract with the liberal, democratic authority, and forfeited his freedom—i.e., his liberal contract—as a result. While this argument may have some reality for the business executive convicted of tax fraud or price fixing, it is of dubious validity for the poor black or white laborer. If there is any implicit contract between them and the state, it is an extremely tenuous one. Some blacks in particular, both within prison and on the outside, see their relationship to the state as lacking any contractual base. They describe themselves as a "black colony" within white America, and when they are imprisoned, they describe themselves as "prisoners of war." To them, the authority of the state is essentially totalitarian, rather than liberal. The important point here is that whether or not the authority outside the prison is seen as liberal or totalitarian, *with respect to the prisoners inside,* that authority as embodied in the prison administration is totalitarian.

individuals who defy authority to individuals who passively conform to authority. From the prison officials' perspective, the
more rehabilitated the prisoner becomes in these terms, the
more freedom he can be given (in the form of privileges) until
eventually he demonstrates that he is "fit" to be released. From
the prisoner's perspective, the more he accepts the prison's
ideals of rehabilitation, the more he must bow down to an
arbitrary authority and the less free he becomes. Every movement toward freedom from the official's perspective is a movement toward submission from the prisoner's.[10]

Such a situation is necessarily precarious. The system functions smoothly only as long as prisoners more or less go along
with the demands of the prison authorities. When prisoners
refuse to conform to those demands, and especially when they
openly resist them, the system breaks down. In this situation,
the prison resorts to the naked use of force by locking prisoners
up, depriving them of their "privileges," gassing them, or shooting them. When this happens, the pretenses of the "liberal"
totalitarianism of the prison are exposed and it becomes clear
that, with respect to the prisoners, authority rests on force and
not on any liberal legitimacy.

10. There are some very difficult ethical issues raised by this discussion.
Prisons are institutions which try forcibly to change people. It is difficult to
justify changing a person against his will, even if the motives for that change
are good ones. Yet, it seems obvious that in certain circumstances, a society has
a legitimate right to say to an individual: "You are too dangerous to live among
us. You must change before we will let you return to the community." The
problem, of course, is in determining what those circumstances are, and in
creating just procedures for assisting the changes. In the present society the
emphasis on changing the individual criminal through "rehabilitation" basically
represents a political alternative to changing the society itself in ways which
would reduce crime. Rehabilitation can be considered in a fundamental sense
a political alternative to eliminating poverty. These issues will be discussed
more fully at the end of Chapter 15 in the section "Humanizing Punishment
and Socializing Society."

PART III

Troubles at Soledad

CHAPTER 8

The Roots of Violence at Soledad

by Frank L. Rundle

Soledad! In Spanish a special sort of loneliness—desolation. An apt characterization of its placement in the wind-swept Salinas Valley and of the spirit-sickening atmosphere which pervades the prison. But Soledad has come to have other meanings— violence, fear, death.

Every inmate within the California Department of Corrections and perhaps elsewhere is aware of Soledad's reputation as a place where one must "watch his back" at every moment, a place where racial tension has tested the endurance and control of even tolerant men. Every prison staff member, correctional officer through superintendent, shares the same awestruck and fearful attitude toward Soledad.

VIOLENCE AT SOLEDAD, 1968–1971

The documented history of violence at Soledad is sketchy before 1970, but inmates who were residents then talked with me about the racial riots of 1964 and 1965. They described events in the late 1960s, when reportedly nearly every inmate had a knife secreted somewhere. Macabrely humorous scenes were described of inmates scrambling to dig knives out of the exercise field when a rumor of impending trouble spread.

A review of newspaper accounts of incidents in Soledad prison indicates the high level of violence in the period 1968–1971. In 1968 three inmates were murdered by other inmates, and three inmates were assaulted by other inmates with serious injuries resulting. Most of these involved racial conflict. One inmate died mysteriously; other inmates say that he was tear-gassed, then beaten to death by guards. There were several major incidents of inmate rebellion, destruction of property, and physical clashes with staff. 1969 was relatively calm with no violent deaths, only two deadly assaults, two racial clashes, and one no-work strike. 1970 started abruptly with the shooting deaths of three black inmates in the adjustment center exercise yard. A new era was ushered in three days later when a guard was murdered by inmates, the first such death in at least 25 years in the California Correctional System. The revolt had begun; the signal had been given that inmates were no longer going to passively submit. In the next 17 months three strikes occurred, six riots of varying proportions, innumerable tear gassings of inmates in the adjustment center, two inmate suicides, three assaults with weapons by inmates upon inmates, three incidents involving guards taken hostage by inmates, three murders of inmates by inmates, two murders of guards by inmates, and the crowning impertinence, the murder of a program administrator by an inmate. This last incident accomplished what nothing else had: it forced the Department of Corrections to act. The superintendent, who had already been designated to move on to an obscure central office job, was abruptly moved out and a new superintendent brought in. An associate and a deputy superintendent were transferred, and several hundred inmates were moved to other institutions. Emergency treatment was finally provided for what Raymond Procunier, director of the Department of Corrections, has described as a "sick institution." A relative calm began to settle on Soledad.

THE EXERCISE YARD SHOOTING

In early 1971, when I assumed the position of chief psychiatrist at Soledad, the walls were still reverberating in the aftermath of the shooting of three black inmates by a correctional officer on January 13, 1970. Inmates who were within the walls of Soledad at the time of that incident described a state of intense racial tension and a great deal of overt conflict between inmates and staff. They reported having heard rumors on January 12 that inmates were to be shot the following day in the O Wing exercise yard. But then rumors of one sort or another are perpetually rife in prison and must usually be discounted or be treated with watchful expectancy. This rumor proved to be prophetic. On January 13, after having been strictly racially segregated, O Wing was to be forcibly integrated. Whether they liked it or not, by administrative order, blacks, Chicanos, and whites were going to mix in the exercise yard and on the cell tiers. The accumulated racial hatred of these men for one another, stimulated or aggravated by deliberate efforts of the staff as suggested in Chapter 6, was to be controlled by the threat of gunfire from the gunman in his cage overlooking the exercise yard. As numerous prison staff watched from behind the chain link fence, the prophecy came to be historical fact, and inmates Nolen, Miller, and Edwards were killed by the guard marksman.

Inmates present at the time believe that the entire event was carefully and deliberately planned by the prison administration; that the three blacks were executed because of the threat posed by their militant political views and their leadership. Many inmates further believe that prison administrators continued thereafter to "set up" inmates for execution at the hands of other inmates or prison staff. Believing this, no inmate at Soledad could trust any other man. Every move was eyed with suspicion and caution, and each prisoner was at the ready to protect himself at every moment, to fight to the death if necessary.

MADNESS IN SOLEDAD

These conditions bred an atmosphere of paranoia which permeated Soledad from the guard towers to the utility tunnel, from the schoolroom to the hog farm, from the superintendent to the maintenance crew. The ingredients of this atmosphere were fear, distrust, suspicion, caution. It varied in intensity from day to day, but was ever present. In O and X wings, which together constituted the so-called adjustment center, the mood was always very tense.

In psychiatry there is an axiom that there is always some fact in any paranoid delusion or distortion. Certainly there was a reality base in the fears of adjustment center inmates that they might be killed. Three of them had been. The presence of loaded guns was always obvious, as was the hair-trigger readiness to use them. I personally witnessed inmates coming into X Wing being advised by the staff that if there was trouble there would be no warning shot; the gunman would shoot to kill. So the primary ingredient of the paranoid atmosphere—fear for one's life—was at an especially high level within the adjustment center.

In addition to this justifiable fear for one's life, the extreme sensory deprivation of solitary confinement meant that these prisoners were especially vulnerable to impairment of their ability to distinguish reality. They had no access to television and little reading material. The cells in X Wing in which they were locked for most of the 24 hours of each day had only one partially obscured window and a door of solid steel. It was impossible to offset this isolation by establishing any trusting relationships with staff members. There was, simply stated, no opportunity to apply the reality-checking logic which is imperative to the maintenance of a rational state of mind. Many inmates slipped in and out of an autistic world of fantasy as a consequence of this isolation.

Some prisoners, after days of such isolation, would become so desperate for relief that they would set their mattresses afire so as to force the staff to open the door and remove them from the torture chamber, even though they knew it would probably be for only a few moments. Others would burst out in a frenzied rage of aimless destruction, tearing their sinks and toilets from the walls, ripping their clothing and bedding, and destroying their few personal possessions in order to alleviate the numbing sense of deadness or nonbeing and to escape the torture of their own thoughts and despair. In this absolutely insane world that was the adjustment center, "madness" was at least partially functional and adaptive. The crazy ones were those who tried to follow the rules of the world outside.

RACISM

The forced integration begun on January 13 was continued not only in the adjustment center but throughout the prison. An effort was made to maintain racially balanced populations in the various living units, which meant generally having about 50 percent white, 30 percent black, and 20 percent Chicano inmates in each wing. Despite this superficial effort at racial integration, no meaningful attempt was made to attack the real sources of racial tension. No effort was made to deal with the prejudices of the inmates or, more importantly, the prejudices and tension-promoting behavior of the staff. As a result, this superficial effort produced only superficial results, and racial tension continued at a very high level.

The dining hall continued to be segregated, and any man sitting out of his racially determined place was risking his life. The television viewing room in each living unit was segregated, proximity to the TV set being determined by which racial group possessed the greatest power at any particular time.

Within the living units, any man who became too friendly with a man of another race would be visited by representatives of his own racial group and pressured into maintaining segregation. If he did not, he would be ostracized from his group and would run the risk of physical attack or even death at the hands of his own race.

Administrative practices maintained racial stratification, competition, and enmity. In the vocational training areas, according to black inmates, the most sought-after assignments went to whites. Desirable work assignments throughout the prison were said to be made on a similar basis. And as previously mentioned, the most potent source of racism, the prejudices and emotions of staff and inmates, drew no attention, unless it was that of studied neglect. The staff aggravated racial tensions in many ways. A case in point was the sergeant in charge of the reception and release unit, who had the opportunity for contact with every inmate who passed in or out of the gates. He was a master of the "Hey you boy" derogation in addressing blacks. Some men on the staff chafed under the order from the director of the Department of Corrections forbidding the open use of any racially denigrating term, and found subtler but still effective means of communicating their hatred. Inmates reported certain officers making remarks to white inmates such as, "I hear the black boys are carrying their shanks [knives] today. What are you and your friends going to do about it?"

OTHER ROOTS OF VIOLENCE

Other factors were important in generating the explosive tensions which resulted in the January 13 triple shooting. The cultural setting of the prison, the Salinas Valley of Monterey County, is extremely conservative, dominated by the power of the wealthy retired, the huge produce farms and vineyards, and a vast military complex. Numerous retired military men, shaped into paragons of resentful submission by 20 to 30 years of service, reside there, and many prison guards are drawn from these ranks. There are relatively few black residents in the county, and almost none in the immediate environs of the prison. The exploitation of Mexican farm workers has been openly condoned in the area for years, and continues to the present. All these factors contribute to making the surroundings of Soledad prison a bastion of right-wing conservative values, with strong racist undercurrents.

In addition, the role of Soledad within the California prison system maximized its problems. It is the one prison to which other institutions can relatively freely transfer inmates in the eighteen- to twenty-five-year-old group, probably the age group most willing to engage in violence. San Quentin is generally restricted to men over twenty-five years of age, usually those committed for the most serious crimes or considered to be security risks. Folsom is generally intended for the older inmates, often "burned out" and nonviolent, but still considered by staff to represent security risks. The California Institution for Men at Chino is only for minimum-security prisoners, and the Deuel Vocational Institute is for the teen-age offenders too difficult to manage in the Youth Authority complex. This leaves Soledad as the "dumping ground" for men eighteen to twenty-five, many of whom are identified as management problems at other institutions. Since, until 1972, Soledad operated a large adjustment center, it drew many inmates identified as the most troublesome, assigned for maximum-security isolation. All of this contributed to developing Soledad as the "School for Gladiators," the prison whose reputation spread far and wide and instilled fear in even experienced convicts.

Another root of violence was the ineffectual, ambivalent administration of C. J. Fitzharris, the superintendent for many years. His administration set the tone of the institution, characterized by uncertainty and unclear expectations, and generated a great deal of anxiety within inmates and staff alike. He disliked and feared inmates generally, and rarely came into direct contact with them. His concerns about inmates seemed to be related to protecting them from what he deemed immoral influences, such as *Playboy* magazine. He would not take a strong stand on important issues, and tended to ignore divisions within the staff. Consequently, the usual conflict between custody and treatment, found in almost any prison, was even more prominent at Soledad. (Treatment is really a misnomer, for there was no meaningful treatment in the sense of psychotherapy. And as in any prison, considerations of custody took final precedence over any other.)

Another significant root of violence should not be overlooked. There is a psychiatric theory that in a relatively closed social system such as a mental hospital, prison, or even a family it is possible for a certain subject to cause other subjects to act out his conflicts and impulses for him. For example, if a guard had strong aggressive and hostile impulses which he had difficulty keeping under control, he might unconsciously manipulate an inmate so as to cause him to assault another person. The same theory has been applied to parents and children: that is, parents might unconsciously promote the "bad" behavior of their children as a means of keeping their own "bad" impulses under control. One of the means of causing this to happen is to repeatedly communicate to the child the expectation that he will be bad. Certainly in prison, inmates are subjected to massive doses of the notion that they are dangerous, untrustworthy, unreliable, and potential murderers. Some fulfill those expectations.

VIOLENCE AND CONTROL

Shortly after I began working at Soledad, I was impressed as I walked the quarter-mile-long mainline corridor by the fact that there were hundreds of inmates walking there, with only eight or ten unarmed guards in view. I suddenly wondered why the inmates submitted to the dreary regimentation, the oppressive power, the unreasonableness and arbitrariness of the prison. Why didn't they just take the place over? At first I thought they obviously were cooperating, which meant they really wanted to be in prison. I had to reject that theory, since it seemed so patently ridiculous. Then I thought: It's because they are essentially passive and dependent people, brainwashed and conditioned. I had to reject that also, since I knew many who were not. Then I thought: They aren't and couldn't be organized because of the racial hatred, subgroup animosities, and competitiveness. But I knew there had been strikes and organized efforts of resistance recently, involving hundreds of inmates. It suddenly dawned upon me that the ultimate enforcer was the gunpower in the hands of the staff, locked in cabinets throughout the prison and at the ready in the gun towers. And everybody knew the guards would shoot to kill. All inmates knew that even if they succeeded in taking over the prison or a section of it, the vast police and military resources of the state, and the nation if necessary, would be brought against them. They knew that if they survived, they would be prosecuted, receive an additional sentence, and their parole date would recede into the distant future. I remember with what chilling confidence in his power and the righteousness of his position Ray Procunier had told me, "Give me a riot anytime —I'll know exactly what to do. We have the guns."

As I gained more experience at Soledad and my understanding of the institution and its inmates developed, I came to know the crushing weight of the total control which was exercised over inmates' lives. The only way to get an early parole was to submit totally to the prison regime. If an inmate didn't play the dumbness of docility but also didn't cause overt trouble, he would simply serve out many years of his indeterminate sentence and eventually be paroled. If he rebelled in minor ways —didn't cut his hair, wore his cap in the hallway, or spoke sharply to a guard—he would be written up for violation of a rule, ground through the arbitrary and unjust disciplinary procedures, and perhaps be sentenced to up to 29 days in the hole. If a man were to rebel strenuously—write writs, denounce the system, refuse to work, get into physical clashes, flout the rules—he would be locked away permanently in the adjustment center. There his remaining humanity would be quickly eroded and he would become a living bomb of rage, hatred, and bitterness. And if he should, in addition, hold and speak radical or revolutionary views, he would be labeled a "dangerous racial agitator" and be accorded special isolating treatment.

It is perfectly clear to me now that the roots of violence at Soledad and other prisons reach deeply into the prison system itself. It is a system which renders a man impotent, denies his individuality, destroys his identity, and grinds him ceaselessly under a heavy yoke of uncertainty and injustice. Such a system generates rage and bitterness which in some men will be turned upon others, whether tormentors or brothers. Prisons, then, are generating the very behavior which they are ostensibly designed to eliminate. They are destroying rather than rehabilitating men. They are promoting violence rather then controlling it.

CHAPTER 9

A Chronicle of Three Years in the Hole[1]

by Thomas Lopez Meneweather

In 1965 I was transferred to San Quentin and associated briefly with several Black Nationalist groups. Guards accused me of being hostile because of my refusal to declare myself a member of any one group. I terminated all these associations when the Adult Authority stated that they would consider me for parole if I entered the prison school program, which I did.

On July 31, 1967, while returning to my cell to get my school books for morning classes, I was arrested by guards and accused of killing a Caucasian inmate who was thought to have stabbed a black. I knew nothing about this incident and told them so. The county prosecutor's office refused to prosecute me, stating that there was no evidence that I had committed the offense or participated in its commission; nevertheless, the prison insisted that I was guilty. The disciplinary committee told me that I would not be let out of prison until I had served my maximum term. They added that I should not plan on getting out even then because I would probably find myself going before an outside court for possession of a weapon, which would increase my maximum term to life. Or I could be killed by friends of the

1. This chapter was made available by the Prison Law Project of Oakland, California.

dead inmate or other Caucasian inmates who just "wouldn't let a nigger get away with killing a white man." Or I would end up in the gas chamber for defending myself against inmates attempting to take my life, because they, the officials, would see that "the word got in the right places." Pictures of the body of the dead inmate were placed in my central file along with the write-up accusing me of the offense and the findings of the committee of prison officials.

In April of 1968, I was transferred to Soledad from San Quentin and placed on the first floor of O wing, commonly known as Max Row. Upon my arrival I was confronted with extremely hostile prison officials who made no effort to conceal their racial hatred of blacks in general and of me in particular. One guard pointed in my face and remarked to another that San Quentin had sent them one of the niggers involved in the July killing and that the inmate who was killed was a fine fellow because he hated niggers.

While waiting to be taken to the classification committee, I watched a black inmate, Clarence Causey (nicknamed Dopey Dan), be set up and cold-bloodedly murdered. He had been assigned to a work group of consolidated Caucasian and Mexican American inmates who both identify themselves and are known around the prison as Nazis. He was the only black. He was immediately set upon with knives and stabbed to death while three guards, including the one who had made the remarks to me referred to above, stood by indifferently and watched until he fell on his face in a puddle of his own blood. Then the guards shot tear gas onto the tier, ordered the inmates back to their cells, and removed the mortally wounded black inmate from the tier. Approximately half an hour later they took him to the prison hospital. After repeated inquiries, we were finally informed that night that the black inmate was dead. No search was made of the prisoners who did the killing until after they had been returned to their cells and given more than ample time to hide or get rid of the murder weapons.

I wrote numerous letters to Mr. Leonard Carter, regional director of the NAACP, Region I, in San Francisco, concerning this matter, but none of the letters were permitted to leave the institution. I received a warning about "trying to make trouble for the prison personnel" which I ignored and was promptly punished by being placed in a "quiet cell" and put on restricted diet for fifteen days. This meant that one slice of some kind of loaf (without meat), served three times daily, was all I was given to eat.

I then wrote letters to George B. Harris, then Chief Justice of the United States District Court, Northern District of California, concerning this matter as well as my personal experience beginning at San Quentin on July 31, 1967. But through the United States Probation Office I was advised that he couldn't intervene. After the family of the dead black inmate started asking questions, three of the inmates involved in the murder were charged. When the trial was in progress the inmates involved would return from court laughing and making racial jokes about how the prison officials hated blacks. They said the guards were going to testify that the black inmate, who was roughly 5 feet 3 inches and about 105 pounds, attacked the inmates with an inkpen and that they overpowered him, took away the pen, and stabbed him to death with it. Having witnessed the beginning of the assault on Clarence Causey and having seen the size and length of the weapons that he was murdered with, I did not take their bragging seriously because I knew that an autopsy would disclose what kind of weapons caused his death and that the knives used to murder him could not be passed off as inkpens.

The prison guards who set up the killing and stood indifferently by were Sergeant Matson, Officer Stone, and Officer Johnson.[2] When I use the expression "setup" I am referring to the process by which a guard or guards select an inmate, virtually

2. The names of all guards have been changed throughout this chapter.

always a black, unlock his door, and lead him to believe that it is his turn to come out of his cell for exercise with members of his own race (this is the usual practice in O Wing because of the racial hostility and violence between black and nonblack prisoners). But instead of coming out with members of his own race, the black inmate finds himself outside his cell on the tier with four or more antiblack inmates who are always armed with knives provided by racist prison officials. The guard locks the door to the black inmate's cell to prevent him from going back in. The antiblack inmates immediately ratpack him and stab him, sometimes fatally, depending on his ability to fight off his attackers.

The killing of Dopey Dan occurred on April 23, 1968. The following day, a black inmate purchased a knife from a Caucasian inmate who was an outcast from his own ethnic group because he had associated with blacks here on the mainline. Following the purchase of the knife, in an effort to avenge the murder of Dopey Dan, certain black inmates attacked and seriously wounded a Caucasian inmate who had been instrumental in Dopey Dan's murder. The guards, enraged by the stabbing of the Caucasian inmate, selected at random a black inmate living on the tier and railroaded him for the stabbing.

The officials knew that the security policies on O Wing made it impossible for black inmates to get possession of a knife except through the Caucasian inmate who was being shunned by his own ethnic group. The officials immediately went to that man's cell and demanded the knife they had provided him prior to his conflict with his own ethnic group. He claimed to have lost the weapon, and was set upon and beaten by Sergeant Matson and four other guards. He was then transferred to X Wing and never heard from again.

After a thorough search of the first floor of O Wing failed to produce the knife, the officials physically segregated the blacks from the Caucasians and Mexican Americans, allegedly to prevent further bloodshed. Over a period of three months the officials on O Wing reduced the number of blacks confined on the east side of the first floor to four, never thereafter to exceed six, and made it a point to keep the remaining eighteen cells occupied with antiblack inmates. The antiblack inmates derived a sense of security from their superior numbers and their open alliance with the most sadistic, racist prison officials (the entire staff of O Wing, without an exception) I have ever encountered during my six and a half years of incarceration. These inmates sank to a complete animal level in their daily obsession with hurling obscenities and racial slurs at us.

After six months without making any verbal responses, and being physically prevented from getting at the racist inmates, we approached the O Wing officials and demanded total segregation. We were laughed at by Sergeant Matson, program administrator Mr. Smith, and other officials in both civilian clothes and guard uniforms. We were first asked, "What's the matter, can't you take it?" and then told they couldn't understand "why niggers sit in and demonstrate to get integrated and when things get a little rough they want to be segregated." They further advised us that they could not segregate us as we had requested because it was against the law, so we should just sit back and enjoy our hard-won right to live next to Caucasians.

The daily verbal abuse continued and was participated in by prison guards, Sergeant Matson, and a host of others. It was punctuated by the throwing of spit, urine, human feces, and any other filth these inmates could get their hands on into our cells and on our persons, bedding, and personal effects every time they came out of their cells. The guards regarded this as an ideal source of amusement and shouted encouragement to them. We used our blankets from our beds to cover our personal properties and held them in front of us while standing at the bars of our cells trying to keep out as much of this filth as possible. Because of the guards' refusal to provide us with clean coveralls and bedding every day, and their refusal to prevent these inmates from throwing filth into our cells, we found ourselves with the daily task of cleaning out our cells and washing our blankets, coveralls, and sheets in our face bowls. We then had to sleep in only partially dry or completely wet bed clothing.

After the trial of the inmates who had murdered Dopey Dan, in which they were convicted of a lesser offense, all three of them came back from court bragging about how Sergeant Matson, Officer Johnson, and Officer Stone had testified that Dopey Dan attacked them with an inkpen and they had overpowered him, taken it away from him, and stabbed him to death with it. They said they could hardly wait for another one to be set up.

At this point I began to think seriously about the threat the officials had made about condemning me to death "by seeing that word got in the right places." I began to condition myself for whatever lay in front of me here at Soledad.

Approximately eight months following the murder of inmate Dopey Dan, a black inmate housed on the second floor of O Wing, known to me only by his surname, Powell, and whom everybody knew to be suffering from mental illness, was tear gassed by Sergeant Matson, Lieutenant Knox, and Officer Cook and left in his cell until he passed out. He was then dragged from his cell all the way downstairs to the first floor where he was left lying on the floor in the officers' area. When he started to regain consciousness he was set upon by these officers with billy clubs, gas guns shaped like a billy club (that shoot twelve-gauge shotgun-shell gas pellets), and five-cell flashlights and beaten to death while inmates Lane, Scranton, and Arthur Anderson and I stood by in horror, hearing the agonized moans and cries for mercy by this inmate.

This killing took place somewhere around November or December of 1968. My cell was not close enough to the front of the building to allow me to witness the killing with my eyes, but there was no way I could avoid hearing the scuffling and agonized moans and screams of the inmate while he was being beaten to death. I asked inmates Scranton and Anderson to write down on paper what they had seen and heard, and to make three copies of it, which they did. I sent one to the Chief Justice of the United States District Court for the Northern District of California, and one to Mr. Leonard Carter of the NAACP in San Francisco. Neither copy was allowed to leave the institution. The remaining two copies I secreted in my collection of legal material. One was later discovered by the officials during shakedown, confiscated, and presumably destroyed. The remaining copy escaped discovery and I managed to turn it over to the County District Attorney when he was here in 1970 with the grand jury covering up the murders perpetrated on January 13, 1970. But nothing was ever heard about it again, so I presume that he either destroyed it or turned it over to the prison guards for disposition. The death of inmate Powell was passed off as a heart attack.

Up until this wanton murder, I still felt that perhaps the savage and rampant racism directed against blacks here at Soledad, O and X wings in particular, was confined to the lowest administrative levels of prison personnel, or consisted of isolated individual beliefs and attitudes. But now I realized that in fact these acts had been concertedly done to terrorize and dehumanize us, before the death blows of selected genocide are finally delivered by either the nonblack inmates or the prison guards themselves.

Immediately following the rigid segregation of black inmates from nonblacks in the manner already described, the guards started serving all of the foods to be consumed by the prisoners on the first floor of O Wing. Later they abandoned this policy and assigned this function exclusively to nonblack inmates, who immediately started putting all of the filth in our food that they had been daily throwing in our cells. They also broke up light bulbs provided by the guards and secreted particles of glass in our food whenever they thought there was a chance of our consuming it without detecting it. After countless requests that the guards serve our meals, which they refused to do, all of the black prisoners in protest just refused the trays of inedible food altogether and started complaining to their families. At this point the guards who censored our outgoing mail discovered these complaints and always returned the letters to the inmates. Thus, few letters if any ever got out of the prison. However, they did have the effect of causing the guards to either bring our meals themselves or force the nonblack porters to stop their activities until the guards could think of some way to avoid the inquiries of family members and other concerned persons.

Presumably out of laziness or sheer hatred, the guards quit serving our food after about three weeks and agreed to rotate the porter job and give blacks a chance to be porters. Before, the job had been completely forbidden us. Upon learning of this, the nonblacks, probably out of fear that they would receive the same treatment at the hands of the black porters that they had so ardently bestowed upon us, refused their meals and threw their metal trays and bowls at the black porters and at the guards. After four or five days of this the guards persuaded them to go along with a program that would divide the porter job into half-day shifts, in which a nonblack would work from 6 A.M. to 1 P.M. and a black would then work from 1 P.M. to 4 P.M., to be alternated on a weekly basis. This was eventually acceptable to everyone, and the food problem was thus solved.

It was solved, that is, until Officer Haste was replaced on O Wing by Officer Drake, who was equal to if not more extreme than Sergeant Matson in his relentless racial harassment of blacks. Drake became very angry with the other guards for instituting the new meal service system. He vowed to see that the system was disbanded by seeing to it that no blacks would want the job. He began by assigning all the work to the black porters' shift.

This was effective with one porter; Drake replaced him with an inmate named Madison Flowers, who at that particular time was not educated in the art of defending himself from the attacks of knife-wielding inmates. A few days after being assigned to the porter job, Flowers was set up by Officer Drake with a nonblack inmate he had selected for the shift and provided with a knife. The inmate attacked Flowers but only managed to stab his hands. At this point the guards decided that the knife the blacks had acquired from the Caucasian inmate a few months earlier in retaliation for the Causey incident had either been destroyed or lost, since Flowers was unarmed when attacked. Thus, the setups became more regular. However, since only the stronger and more experienced blacks remained, none of the setups terminated in death or serious injury.

The incident that resulted in the removal of Officer Haste from O Wing to another area of the institution began when he secreted a knife in the cell of a black inmate named Willard Walker while this inmate was out of his cell. Haste then went to court and testified that he had found the weapon in the inmate's possession. Walker was convicted. While he was in the process of going back and forth to court, Officer Haste again entered the inmate's cell and allegedly found another knife. All the black prisoners knew this was a lie because none of us had any knives or any way to get one. The other guards also knew that the inmate was innocent both times. He was going to be convicted of the first frame-up, and the Adult Authority and the Department of Corrections would be given unlimited jurisdiction as to how long they could keep him, since he had a life top. Therefore there was no need to frame him a second time. Upon learning of this second frame-up by Officer Haste, Walker became extremely upset and exchanged a few heated words with Haste. He was then attacked by Officer Haste with a gas-gun billy club and beaten about the head while he was handcuffed and held by Officer Berger. After his head was stitched up, inmate Walker was rushed to Folsom prison. Officers Haste and Berger were removed from O Wing and replaced by Officer Drake.

Several nonblack inmates welcomed Officer Drake's arrival on O Wing with whistles and applause and commented that they had known him from his old job on the mainline. They said he was all right, just like Haste. While being a wing officer on the mainline, he had unlocked the cells of numerous black inmates and assisted in cell robberies. (This meant waiting until the inmates left their cells for work call or some other reason, then unlocking the cells of black prisoners and helping the Caucasian inmates steal such items as cigarettes, pastries, candy, cigars, shoes, watches.)

When he came on O Wing, Officer Drake proceeded down the tier, pausing at the cells of all the nonblack inmates for introductions and to talk over old times with those he had known on the mainline. There were comments about his participation in cell robberies and about how he had caught some of them with weapons, cash money, and other contraband and not reported them or written them up for it. When the subject of blacks came up, he started bragging about how he was a true southerner and had given the blacks bum beefs so the board would deny them parole. He said he hoped they would all be put into concentration camps and killed.

He then asked if Nolen was in X Wing or there on O Wing. Nolen had fought with guards at the various prisons he had been in, and Drake said he had been scheduled to be killed by Nazi sympathizers, but someone had tipped him off. Now he was trying to get some clean time, a parole, and get home. So he had left the mainline and gone to X Wing to avoid trouble and keep his record clean. But they had some of the right boys in X Wing, Drake said, who would do the job.

Having met Nolen at Tracy in 1962, and having seen him later at San Quentin, I of course knew whom Drake was referring to. I was able to listen to the conversation without difficulty because the inmate he was talking to lived next door to me. Following this conversation the officer passed my cell on his way to the end of the tier, but observing me standing at the bars he knew I had overheard all that was said. He stopped and gave me a dirty look, which I returned. He asked me if my name was Meneweather and I replied that it was. He then asked me if I had come down from San Quentin and whether or not I was a "writ writer." To this I did not reply. He remarked that he had already read my jacket and knew all he needed to know about me, and went on down the tier. During a brief conversation he had with the Caucasian inmate in the next cell, I again heard Nolen's name mentioned. This inmate remarked that Nolen was on the other side of the tier in isolation because he had been attacked in X Wing by Caucasian inmates with knives and a pipe. Nolen would be moved to Max Row some time during the following month (December, 1968) when his isolation time had expired. Upon hearing this, I began to worry about Nolen's safety and decided to warn him as soon as possible.

In December Nolen was moved to Max Row, and I immediately explained to him all that I had heard. He informed me that he had indeed been set up in X Wing, attacked by three Caucasian inmates with knives and something that resembled a metal pipe. He had suffered a minor knife wound in his head, which was stitched up, as well as a couple of similar wounds inflicted by the pipelike object. After Nolen knocked one of his assailants to the ground the other two had taken to their heels and fled, abandoning the attack. The one he had knocked to the ground got up and followed his companions, thus terminating the altercation.

This so angered and outraged the officials that they wrote Nolen up. They told him at disciplinary committee that in their opinion the attack on him had been provoked by an altercation he had had at Folsom prison with a friend of the inmates who attacked him. Subsequently they found him guilty as charged in the write-up. They accused him of being violent and advised him to let the matter drop and be thankful that he had survived the attack. He would be placed in isolation, they said, and thereafter, for the protection of himself and his enemies, transferred to Max Row, also located on the first floor of O Wing. Because he had threatened them with a federal civil rights action in connection with the incident, they told him he would probably be a long-time resident of Max Row. However, since preparations were being made to open the Max Row yard in the near future, life on Max Row would probably not be so bad after all.

A few days after he was placed in isolation, prison guards set Nolen up with a Caucasian inmate who, as rumor had it, was credited with five assaults on unsuspecting blacks by command of prison officials. However, knowing that Nolen was "exceptionally good with his hands," the Caucasian inmate, though armed with a knife provided him by prison guards, could do no more than stand at a distance and try to taunt Nolen into attacking him. This Nolen refused to do, and braced himself for the expected attack. The attack never came, and the incident terminated in a stand-off.

In December, 1968, Nolen was moved from isolation to Max Row and about a month later was assigned to the porter job for the half-day allotted to the black inmates. Nolen was set up by Drake two times during the next three months; both incidents terminated without injury to Nolen.

At this point, the guards decided that none of the antiblack inmates on Max Row were firm enough in their feelings, even with the encouragement and weapons offered by the guards, to risk further attacks on Nolen. So they fired him from the porter job.

Eventually, I was assigned the job of half-day porter for the black inmates and was set up several times. With the exception of two times, however, none of the Caucasian inmates would come out of their cells to attack me, being forewarned by guards and inmates alike of my knowledge of karate.

The two exceptions came in August, 1969. Two Caucasian inmates came out of their cells with knives and stood looking at me. One finally came toward me. When I rapidly disarmed him, he and his companion ran back to their cells. I was then ordered to return to my cell by the relief officer. Before doing so, I picked up the knife from the tier. In my cell, I bent it so it would fit into my commode and flushed it down. The guard became very upset and demanded that I either give him the knife, return it to its owner, or destroy it in his presence. I explained that it had already been destroyed, which he refused to believe. He told me that I was fired and no other black inmate would be assigned to the porter job until the knife was produced.

I wrote Officer Drake a letter requesting that another black be assigned the job of half-day porter. He advised me that no blacks would be given the porter job and that he would not serve us our meals but would leave this to the nonblack porter. I protested that I had indeed destroyed the weapon, but they chose to believe that I had given it to other black inmates. Immediately after being told by Officer Drake that there would be no more black porters, the nonblack inmates resumed putting urine, feces, spit, and whatever other filth they could get into our foods.

At this point I prepared and filed a federal civil rights complaint against Officer Drake which was signed by all of the blacks on Max Row who were not frightened by his threats of retaliation. In October, 1969, the blacks who did not sign the complaint were moved off Max Row. In addition all of the nonblack prisoners, with the exception of nine, were moved out. Immediately thereafter, Hugo Pinell, Edward Whiteside, and Eugene Grady were transferred from Folsom to Max Row under circumstances similar to those in which I was transferred here from San Quentin. Each was marked for death by the officials at Folsom in the manner planned for me by the officials at San Quentin.

During the first weeks of November, Nolen was attacked by Officer Drake and other guards who had entered Max Row under pretense of making a security check (shakedown) of all of the cells in the section. The attack occurred after Nolen had been securely handcuffed and surrounded by a group of guards. Cleveland Edwards, Hugo Pinell, and I protested the attack by throwing liquids on Officer Drake whenever he came on the tier. After being tear-gassed virtually into unconsciousness, we were handcuffed and transferred from our cells to isolation, written up, and sentenced to 29 days of isolation, with 15 on restricted diet ("SID").

Prior to appearing before the disciplinary committee and being placed on SID, we were allowed our regular full meal. After consuming a small portion of the food, I discovered that tear gas in powdery form was mixed with the powdered potatoes. I immediately warned Pinell and Edwards who also discovered it and didn't eat the food. A few minutes later my stomach felt like I had consumed fire. I requested that I be taken to the hospital or that the prison doctor be informed of my condition and bring me something to relieve the pain. The guards all laughed, and told me to lie down and be quiet, and I would soon feel better.

The following morning we were taken before the disciplinary committee. Having saved the tear gas filled food for the occasion, I carried it to the committee with me and explained everything to the program administrator and other prison officials. I offered the food as proof. They sniffed it and acknowledged the presence of tear gas but insisted that no guard would do such a thing and advised me to forget the whole matter. At my first opportunity to secure stationery, I wrote to attorneys informing them of the matter and requesting assistance. For this I received a write-up for defaming the reputation of prison guards and falsely accusing the institution. When I appeared before the prison disciplinary committee on this write-up, they warned me and threatened me with retaliation.

After completing the 29 days in isolation, we were all returned to Max Row in December, 1969. While on isolation, we had learned that Alvin Miller, G. W. Randolph, Earl Satcher, and a prisoner named Nance were serving time in isolation stemming from a racial fight on the second floor of O Wing. They were to be sent to Max Row, raising the number of blacks there to eight for the first time since the weeks following the murder of Clarence Causey.

Immediately following our return to Max Row from isolation, a group of prison guards appeared at Nolen's cell and told him the committee wanted to see him. Approximately fifteen minutes later he was returned, and two nonblacks were taken from their cells in the same manner and returned approximately thirty-five to forty minutes later. Nolen was then permitted to leave his cell and visit the cells of all the black prisoners on Max Row. He told us that upon entering the committee room he asked why he was being brought back to the committee. They told him that they knew him to be a very intelligent individual, and noted that he had been in frequent communication with a black guard, known to us as Officer Williams, who was then conducting an Afro-American study class that used books by Eldridge Cleaver, Malcom X, G. A. Rodgers, and a host of other black writers, historians, and contemporary leaders.

They also expressed their belief that the black inmates of Max Row regarded him as their leader and, judging from the respect and brotherly affection given him, his opinions and advice would be accepted by all the black inmates on Max Row. They went on to say that they were aware of the treatment we had suffered since April of 1968 at the hands of the nonblack prisoners and some guards who were a little overemotional when blacks and Caucasians were in conflict. They knew that all the blacks were waiting for a chance to get the nonblacks physically. They felt certain that if Nolen went to the yard, which they thought would be opened on December 30, 1969, he could control the blacks and prevent them from fighting.

They asked him what he was going to do on the yard. Nolen replied that he did not consider himself anybody's leader or spokesman and did not aspire to be. He planned only to exercise when he went to the yard, and all the brothers were men and made their own decisions. The respect and affection afforded him, he said, was a mutual feeling among all of us. At this point the conversation was directed solely to the issue of making sure that Nolen was going to the yard and what he would do if a fight broke out. He told them that he was going to the yard and would not start any trouble but would defend himself if attacked.

Thereafter, Officer Drake and Sergeant Matson in particular made it a point each day to ask Nolen, myself, and all the other black inmates if we were going to go to the yard like men or stay in our cells. With knowing smirks on their faces, they commented that they would like to see some action. On the morning of January 13, 1970, Sergeant Matson came on the tier and walked directly to the cells of every black and challenged us to go to the yard. Then he remarked to another guard that "it looks like the hammers (niggers) are going to come out after all and get what's coming to them." Knowing that he was under the illusion that we would lose the fight if one occurred, I didn't mention the remark to any of the brothers, although others had heard it too.

Matson ordered everyone to strip down to shorts and T-shirts and carry only towels and soap to the yard. The release process began, which consisted of letting out all the inmates one at a time: one Caucasian, one black, one Mexican. When my turn came to be released, I observed upon leaving my cell that the corridor was congested with prison officials of all ranks, numbering approximately thirty-five. All were armed with an assortment of tear-gas guns and containers, billy clubs, five-cell flashlights, and handcuffs. They wore an assortment of expressions from sneers, smirks, and nervous expectation to outright malicious smiles. I proceeded to the cage known as the sally port, where I was ordered to remove my socks, shower thongs, shorts, and T-shirt and hand these items to a prison guard. He searched them for weapons or other contraband while another guard inspected my person: mouth, ears, underarms, hands, bottoms

of feet, beneath my privates. I was then cleared to proceed to
the yard.

Upon passing through the door leading to the yard, I automatically looked up at the gun tower and found myself looking into the barrel of a carbine (automatic rifle) which was
loosely pointed at me by a guard leaning out of the window of
the tower. He yelled that I should go to the other end of the
yard, where the rest of the blacks were located in the area of
the handball court. After arriving there and greeting brothers
Nolen, Whiteside, Randolph, and Satcher, I remained to play a
game of handball with Randolph while the others engaged in
conversation or drifted to the punching bag or the pull-up bar.
After losing interest in the handball game, I joined Nolen, and
we started walking toward the large punching bag located in
the front of the yard just across from the basketball goal. We
were discussing his court case, which I helped him prepare, and
were speculating on his chances for getting a motion for bail
granted.

At the punching bag, Nolen started punching on it. While he
was resting, I punched the bag a few times and started for the
chin-up bar to do a few chin-ups. Satcher passed me then,
headed in the direction of Nolen and the punching bag up
front. After doing a few chin-ups I paused to rest, facing slightly
toward the hospital side of the yard where the nonblacks were
congregated and slightly toward the front of the yard where
Nolen and Satcher were located. I noticed a nonblack inmate
who had just been released from Max Row to the yard. The
night before, he had shouted racial slurs and threats to Nolen.

Immediately, a flash of movement caught the corner of my
eye and I turned to fully face Nolen where he and this inmate
had started fighting. After two or three punches were thrown,
a shot rang out, and Nolen fell to the ground. As I started toward
Nolen to see if he was badly hit, and to protect him from being
attacked while he was on the ground, a voice rang out to me to
"watch it." I looked to see two Caucasian inmates running to-

ward me. Edwards told me as he ran by me that he would take care of Nolen. I then shifted my position to face the Caucasian inmates running toward me. Immediately another shot was fired, and Edwards, running toward Nolen, slumped to the ground holding his stomach. At this point I became temporarily preoccupied with the two Caucasian inmates who had run toward me. I knocked the first one to the ground and shifted my position to face and dispose of the remaining attacker, leaving the one I had knocked to the ground at my back. Miller warned me that the inmate was getting up from the ground and that he would take care of him. Miller started toward us, but before he had gone more than four steps another shot rang out and he fell to the ground holding his chest. Another shot was fired, and the Caucasian inmate whom I had knocked to the ground, having gotten back on his feet, fell back in a sitting position. Another shot brought blood squirting from one of the fingers on my left hand, which I was using to block punches directed at me by the inmate with whom I was still fighting. He backed off, terminating the fight.

I looked at my bleeding hand, put it in the pocket of my coveralls, and started to survey the situation. I heard Randolph yell to Satcher to come and help carry Miller from the yard to the prison hospital. Satcher declined, then yelled to me to go to Miller. After responding that I would, I looked up at the guard in the gun tower and pointed to myself and then to Miller and started to move slowly toward where Randolph was kneeling. The guard raised his carbine as if to fire at me but must have changed his mind because he didn't fire.

After Randolph placed Miller on my shoulder I started in the direction of the emergency exit to the prison hospital, looking at the guard in the gun tower. He again pointed the gun at me and shook his head in denial. At this point some guards started yelling out the Max Row windows from the catwalk inside the building. Approximately five to seven minutes later a guard appeared on the yard armed with a tear-gas gun, pointed in the direction of the inmates. I started to walk very slowly toward the door leading from the yard back onto Max Row, with Miller still on my shoulder. The guard in the gun tower again pointed the gun at me and told me to stop or he would drop me. I paused a moment to reflect on his threat and decided that he probably wouldn't shoot me with an injured man on my shoulder. As I started to move again in the direction of the door leading from the yard, the guard with the tear-gas gun in his hand (presumably because of the shouts and curses and pleadings of some of the uninjured inmates from both sides that we be allowed to remove the wounded to the prison hospital) waved the guard in the gun tower off. Eventually I was allowed to leave the yard with Miller on my shoulder.

When I arrived in the sally port, I found myself surrounded by a large crowd of prison officials who ordered me to lay Miller down on the floor and go to my cell. I refused to do so and insisted on taking Miller straight to the hospital. At this point an official in the crowd remarked, "Who is that, Meneweather? I thought they got him too." A few seconds later the MTA (medical technical assistant), Mr. Henderson, worked his way through the crowd of prison officials and asked me to put Miller down so he could examine him and get him moved to the hospital. I obeyed, and as he unbuttoned Miller's coveralls I saw him put a Band-Aid over a hole in Miller's chest. He then stopped the flow of blood from my finger and bandaged it as best he could.

Again I was ordered by prison guards to go to my cell, but I declined and insisted that Miller be taken to the hospital. They then informed me that they could not take anyone to the hospital until after they got all of the uninjured inmates back in their cells. I moved out of the sally port onto the tier of Max Row. At this point Satcher came in off the yard carrying Edwards and was ordered to lay him on the floor and go to his cell, which he also refused to do, demanding that Miller and Edwards be taken to the hospital first. The officers advised him that nobody would be taken to the hospital until after the uninjured inmates were all back in their cells. Satcher too then left the sally port and started to argue with the MTA concerning the removal of the wounded to the hospital.

Sergeant Matson and some other guards intervened, demanding that Satcher and I go to our cells. Not wanting Miller and Edwards to be left there on the floor to bleed to death, as I remembered in the case of Clarence Causey, we continued to insist that they be removed to the hospital in our presence. Immediately the guards started taking up threatening positions, brandishing billy clubs, expecting a battle. I removed my coveralls to give myself more freedom of movement and to avoid their being grabbed by prison guards in the anticipated battle. They didn't attack, however, because Nolen was brought in from the yard at that moment by Randolph and Whiteside and was placed on the floor, followed closely by two nonblack inmates carrying the wounded Caucasian inmate between them. After placing the Caucasian inmate on a waiting gurney, one of the nonblack inmates was pushed against Whiteside by a guard, and Whiteside, presumably thinking that he was being attacked, immediately turned his attention from Nolen, Edwards, and Miller and started punching with the inmate who had been pushed against him by the guard.

He and Randolph were set upon by prison guards with billy clubs. Satcher and I, by this time on the tier and separated from the altercation by a locked gate, could not go to the aid of Randolph and Whiteside other than to demand that the attack be immediately halted or we would retaliate on the guards who were on the tier supervising the lockup. Thus the attack was terminated without any serious injuries inflicted on either of the brothers in that incident. But Nolen, Edwards, and Miller lay dead from the shootings in the exercise yard.

Three or four days later, I was taken to the prison hospital, where I received an X-ray by a prisoner hospital attendant which revealed a break in one of my fingers. He put a splint cast on my hand and I was returned to my cell. A few days later all of the inmates on Max Row were taken before the prison disciplinary committee for the fighting on the yard. As usual, the blacks received the harshest punishment (a number of days of cell confinement, the only punishment meted out on that occasion by the prison officials). The entire blame for the violence was placed on the black inmates.

The murder of the three black inmates was ruled "justifiable homicide" by the Monterey County Grand Jury. Yet, at the event on January 13, 1970, there were more than twice as many prison guards present as inmates from the minute the first inmate was released to go to the yard until the last survivor was locked back in his cell. At all times they were armed with an assortment of tear gas, mace, five-cell flashlights, and billy clubs. They also, of course, had the support of the guard in the gun tower armed with the carbine semiautomatic rifle. There was no reason why they could not have terminated the altercation without the loss of a single life and possibly without the firing of a single shot by the guard in the gun tower. Yet they deliberately chose a course of action that resulted in the wanton murder of three black human beings. I cannot believe that anyone could not have foreseen violence or a high enough potential for violence to take steps to suppress it in advance and without the loss of life.

Sometime during the latter part of January, 1970, the word came into O Wing through the guards that a guard had been killed on the mainline and that it was believed by the officials that the killing was an act of retaliation for the murders of Nolen, Edwards, and Miller. Immediately thereafter three black inmates, George Jackson, Fleeta Drumgo, and John Clutchette, were selected and locked up in various parts of the institution's O and X wings.[3] Eventually they were all brought to Max Row. One of them I had previously met at San Quentin.

3. George Jackson was killed by guards at San Quentin prison during an alleged escape attempt in August of 1971. Fleeta Drumgo and John Clutchette were acquitted of the murder of the Soledad prison guard after a lengthy trial ending in early 1972.

A few days after their arrival, while I was being searched prior to a visit with my attorney, I heard the two guards who were to escort me to the visit discussing the incident in which the guard was killed. From what was said I soon gathered that one of the guards had not been at the prison on the day the incident occurred, but he had heard or read in the papers that the killing of the guard had been an act of retaliation for the murders of the three black inmates on the O Wing yard on the morning of January 13, 1970. The other guard told him that he had been told by the brass that no prison personnel witnessed the killing, and that they had learned from inmate informers that the dead guard was attacked by a crowd of racially mixed (black, Chicano, and Caucasian) inmates. Further, he continued, the identification of the inmates involved in the attack could not be ascertained. Nevertheless three niggers were going to ride the beef for it as a warning and an example to all of what they could look forward to for attacks on guards.

At this point I was drawn into the conversation by one of the guards who asked if I knew the one inmate who had been at San Quentin. I replied that I knew him there by name, sight, and reputation and that I had talked to him briefly on four or five occasions, maybe less. The guard then told me that I had better take a good look at him now if he was my friend because the next time I would see him he would be sniffing cyanide in the gas chamber. I pointed out that according to what he had just finished telling the other guard, they all knew the man didn't know who was responsible for it. With an arrogant sneer on his face he went on to point out to me that a few paroles or discharges in the right places would produce inmate witnesses to testify to anything the brass wanted said. Then they started to curse me for fingering the guard who murdered Nolen, Miller, and Edwards to the attorneys who were going to interview me, and remarked how I wouldn't get away with it.

Following the interview, I told the inmate in question about this event, and he suggested that I tell it to his attorney, who would know how to handle the matter. I wrote to his attorney and repeated the entire matter and included the name of the guard who had done most of the talking. Having been informed at an earlier date that the law and the institutional rules had been changed, permitting inmates to personally seal communications to attorneys before mailing, I sealed the letter and sent it off.

Nevertheless, it was opened by the officials at Soledad. Photostat copies were made of it, and it was placed in my central file for the Adult Authority to see before considering me for parole. Presumably the district attorney's office was provided a copy of the letter too, since they were prosecuting the inmate and two alleged codefendants for the offense.

I was scheduled to appear before the Adult Authority in April, three months after the incident. I was told by the O Wing counselor that my injury from the gunfire would not be made public during the investigation into the deaths of Nolen, Miller, and Edwards. If I refused to discuss the incident with the various people who would be making inquiries on the grounds that I didn't want to get involved, he said that he would take appropriate steps to see that I got cut loose when I got to the board. He went on to point out that I had tried to cause trouble for the staff over the deaths of Clarence Causey and Powell, and that although I had had direct knowledge of or had witnessed those two events, in neither case had I been successful. I should know by now, he concluded, that I was fighting a losing battle, and I should just do the sensible thing and take advantage of this once-in-a-lifetime opportunity and go home. He added that the staff's tolerance of me had about worn itself out.

At this point I interrupted him and pointed out that I had no illusions about Soledad or anyone who worked here. Common sense, aided by my experiences at this place, forced me to believe that the entire administration of Soledad was aware of the unlawful and inhuman acts perpetrated here against blacks

by guards and nonblack inmates. The deaths and injuries inflicted on blacks here amounted to Soledad's being a death row
or a holding pen where selective genocide is practiced against
black humanity by the cruelest and most sadistic racists that
ever preyed on mankind. What was really being offered me was
a temporary escape in exchange for sharing their guilt for all the
crimes committed against blacks here at Soledad prior to and
following my arrival, something I could not go for and still
respect myself as a human being, not to mention as a man. He
responded that I should not expect to get out of prison until my
maximum term expired, if I was lucky enough to live that long.
I was then escorted back to my cell on Max Row.

In April of 1970, I went before the Adult Authority. Having
reviewed my central file before I entered the room, they immediately informed me that they could not consider releasing
me. They then asked me a few questions, and I returned to my
cell. A few days later I received my board results, informing me
that they had denied me parole and that I would not be brought
back for three years. The following week I was taken before a
committee of prison officials for classification and post board
review, at which time the three-year denial was confirmed. The
counselor pointed out to me that the board had stipulated that
the officials could refer me for parole consideration whenever
I got a year's clean time, but that they did not think I would be
capable of getting a year clean. Considering the racial situation
among the inmates and the agitation encouraged by the guards,
I myself did not see how I could possibly get a year's clean time.
I just decided to live each day at a time.

In July, 1970, I again appeared before the committee of
prison officials for review and was told that I could move up to
the second floor. Since they had confined me to Max Row since
April, 1968, and refused me transfer to any other prison, the
mainline here, or any place other than the first floor of O Wing,
I of course thought they were joking and asked them not to play
games with me. Finally I became convinced that they were

serious and went back to my cell to pack my property for the move to the second tier. Upon arriving on the second floor, I was assigned to the very first cell.

Approximately ten minutes later two large Caucasian inmates were moved in the second and third cells. While moving their property they each looked into my cell at least four times, which didn't alarm me at the time because that was normal behavior for new arrivals. A few days later I was assigned to the porter job reserved for blacks on the same half-day basis that existed on Max Row. (Blacks were segregated from the other races on the second floor too. The only difference was that on cleanup days the porters were allowed to integrate with the Caucasian and Mexican porters to clean the tiers.)

The inmates on the second floor, without regard to race, soon learned through observation or contact with me that I was a naturally courteous and respectful person toward everyone, until forced to be otherwise. Eventually communication was established between me and the inmates in the second and third cells. In September, 1970, the inmate in the second cell told me that they had been propositioned by officials to kill me. At this point I thought back to the third week that I had been given the porter job. At that time a Mexican inmate porter whom I hardly knew had informed me that a guard had approached him and told him that I was talking bad about him and that he, the guard, would not beef him if he got me for it. I dismissed the incident at the time as a mistake of no importance. However, after listening to what these two inmates had to say, I began to see just why I was allowed to move to the second floor, and I decided to be more cautious.

I asked the inmates to write down on paper what they had told me. I showed them how to make a perjury oath, in order to make their statements legal affidavits, and I received their permission to turn the affidavits over to an attorney or someone else who would know how best to handle the situation. Then I hid them in my legal materials and other personal effects so that they would not be found and confiscated by the guards during a shakedown or when my property was sent home in the event that someone was successful in collecting the bounty placed on my life by the officials. Eventually, I decided to turn the statements over to an attorney I thought trustworthy enough to advise me what to do. I took advantage of the first opportunity to get the statements past the prison officials, and the statements were mailed to the attorney for me.

The officials became very angry when they found out that their selected assassins had betrayed the plot against my life and had cooperated in bringing the matter to the attention of concerned people and eventually the general public. They immediately transferred one of the intended assassins to another institution and thereafter moved me to the east side of the second tier on O Wing, where, in February, 1971, I sit writing this document of my life and experiences at Soledad.

CHAPTER 10

The Soledad Seven: Attempted Murder in Monterey

by Eve Pell

On July 13, 1970, a white guard named William Shull was stabbed to death at North Facility, a minimum-security section of Soledad. He had been stabbed more than 50 times while in his office in a small shack near a baseball diamond. Guards locked all inmates in North Facility in their cells, searched them and the cells, and questioned them. The yard shack where Shull died was tested for fingerprints, footprints, and other evidence by representatives of the Bureau of Criminal Identification and Investigation (CII), a state equivalent of the FBI.

Records of the investigation show that prison officials at first suspected a conspiracy of Mexican Americans. They knew that Shull had had serious difficulties with Mexican Americans near the time of his death. However, after interrogating Mexican Americans without being able to establish a good case, prison officials began to interrogate blacks, and the focus of the investigation shifted. Why to blacks? Possibly because Shull's death could be regarded as a second act of retaliation for the shooting of the three black inmates in the O Wing yard; possibly because groups of black inmates gathered daily to talk around some picnic tables near Shull's office. Perhaps, also, prison authorities felt they could use this murder as a pretext for destroying black organization within the institution.

INVESTIGATION AND INTERROGATION

"We do not charge people who are innocent with crime. I
have been in this business for a long time and I have never done
that. . . . There is nothing in the world that will make me charge
an innocent man of a crime," one investigator assured an inmate suspect.

Black prisoners had organized a tutoring class which met on
Wednesday nights in North Facility. Prison officials and investigators focused on this class as a center of black militancy and
the place where a conspiracy to kill the guard had originated.
They interrogated suspects extensively about what went on in
the class. Despite requirements that attendance records be
maintained, prison officials lost or destroyed the attendance
records of this particular class. Thus, blacks who had never
attended the class were unable to prove statements to this
effect, and an important means of testing the veracity of certain
witnesses mysteriously disappeared.

A team of officials was assigned to prosecute the case: Norman
Card of CII, Captain Clifford Rodgers of North Facility, Captain
Charles Moody, head of the Security Squad and special investigator of the district attorney, and Assistant District Attorney
Edward Barnes of Monterey County. These men, along with
prison staff, interrogated inmates and took charge of those who
claimed to be witnesses.

The interrogators were required by law to read each suspect
a statement of his rights before questioning him, advising him
that what he said could be used against him and that he had a
right to counsel. Transcripts of the interviews reveal that in
many cases this advice was never given. In other cases, the
rights were read, but when the prisoner attempted to exercise
them, he was overruled.

For example, note the following excerpt from the transcript

of an interview with Jesse Phillips, a nineteen-year-old black. Several times earlier in the interview, Phillips had requested an attorney. The interrogators overrode his requests and continued to ask him questions; Phillips said he would talk if so advised by an attorney.

Q: Are you really half as interested in let's say—
            completely clearing yourself of this thing as
            we are?
Phillips: Interested in clearing myself? Yes.
Q: We can shake you out of this situation as it now
            stands—do you understand we want to do
            that?
Phillips: No, I don't. If you did, you would have a law-
            yer here.

And the questions continue.

In another session with Phillips, one of the interrogators stated: "You have the right to refuse to talk to us. I also have a right to assume that if you do refuse to talk to us you do it because you feel that you are implicated or something. . . . If you want a lawyer, you are certainly entitled to have one."

But no lawyer ever is present during the questioning, and the grilling continues, with the constant implication that asking for a lawyer implies guilt.

Another technique used by the interrogators with the inmates most suspected of involvement was deception: "We only want to clear you." "You are not really under suspicion." "Don't you want to help yourself?"

Interrogators pressed inmates to take polygraph tests and Sodium Pentothal, again with the implication that refusal indicated guilt: "How about a little Sodium Pentothal? They call it a truth serum. It liberates your mind."

The interrogators often threatened to unleash the "inmate code"—a major canon of which is that "snitches" or "rats" get stabbed—on those who would or could not answer their questions. After one terrified inmate refused to talk, Captain Rodgers threatened to send him out into the halls and loudly thank him for the information so that inmates within earshot would spread the word that this inmate had snitched. This prisoner was repeatedly called in for interrogation so that inmates would think he was talking, even though he said he knew nothing.

Carrot as well as stick was applied to this man. He said that he was offered $500 and a reduced sentence for saying that he had seen a certain black inmate with a knife before the killing. He was also offered help with the pending appeal of his own case.

Several days after the murder, prison staff posted reward notices. A prisoner who inquired about the poster later described it: "It said $500 reward for information leading to arrest and conviction of any person involved in the killing. . . . It was signed by D. B. Cole. Written up in longhand. I asked him about it. He said they will probably parole the dude." Prison officials later denied that these posters had existed. However, the tape recording of an interrogation picked up a background conversation in which one staff member told another to go and take down the reward posters.

Threats of doing extra time or time in the most severe prisons occur frequently in the transcripts. One inmate was told, "You are close enough to the fire and you might get burned. . . . How much time do you think you will do if you get completely resolved of this thing?"

"About seven . . ."

"The way it stands right now, exactly at this point, this tenth day of August at 1:35 P.M., I can see more than seven years. I think it is important that you stay and clean yourself up. You are not clear. You are implicated. . . . I don't know if we ever can clear you." And they continue to ask for information.

One white inmate was unloading a truck at the time Shull was killed. At 2:30 the following morning, guards took him to be questioned. He described that questioning:

They asked me if I knew what happened and who did it. I told them no. And they told me I must know who did it. Then they showed me some pictures of some black inmates and told me that they think they did it. But they don't have any proof and they would like to know if I was interested in a parole or discharge in exchange for my testimony against the inmates in the pictures that they showed me. I told them that I didn't know anything and they told me it did not matter, that they would tell me what to say in court. All they wanted was a conviction. They was willing to give me my freedom in exchange for my cooperation. I refused to lie on those inmates.

Then they told me they could really make things tough for me and that I had no sense of responsibility toward my race and the officer who was killed was killed by niggers and who knows I could be next because they are trying to kill all white people. Therefore I should not care what happens to them.

THE WITNESSES

On September 18, two months after Shull's death, seven black prisoners were charged with murder and conspiracy: James Wagner, Jesse Phillips, Roosevelt Williams, O. C. Allen, Walter Joe Watson, Alfred Dunn, and Jimmie James. Because they were all serving indeterminate sentences with a maximum term of life, they were subject to a mandatory death penalty if convicted. All seven were indigent, with no possible means to pay lawyers.

The families of the defendants contacted Berkeley attorney Fay Stender, well known for her work in prison reform. Stender arranged with San Francisco attorney Patrick Hallinan to take the case. For a while, Hallinan represented all seven defendants.

According to the report filed by Special Agent Norman Gard of CII, the charges against the seven were based on statements by the following inmate witnesses: Anthony Bianco, William

Brizendine, Rodney Catsiff, Arnold Chase, Francis J. Indino, Herman E. Johnson, Don Lamontagne, and Warren Miner.

Who were these witnesses? How did they come forward? Curly-haired, flamboyant Patrick Hallinan gave his explanation at the opening of the trial. He described how the prison authorities had first investigated the Mexican Americans but had not been able to make a good case. Then, he said:

> Now, amongst hungry starving men, they dangle a piece of chocolate cake and they get results. They appeal to two kinds of men and these are what the witnesses are, ladies and gentlemen, who will testify on this stand. The first group of people they appeal to are the Nazis, white racists in the penitentiary who call themselves Nazis, who tattoo themselves with thunderbolts and swastikas and who feel that any chance to get a nigger is a strike for the cause . . . and they say, let's lay it on the black man. . . .
>
> The other kind of witness is the ordinary home-grown style of opportunist which the prison is full of, who will take advantage of the opportunity to get himself special privileges and to get himself rewards or to get himself a parole. And those witnesses, ladies and gentlemen, as we develop their testimony, will almost invariably, almost to the man, bloom in this manner, that on their first interview and first occasion they are talked to, they know very, very little and they have very little to add to the prosecution's case. And then as they are segregated and isolated and put amongst themselves where they can talk between themselves, and as they are interviewed time and again and time and again and time and again by a particular few correctional officers who, I will say right now, we will say coached these witnesses, their testimony blossoms and blooms into the case which will finally be brought into this courtroom.

By the end of the trial, Hallinan's opening charge that the witnesses were coerced would return to haunt the prosecution and provide a stunning climax to the trial.

One of the witnesses, Rodney Catsiff, described in a letter how he happened to become involved.

I was associating with a known homosexual *black* inmate, and when the officer was killed the staff called me in and advised me they are ready to send me to San Quentin as an undesirable inmate. Lt. William Merkle, Captain Clifford Rodgers, Assistant Attorney General Norman Gard and Mr. Barnes, Chief Deputy, Monterey County, were at the institution. Lt. Merkle said, I can save you if you'll go into the Adjustment Center and be placed between the suspects as a "plant." I reluctantly agreed, as San Quentin was not very good.

James Wagner, one of the accused seven, reported that Catsiff had been placed in the hole with him and constantly said that he was going to set Wagner up for the murder of the officer.

Catsiff was promised "a nice place with no other inmates," and "Lt. Merkle told me we'd be released after trial." However, once Catsiff had given a deposition against the defendants, the tone changed. While being transferred from one prison to another, Catsiff reported, "Captain Rodgers from Soledad said, 'Don't you forget we got your depositions and really don't need you. Don't ever cross me—you'll regret it.' Then the Captain told us, 'If you escape, *I'll* hunt you down and *I'll* find you.' "

Catsiff, who had a reputation among prisoners as a snitch and a homosexual prostitute, marked himself as a witness for the prosecution and had to be kept in protective custody.

Francis Indino, an inmate with whom Shull had argued on the morning of his death, described how he came to be a witness. Immediately after Shull's death, officers questioned him for seven hours, then left him in a holding cell. A lieutenant threatened to use a rubber hose on him "if the right answer wouldn't be used." The next day he went for a lie detector test. The polygraph operator, Indino reported, threatened him with his maximum term in prison. Indino then took Sodium Pentothal. In a later account of his experience he wrote that before he took it, ". . . they showed me pictures of the defendants and somehow they had worked on my mind before I went under the sedation."

The transcript of his testimony under the Sodium Pentothal, as well as the actual tape, had to be delivered to defense lawyers representing the inmates accused of murder. Comparison of tape and transcript reveal significant differences between what was said and what was transcribed; sounds of slaps and "Wake up, Indino" recur throughout the tape.

When asked if he had ever had any trouble with Shull, he answered, "No." He said that he had seen Phillips and Dunn enter the yard shack. His answers contain inconsistencies: he did and he did not see Shull's body; he saw Phillips and Dunn before, then after, he went to the canteen; he does know, he does not know, anything about the case.

After he recovered consciousness, the tape was played back to him once or twice. Like Catsiff, he was promised safe, non-punitive confinement and was threatened with violence if he double-crossed the interrogators.

Arnold Chase, a black inmate who had attended the tutoring class, told defense attorney Laurance Moran how he came to testify in the case:

> They asked me, did I know what was going on. I didn't. I knew of rumors, of course. . . . Then Lt. Shumaker kicked me in the back and I just went along with what they were saying. . . . Captain Moody said if I didn't go to court to testify that they would never get me released. . . . They kept telling me to say Jesse Phillips was there. He wasn't at the class. If I was to tell it like it is they might harm me. They kept threatening me. . . . They had some pictures and they laid this on the table and said, "Wasn't this the one there" and Shumaker said, "The man showed you," and I said, "Man, I don't know." Shumaker hit me on the head with his keys and told me to pick someone and I closed my eyes and picked one.

Chase said that he had been offered $1,000 and immediate parole to testify. They told him that whatever he said would be held confidential and that no moves would be made that might jeopardize him.

In that conversation, Chase seemed uncertain about the name of the man he was supposed to be incriminating, James Wagner, nicknamed Punchy. Chase said that a man in the tutoring class had said that an officer "had to go," and that the man was: "It's, uh, what is it, I forgot who, uh, Pooky. His nickname is Pooky."

Q: Pook?
Chase: Yeah, they call him Pooky.

A little later, Chase called him "Poochy." Still later, he said, "Hey, that name ain't Pooch, it's Punchy." But further on he referred to Poochy. "Punchy," corrected an interrogator. "Punchy," repeated Chase.

When asked if he knew Roosevelt Williams, another of the seven, Chase replied, "The short, dark-complexioned brother?"

Q: He, he's pretty tall—I think he's a weight
          lifter. Big guy, big guy, they call him Rosie.
Chase: I could picture a brother. . . . He comes to the
          meetings all the time. . . . He's big, you know.

Throughout, Chase appears to try to follow the leads held out to him by the questioners, to give the right answers.

Chase told an investigator for the defense attorneys that he expected an early parole in exchange for his testimony; that the usual period of time served for his crime is two and a half to three years, but he expected to be out soon, having served only one. A notice was placed in Chase's file that he ". . . voluntarily and with knowledge of the great peril to his physical well-being and for his life, has given various statements and submitted to numerous examinations resulting in his becoming a prosecution witness." Before long, Arnold Chase was out on parole.

The other prosecution witnesses, whose names had spread throughout the prison system, required special care and treatment. They could not be allowed into the general population of any institution, for fear that an inmate would kill them. Yet the witnesses complained and grew restive if they were kept in lockup all day.

In October, presumably for safekeeping, the group was transferred to Palm Hall, the maximum-security section of the California Institution for Men at Chino. The prisoner porter responsible for cleaning up the area near them observed the special treatment they received.

> No one was allowed on the tier but me to sweep. They got supplies, they were afraid of poison. . . . They were given $80 apiece to testify, and all they had to do was ask for anything from the canteen and they would get it. Witnesses were given decks of cards and special chess sets— I passed them out. . . . They got special contact visits, while other people had to visit through a telephone.

The porter reported that Warren Miner, one of the group, said that the statements he had made to the prosecution were false, that all he knew is what Captain Rodgers at Soledad had told him, that Rodgers had promised an early parole date, $500, easy time, and unlimited canteen supplies. According to the porter, some of the witnesses were anxious and wanted to change their testimony, but they were afraid to, and Captain Moody, an officer known for his cruelty at Soledad, came to check on them every week.

Among the many Chino inmates who confirmed the free canteen and special privileges given the group was Robert Morris, who overheard a sergeant asking Miner if the free canteen had made him happy. Another inmate wrote his lawyer in fury: "This is self evident, that those guys are willing to send [the seven] to the gas chamber just to obtain their release and not because they know anything."

Witnesses received less desirable treatment than they had been led to expect, however. Warren Miner had a friend in another section of Chino with whom he kept in contact. In one of his "kites" (illegal messages) he wrote: "I am kind of scared to write anything that might be intercepted but you cats got a right to know. It's bad bad. They are so much in a panic that they can't show no heart. . . ." He reported that prison staff handcuffed him with his hands behind his back, then pulled up on the cuffs until his arms could go no farther, asked him questions, and pulled up still more. "I ain't never felt so much pain as that." In his correspondence, Miner went to some lengths to try to convince his friend that he was a good guy, that he was not really on the side of the prosecution.

Miner described his keepers with feeling: "They're worse than the syndicate. I mean it; they're cold blooded aminals [sic]. I fear them more than getting stuck. . . . They hint around they could go to your family and make you look like some rat, some punk in the joint, if they wish."

Terrified of the prison staff, knowing their lives were in danger from inmates, the witnesses stewed and fretted. In November they were moved from the strict confinement of Palm Hall to the more comfortable California Men's Colony West at San Luis Obispo. A curious series of flip-flops took place there.

A renowned "jailhouse lawyer," a prisoner named Richard Lewis, wrote a Berkeley lawyer that he had important information on the case. When the lawyer visited CMC West, he was met by Associate Superintendant Russell, who, in a highly unusual procedure, served him with a judge's order forbidding publicity about the case. Lewis told the lawyer that Russell had tried to forbid him to come out for the visit and had threatened that he would be in violation of a court order, in a "precarious" position.

The reason for Russell's anxiety was shortly made plain. Lewis told the lawyer that three of the prosecution witnesses, Indino, Catsiff, and Brizendine, had come to him requesting protection and help. They had dictated and signed a deposition saying that they had been coerced into testifying and, in fact, knew nothing about Shull's death. The deposition, dated November 12, said:

The methods employed to compel us to give false testimony were injections of various drugs, psychological stress and strain induced through the employment of deprivations and long hours of constant, cruel interrogation whereby we were advised that if we did not do as we were instructed and sign statements dictated to us, we would be housed in the regular cell blocks and that the California Department of Corrections officers would then promulgate to the other inmates that we were informers, which would surely result in our demise. . . . Our lives are in constant danger; the Department of Corrections will not afford us protection. It is therefore imperative that we either secure Federal protection or escape. This is a true statement given of our own free will.

Correspondence between staff members at CMC West shows that Catsiff had requested immediate FBI protection on November 10, two days earlier. When that did not arrive, he turned to Lewis. When an FBI agent visited him November 13, however, Catsiff told him about the deposition he had given to Lewis and again requested protection. Appealing to the agent for help, Catsiff said he had been threatened into making that deposition. Catsiff was rushing from one side to the other, terrified for his life.

James Willis, a prisoner at CMC West, was one of several who said that the three prosecution witnesses had voluntarily given Lewis the statement, but had become wildly frightened of Corrections personnel after they had done so. After prison authorities found out about the deposition, said Willis, they threatened the witnesses and forbade them to communicate further with Lewis. The witnesses were pressed back into line; Captain Moody of Soledad continued to check on them periodically.

Indino described the most notable of these visits. "It was Christmas. When he came in, Captain Moody was under the weather. He came in and gave us our Christmas pack-cakes, stuff that was contraband, figs and stuff—mmm that was good stuff."

Some of the witnesses complained to Moody about having to get up early in the morning and about having insufficient food. Pulling out a gun, the drunken Moody became enraged and moved next to Bill Brizendine.

"You will [testify] or else, Brizendine," threatened Moody, holding the gun to the witness' chin.

"I will, I will," said Brizendine. Moody then glowered at the group.

"If any of you men try to cross me I will lock you up in Central Soledad and bury you."

Bringing firearms into certain parts of a prison is a felony. Moody, who had violated that law, was never prosecuted and continued his employment with the Department of Corrections, later riding herd on witnesses in the Soledad Brothers case.

Brizendine, in an interview with a lawyer defending one of the seven accused, reflects something of his state of mind: "Anything said here will not be given to the District Attorney, will it? I could tell some things, but I would be dead in the morning. . . . If I tell, I would catch the wrong bus going to the wrong institution and be killed. Moody pulled a gun and threatened to kill me. . . . I am trying to get someone to help me so that I can tell my story, otherwise I am dead."

The lawyer asked, "Who is threatening you?"

"The Department of Corrections."

"How are they doing this?"

"Threats. . . . I cannot say more until I get some help. If I say more I am dead."

In January, 1971, a final witness came forward for the prosecution. When first interviewed, he had said he was in school when Shull was murdered; later, he said he had gone to class, but had left shortly after it began. In January, he said he had stayed in his cell all morning after bribing a clerk to mark him present. From his room, he had an excellent view of the yard shack. This witness, Thomas Brenson, was interviewed by prison staff and representatives of the prosecution on January 26.

After congratulating him for having the courage to admit that he initially lied, the questioners proceeded:

> Q: Let me assure you of one thing, if there's any-
>   thing that you have to contribute in this affair,
>   you'll be properly looked after, as have other
>   people, you know.
> Q: We can split you out of here right now, it's up
>   to you. . . .
> Q: Do you remember the nationality of the peo-
>   ple coming out of the yard shack?
> Brenson: Right, they were black. See I'm white
>   and . . .
> Q: We realize.
> Brenson: Yes, he was one of them. I don't know his
>   name.
> Q: Maybe it's better that you don't for right now.
>   Hey, rest easy man, it'll be taken care of.

The questioners then showed Brenson photographs of the accused.

> Q: We're going to ask you, Tom, we're going to
>   put those pictures back in there, there's a cou-
>   ple of guys that look very similar in there; I
>   don't know that you looked through all of
>   them or not, we'll keep this one of Wagner out
>   and look through that group again. . . .

Brenson, not surprisingly, identified as James Wagner one of the two men he said he had seen emerging from the yard shack. The other he named as *Theodore* Williams, a black inmate not related to Roosevelt Williams.

> Q: . . . if you were to go back out, do you think
>   there would be any heat on you?
> B: I'd feel unsafe, let's put it that way.

The interview ended with assurances to Brenson that he would be protected.

THE DEFENDANTS

All fifteen suspects in Shull's murder were sent directly to O Wing, the maximum-security section of Soledad. The first to go was Roosevelt Williams, whom I interviewed later at Folsom prison. Tall, handsome, and athletic, Williams had been a model prisoner in minimum security when Shull was killed. He kept smiling as he described his experiences, moving his head from side to side ruefully as he described horror after horror. He spoke as though he could not believe these things had happened.

He was sent from his cell to the hole without being told why. A lieutenant merely told him: "You're going to the gas chamber." In O Wing, said Williams, "I just lay there. I thought, they're going to kill me. The first days officers kept coming by and looking: we were just like art exhibits. I was thinking what to do—I can't protect myself, they're going to win." He told how white racist inmates took torn strips of sheets, rolled them into knots, set them afire and threw them to burn in front of his cell and the cells of the other blacks who had also been sent to the hole. Mail was not delivered.

Williams described what O Wing was like for him:

> When first placed in the hole, I was stripped down and remained without clothing for two to three weeks. I had no shoes. I was given none of my personal property for over a month. Eating and sleeping were extremely difficult and much of the time completely impossible. With no clothing and skimpy blankets, the nights in the cell were too cold for decent sleep. Tear gas is used frequently in O Wing, and when used in any cell on either of the two connected tiers, all of the cells receive gas. Food served me by white inmates often had urine and excrement in it. Racial taunts and names were yelled to me day and night.

The other suspects in the hole suffered similarly. They were not told why they were being held; they were isolated in their cells twenty-four hours a day except for a shower once or twice a week. Guards stood by and silently stared at them, and the racial harassment continued constantly.

In February, 1971, a new district attorney took office in Monterey County. Without any explanation, he dropped the charges against four of the seven, leaving Roosevelt Williams, James Wagner, and Jesse Phillips to go to trial. After complicated maneuvering, the court appointed lawyers. Richard Hodge of San Francisco represented Williams; Laurance Moran of Monterey, a former OEO official, represented Phillips; and Patrick Hallinan of San Francisco, in the case from the start, represented Wagner.

During the months before trial, the lawyers and a team of investigators interviewed inmates and collected evidence of the bribery and coercion of witnesses. The lawyers were not afraid to challenge the Department of Corrections, to accuse them of railroading innocent men to the gas chamber, or to condemn the dreadful prison conditions in which their clients were held. The lawyers and their investigators interviewed each witness several times, driving many miles to remote prisons throughout California, and thus were able to detect and document the bribery and coercion attempts by Corrections personnel.

Hodge, the tall, blond lawyer for Williams, prepared a motion to suppress all statements made by defendants and all statements made by witnesses and to dismiss the case on the ground that since all witnesses had been bribed or coerced, there could be no truthful testimony and no fair trial. "This case represents the most outrageous denial of due process any court has seen in the history of jurisprudence," he claimed. "No witness who takes the stand can be deemed to be reliable or trustworthy." Judge J. Francis Good denied Hodge's motion, and the case went to trial.

It lasted nine days. After several days of testimony from investigating officials and custodial personnel, the key inmate witnesses for the prosecution were called to the stand. The first of these was Francis Indino, who had given testimony incriminating Jesse Phillips while under the influence of Sodium Pentothal. Under questioning by Assistant District Attorney Barnes, Indino reported seeing Phillips and Dunn at the picnic tables and overhearing a remark about offing a pig or bull; he described his activities during that morning.

On cross-examination, Hallinan asked Indino about the testimony he had given while drugged. "Was there anything in the tape that you did not personally remember before you went under the drug?"

"Yes, sir," replied Indino. "Mostly all of it."

Hodge inquired about Correctional personnel's threats to use the rubber hose.

Hodge:	I take it at that time, after you had been threatened, you were a little bit worried about your own welfare, were you not?
Indino:	Yes, sir.
Hodge:	As a matter of fact, at that time you thought it would be important for you, as a witness, to come up with something that would point the finger of suspicion away from yourself to someone else, did you not?
Indino:	Yes, sir, I would have to say that.
Hodge:	Isn't that the reason, Mr. Indino, that you mentioned to Mr. Barnes that you saw another person by the name of Jesse Phillips at the picnic table?
Indino:	Yes, sir.

Indino told of other threats and of his fear of doing the maximum amount of his sentence. He said that Barnes had been trying to get him to lie on the stand. One attempt by Barnes to discredit Indino was ludicrous. Hodge was asking about Captain Moody.

Hodge:	You actually observed Captain Moody take a gun and put it to Mr. Brizendine's head?
Indino:	No, chin.
Barnes:	Objection, Your Honor. I ask that the defendant's answer be stricken because there is no showing of any threats made to this witness. . . . He said the gun was pointed at another witness' head.
Hodge:	In his presence, I might add.
The Court:	In his presence.
Barnes:	There is no showing as to whether this witness was intimidated by that or not. (Laughter)
The Court:	Objection overruled.

Indino's performance on the stand shook the prosecution. Most of the spectators at the trial were members of local law enforcement agencies. Silences of despair and dismay filled the courtroom as Indino came apart under cross-examination.

More shocks for the prosecution were forthcoming. The next day Arnold Chase, the black on parole in Los Angeles, took the stand. Under questioning by Barnes, he testified about events which had taken place prior to Shull's death, the only significant allegation being that he had heard Punchy Wagner say in the tutoring class that "a pig had to go." He answered Barnes's questions, seemingly without difficulty.

He changed when under cross-examination. Mumbling and nervous, he refused to remove his dark glasses when Laurance Moran requested him to. He said he was utterly unable to recall a long interview he had had with Moran in Los Angeles the month before; in this interview he had told Moran about the coercion to which he had been subjected. He gave contradictory answers, refused to recognize as his own words the transcriptions from the interview which Moran read into the court record, and said at one point, "I don't want to remember anything I said to you." Barnes even asked him during redirect examination, "Are you telling the truth now or when you talked to Mr. Moran?"

Chase's two-and-one-half-hour series of evasive responses further damaged the prosecution's case. Later that same day, the whole house of cards fell in, like a scene from Perry Mason.

Thomas Brenson was called by Richard Hodge. He testified that he had seen Punchy Wagner leaving the yard shack, presumably after the death of Shull. Brenson was asked to identify Wagner, sitting at the defense table before him. After much hesitation, in the hushed courtroom, he picked out Jesse Phillips.

Brenson went on to testify that he had identified a second person leaving the yard shack, then added lightly that he had lied about it. He explained that he held a grudge against Theodore Williams, a black inmate whom he had identified as leaving the yard shack with Wagner. Brenson admitted, as Wagner stood for all to see, that he was not the man who had left the yard shack.

Hodge inquired why Brenson had waited a full six months before coming forward with his testimony. "There is just something on my conscience," he responded.

"And what part of your conscience," continued Hodge, "caused you to name Theo Williams and place him in a position where he would be executed if he were convicted?"

Silence from Brenson.

Hallinan began to pound questions at the witness, who was by this time flustered and shaken.

> Hallinan: You told [the officers interviewing you] that you are known as a staff snitch and will tell anything you know, correct?
> Brenson: Yes, sir.

Hallinan established that Brenson had been confined in a special lockup cell in North Facility at the time the crime occurred.

Hallinan:	Tell me, Mr. Brenson, was not the reason you were down there because you were heavily in debt?
Brenson:	Yes.
Hallinan:	Now, what I would like you to do, Mr. Brenson, is tell the jury what it means to incur heavy debts in prison. . . .
Brenson:	It is, let's see, I would be turned out as the phrase is used, or stabbed.
Hallinan:	Doesn't turned out, Mr. Brenson, mean that whoever you are obligated to or indebted to, uses you as a male punk or homosexual to have relations with other inmates?
Brenson:	To a certain degree, it depends on the other individual, sir.
Hallinan:	Brenson was so heavily in debt that he relied upon the protection of the institution and as payment for that continued protection, became a witness in this case.

Moran followed Hallinan on the cross-examination. Gentle and compassionate where Hallinan had been severe, he asked Brenson again about his identification of the man he had seen leaving the yard shack. He showed him a photo of Jesse Phillips.

"Is this not the man you saw coming out of the yard shack, Mr. Brenson?"

"No, it isn't," he finally answered.

Moran, gently, "Mr. Brenson, do you have any idea what the effect of your testimony in this case can be?"

Brenson then went on to explain that he wished to be transferred out of Soledad, that his own information was inadequate to achieve a transfer, so he invented names in order to make the information more valuable.

Hallinan:	And that was so you would get paroled, wasn't it?
Brenson:	No, sir.
Hallinan:	It was so you would get out of the institution, wasn't it?

Brenson: Correct.
Hallinan: I—I really have no further questions.

The court case was finished, after only the tip of the iceberg had surfaced. The next day, the district attorney himself asked that the charges be dismissed. The judge complied, with a short homily to the defendants to the effect that although they were innocent of the charges lodged against them, they should note that justice had been done.

The defense attorneys, by now wise in the ways of prison personnel, asked the judge to write a letter to be placed in the records of the three defendants stating that they had not been found guilty and ought not to be discriminated against in prison on account of the charges lodged against them. The judge agreed, yet when I first interviewed Roosevelt Williams and Punchy Wagner at Folsom after the trial, I found that the effect of that letter had been virtually nil. Guards made remarks to them such as, "You got lucky once, but I'm watching you," and often fixed them with hard, hostile stares. Wagner and Williams had been sent to Folsom and Phillips to San Quentin, directly from the Monterey County courtroom. All three, who had been in minimum security before this case, were sent to the hole at their new prisons and spent many, many weeks there before being released to the general population after much pressure from lawyers and further inquiries from Judge Good.

I asked Punchy Wagner what the effect of the case had been on him. He could barely answer. "I was bewildered," he said. "Hallinan would bring me transcripts and I would get confused. I'm still confused as to what happened, the change was so sudden. I was a model convict." With his young, bland face, he looked about twenty, glasses askew on his broad nose. "The police [convict word for guards] have not forgot what happened in Soledad. I think there is going to be a setup; no telling what these people are capable of doing. I feel paranoid, all these police officers knowing who Wagner is and what he was charged with and letting their personal feelings interfere with their jobs."

Wagner added, slowly, "This case caused me to lose my family. My wife stopped corresponding and would not bring our two sons to visit me. She just thought me capable of doing that. I was trying to fight for my life at the same time I was trying to fight for my family, my wife and my children." Wagner's face clouded with pain. "I tried to convince my first lawyer, the public defender, that the evidence was being trumped up. But he would not believe me; he was a friend of Barnes."

I asked Patrick Hallinan whether he thought the conduct of prison officials in this case was an aberration or whether it was representative. "The testimony, the manner in which it was collected, put together, and prosecuted is on a par with almost every prison case I have seen," he replied. "Most of the cons who were prosecution witnesses have in their files evaluations from prison psychiatrists as pathological liars. The Corrections people were relying on the testimony of pathological liars to send seven innocent men to the gas chamber!"

The behavior of prison staff—selecting defendants, coercing witnesses, eliciting testimony with bribes, threats, and coaching, harassing the men found innocent—illustrates the absolute power these men exercise over the lives of prisoners.

Constitutional rights and due process under the law were annihilated by officials desperate to obtain conviction. Representatives of the California Department of Corrections and the district attorney preyed on the opportunism and racism of prisoners willing to see others executed so that they might go free or get transferred to a safer prison. Inmates who could not be enticed by rewards were threatened with physical harm and parole denial.

For all that was done to coerce, bribe, and threaten the inmate witnesses, no Correctional officer will be tried for assault, no prosecutor will be tried for tampering with evidence, no warden will be fired. Indeed, the warden was promoted and Captain Moody went on to further custodial care of the alleged prosecution witnesses in the Soledad Brothers case. The Department of Corrections fully lived up to the name inmates have bestowed upon it—the Department of Corruptions.

Every inmate of the California Prison System who knows about the Soledad Seven case has one more coal to add to the fires of his rage, one more flagrant example of the law's hypocrisy, one more reason to act with violence, because he knows how high are the odds against him. And for all that the defendants were acquitted and the prison authorities discredited, the shame of the moment will pass; the reporters and the lawyers will return to their offices; prisoners will remain powerless in their cages; those who stood against the power of Corrections will pay, in paroles denied and endless small harassments, until prison authorities are stripped of the absolute power they now possess.

CHAPTER 11

Violence and Lawlessness at Soledad Prison[1]

by Fay Stender

The California prison system was shaken by unprecedented levels of violence in the years 1970–1971. In the course of two years, 9 prison guards and 24 inmates were killed. More than 100 nonfatal assaults against prison officials were reported, and nearly five times that many assaults against prisoners.[2] Prison officials in the state have looked everywhere for explanations of this violence except to the conditions within prisons themselves.

The president of the California Correctional Officers' Association, in testimony before a Congressional hearing on prisons, explained the causes of violence this way:

> Prison violence and murder in California, if not throughout the United States, will continue to increase unless and until we accept the cold, hard fact that a conspiracy exists to destroy our penal system and are willing to deal accordingly with those who are responsible.
>
> And those responsible include not only a small portion of our inmate population, but a segment of our free society

1. The author is indebted for editorial assistance to Elsa Knight Thompson, former public affairs director, station KPFA, Berkeley, and presently consultant to the Prison Law Project.

2. From 1953 to 1970, a total of four prison employees were killed on duty.

that encompasses professional people and lay citizens, as well, apparently, as a few members of our legislature. . . .

We find that the most commonly employed approach of inmate revolutionary recruitment and agitation is provided through inmate contact with members of the legal profession. Radical attorneys appear to provide the ideal pipeline between the outside and the inside revolutionary movement. . . .

Our Association has uncovered a countless number of incidents involving plots of violence that are directly related to outside sources, some of whom we understand are here today to provide testimony to your committee.[3]

The Board of Corrections, in a special report to the governor, presented a similar view of the scope of outside agitation responsible for the violence within prisons:

It became reasonably clear that some type of inmate organization, probably involving a relatively small number of prisoners, did, in fact, exist. Information from several sources alleged that some outside attorneys had encouraged disruptions in prisons such as hunger strikes and riots, as a means of generating unfavorable publicity.

Information was obtained indicating that some investigators and aides for lawyers were acting as message carriers between prisoners. These same lawyers and legal aides often appeared at outside events and made false and inflammatory statements about prison conditions.[4]

The Department of Corrections itself, in addition to seeing prison violence as the result of outside agitation, felt that much of the problem was rooted in neurological brain damage of prisoners. The director of the Department proposed the development of psychosurgical techniques to "cure" the "violent

3. Testimony of Moe Camacho, reprinted in hearings before Subcommittee No. 3 of the Committee on the Judiciary, House of Representatives, Ninety-Second Congress, First Session, "Corrections, Part II: Prisons, Prison Reform and Prisoners' Rights: California," October 25, 1971 (Serial No. 15), pp. 142–144.

4. *Ibid.*, p. 321.

inmate" of his aggressive tendencies through brain surgery (see p. 330 for the text of his proposal). Nowhere, to my knowledge, has the Department of Corrections ever hinted that the violence of prisoners could in any way be related to the conditions within prison, to the absence of enforceable prisoners' rights, to the total powerlessness of prisoners, or to the treatment of prisoners by guards and officials.

This chapter will examine the relationship of prison violence to prison conditions, particularly to the quality of lawlessness in the administration of American prisons. My understanding of these issues is based on my experience as an attorney for hundreds of prisoners in Soledad and other prisons during the period 1970–1971, and on information from other attorneys who have worked with prisoners throughout the California Department of Corrections.

LAW AND LAWLESSNESS

"The essential element of the rule of law," Phillip Selznick has written, "is the restraint of official power by rational principles of civil order. . . . Legality imposes an environment of constraint, of tests to be met, standards to be observed, ideals to be fulfilled."[5]

The irreducible requirements of any system of law include standards of procedure, some degree of reliability and enforceability, and some real mutuality between the enforcers of the law and those upon whom the law is enforced. The rules and the enforcement of the rules must have some claim to legitimacy beyond the existence of naked and total power. There must be some rational relationship between the severity of the punishment and the behavior being punished, and some reliable procedure for the determination of guilt or innocence. Above

---

5. Phillip Selznick, *Law, Society and Industrial Justice* (New York: Russell Sage Foundation, 1969), p. 11.

all, there must be some meaningful restraint upon the enforcers of the rules as they act upon the subjects of their enforcement.

The notion of restraint upon the enforcers is at the heart of what is meant by the "rule of law." It is only when institutionalized restraint exists that the individual can be protected from the arbitrary exercise of discretionary power by the enforcers of the law. For such restraint to have any meaning, it cannot be based on the benevolence of the enforcers, on their feelings, whims, or subjective judgment. Restraint must be grounded in the basic structures of the legal system which provide the subjects of enforcement with real opportunities for appeal of actions, channels for redress of grievances, and power to punish the enforcers themselves for violations of the rules.

When no reliable, workable channels exist for redress of grievances or appeal of decisions, when there is no enforceable restraint upon the behavior of the enforcers, then there is no "law." A relationship exists which can be described in terms of power and powerlessness, but there are no attributes of law and legality, in either a philosophical or a commonsense understanding of the term. Such a situation is one of "lawlessness."

In the American legal tradition, the United States Constitution, with its backdrop of English common law, provides the basis for the rule of law. The Constitutional concept of "cruel and unusual punishment" is directed specifically at preventing the enforcers of the law from using certain kinds of sanctions against offenders. The Bill of Rights restrains officials from abridging the freedom of speech, assembly, religion, and petition for redress of grievances. These substantive rights are intertwined, in the Constitution, with procedural rights: the right to assistance of counsel, confrontation of accusers, cross-examination, examination of evidence submitted by the prosecution, opportunity to be heard and to prepare a defense, right to a decision based only on the evidence produced at the hearing or trial, and the right to some form of appeal and review. These procedural safeguards constitute the "due process" which sustains the rule of law in the courts.[6]

These fundamental elements of the rule of law are almost totally absent from American prisons. Prisoners are denied, either by statute or by prison practices, virtually all substantive Constitutional rights. They are granted very limited freedom of speech and assembly, and only recently, freedom of religion. Within the prison, there are no procedural restraints on the administrators. Not only do they have total power to create the rules the prisoners must obey, but they have total discretion to ignore those rules in the name of expediency. Prisoners have no effective channels for redress of grievances. They are denied even the most rudimentary elements of due process in disciplinary and parole hearings, and they have no legal power whatsoever to obtain sanctions against the enforcers of the rules for arbitrary violations of the law.

For these reasons prisons can be called lawless institutions. While discretionary power pervades the criminal justice system from arrest to plea bargaining, to imprisonment, to probation and parole, only in prisons is it totally unrestrained.[7] The very essence of American prisons is lawlessness.

6. Even these processes are, of course, open to very serious question. The effective disenfranchisement of a whole class of people, the availability of better legal counsel for the rich than for the poor, raises the question whether conduct can be justly considered "criminal" when it violates rules which protect the economic, political, and social privileges of the owners of property in its various forms. These issues and questions cannot be ignored if we wish to pursue a thorough examination of American justice and American society, but they must fall outside the scope of the present discussion.

7. In many respects the precepts of the rule of law are frequently violated in the courts in America. Nevertheless, in spite of the racial, social, cultural, and economic biases of the courts, criminal law still operates within the procedural *framework* of the rule of law. However unevenly these procedures are enforced, they are potentially enforceable, and they do provide some real safeguards for the subjects of the law. Prisons lack even these formal attributes of a system of law. For a particularly good analysis, see Michael Feit, *Prison Discipline and the Inmate Sense of Injustice* (State University of New York at Albany: School of Criminal Justice, 1972).

LAWLESSNESS AT SOLEDAD PRISON, 1970–1971

The lawlessness which characterizes American prisons in general has been particularly intense in Soledad prison, especially in the period 1970–1971. As an attorney working with the inmates at Soledad, I was struck by the fact that there were almost no consistent rules in the prison. Rules and regulations seemed to change the moment prisoners and their attorneys had adjusted to them. Visiting hours were changed at the time of a proposed visit. Regulations concerning mail, the right of lawyers to discover documents, the use of tape recorders, and the receipt of reading materials were changed frequently, with no warning. There was *nothing* that the inmate or the attorney acting on his behalf could rely on. There was not even the consistency which in a desperate situation can lend at least the security of foreknowledge.

Whatever frustrations attorneys felt when confronting the lawlessness of the prison regime were suffered infinitely more intensely by the inmates. Prisoners at Soledad (as in all California prisons) are expected to accept everything that is told to them about their own unworthiness. They are expected to confess to crimes which they did not commit—including offenses with which they had been charged and acquitted, and even offenses with which they have never been charged but which prison officials or the parole board think they committed. Officials require prisoners to walk between white lines down the corridor and have their hair cut to rigid specifications. In the dining room, prisoners must never take an extra slice of bread (although at Soledad extra bread was thrown away regularly); and they are required to take the next seat at tables (moving out of line to sit next to a friend, or leaving one seat empty and taking the next one, constitutes an in-prison offense which is written up and placed in the prisoner's central file for the parole board to see). Those few prisoners who can get shop placements are assigned to an available position regardless of whether it fits the inmate's previous education, experience, aptitude, or his plans for when he will be released. A prisoner is placed in solitary confinement for the most trivial of infractions, or simply because a guard has a grudge against him. Once he is in isolation, the prison authorities can impose a special restricted diet consisting of a food loaf looking somewhat like dog food and almost inedible due to smell, taste, and texture. And of course, each prisoner must contend with the ever-shifting Adult Authority. He never knows when the board will decide that he has the "right attitude" and can be released. He could wait two years, five years, ten years, his life.

Into this atmosphere, already strained almost to the breaking point, came the murder of the three black prisoners in the exercise yard on January 13, 1970. The white guard responsible for the deaths was promptly exonerated without even being taken off duty while his innocence was being "established." Harassment and intimidation of prisoners, especially in the Soledad adjustment center, became increasingly frequent and intense. Inmates have insisted (and staff denied) that some guards spat into the food of the prisoners confined in O wing. Prisoners were tear-gassed and beaten in the cells for causing even the slightest commotion. It became increasingly common for prison officials to try to bribe or threaten inmates to get them to testify against prisoners accused of violent acts within the prison. The prison, supposedly designed to enforce the law, became a complete negation of every principle of legality.

Could an inmate in this situation possibly conceive of himself as a legitimately confined prisoner who had been duly committed to an institution which upholds the law? Could he possibly see the prison as a just institution which has no special interest in his humiliation and degradation? Could an inmate in these circumstances feel that there was any possible reward in continuing the passive acceptance of endless humiliations, harassment, uncertainties? What is surprising in such a situation is not that so much violence occurred in Soledad prison, but so little.

VIOLENCE AND LAWLESSNESS

Violence is not new in American prisons. Although assaults and killings became much more frequent in the early 1970s, they have always been a fact of life in prison. What is distinctive about the violence that occurred at Soledad after the January 13, 1970, shootings is its overtly political character.

Violence in prison can be broken down into four interrelated categories. Each of these is directly or indirectly related to the lawlessness of American prisons:

1. *Violence as an expression of conflict among prisoners.* In the past, this has been the most common form of violence in American prisons, and the kind of violence that is best documented in the literature on prisons. It includes such things as stabbings that are the result of unpaid drug and gambling debts and, more rarely, violence that stems from struggles for power within the inmate society. Much of this kind of violence stems from the extreme deprivations of prison life and the manipulation of those deprivations by prison officials. The number of reports by prisoners of guards who promise early parole or special privileges in exchange for "setting up" a disliked prisoner are too numerous to be discounted as pure fabrications. Involvement by prison officials in racial conflict, in the drug traffic, and other illegal activities also increases violence among prisoners.

2. *Violence as a product of frustration and despair.* This kind of violence is also a traditional part of prison life. The sense that nothing one does makes any difference and that one has no control over his own life can generate rage, personal disorganization, and a constant sense of panic. Under the most trivial of circumstances, such frustrations can lead to aggression. Much of

this tension is directly the result of the total powerlessness of the prisoner and the arbitrary manner in which he is treated.

3. *Violence as an affirmation of autonomy.* Violence on the part of the prisoner, especially when directed against the prison system itself, can be a way of affirming the self, of striking back at the oppression of the prison instead of being destroyed as a person. This form of violence is not merely a product of lawlessness within the prison; it is a psychological defense against that lawlessness. Lawlessness is not only an attack on individual freedom, it is a profound attack on individual dignity; violence can be a highly individualist form of rebellion by the prisoner to defend his dignity from that attack.

4. *Violence as a substitute for law in prison.* Violence by prisoners can be a self-consciously political act. In addition to being a psychological self-defense against the dehumanization of lawlessness, violence can become an attack on that lawlessness itelf. Inmates can see themselves as the upholders of "law," and even of "order," within the prison by attempting to use violence, and the threat of violence, as a check on the exercise of arbitrary power by the prison regime.

Until the 1960s, the use of violence as a self-consciously political weapon rarely entered into prison disturbances, and then generally in a limited way. Since then, however, prison violence has become increasingly politicized.

Much of the violence in Soledad Prison during 1970 and 1971 was of this political variety. The ruling by the Monterey County Grand Jury that the January, 1970, killings of the three black inmates in the adjustment center exercise yard were "justifiable homicide" was the clearest possible statement that the power of the guards is absolute and unrestrained, that prisons are utterly lawless institutions. Shortly after the news of the grand jury decision was announced in the prison, a guard was killed, allegedly by a group of prisoners. That act may have been a declaration by the prisoners involved that they were willing to resort to the use of force to "punish" the prison for the murder of the three prisoners. The act would appear to be not simply an expression of the rage felt over the murders, but an attempt to establish a new pattern of power relationships within the prison. The prison could no longer freely exercise unlimited power without fear of retaliation from prisoners.

The prisoners who actually committed acts of violence against guards were, of course, a small minority. They knew that the consequences of their actions would be continued imprisonment in the most punitive sections of the prison. They knew they would be subjected to new trials, new convictions, and possible death sentences. They knew they would have almost no hope of getting a parole under the indeterminate sentence. While many prisoners silently supported the courage of these defiant prisoners, relatively few were willing to accept the enormous risks of fighting the prison regime.

Lawlessness has always been a reality at Soledad prison; why did a pattern of political violence emerge in 1970? Two issues are especially important in answering this question. First of all, the steady growth during the 1960s of political sophistication and organization of blacks in America had an important influence on the ways in which prisoners saw their imprisonment. Many prisoners, especially minority prisoners, gradually developed a radical understanding of prison and as a result became less willing to accept passively the lawlessness of the prison regime. Soledad prison was a dumping ground for young men who were considered management problems in other institutions and therefore had a higher concentration of defiant prisoners than most other prisons in California.

The second ingredient in the explosiveness of Soledad was a clear increase in lawlessness on the part of the prison in 1969–1970, particularly in the adjustment center. As Meneweather has recounted, the prison guards were systematically increasing racial tensions among prisoners in O and X wings in the months prior to the shootings in the exercise yard. With the shooting in January, the prisoners were notified, in effect, that their lives were worth nothing and that they would be shot with impunity at the discretion of the guards. The prisoners responded by telling the prison that such actions would be responded to in kind. The conflict increased steadily in the year and a half following the shooting in the O Wing yard. By the spring of 1971 tear-gassing of prisoners in the adjustment center was an almost daily event, and attacks on prison officials became relatively common occurrences.

It was only with the replacing of the prison superintendent and the drastic reduction of the number of prisoners in the adjustment center that the level of violence in Soledad began to decline. By early 1972, Soledad had become quieter. Yet, the same official lawlessness continued, if perhaps more carefully concealed under the guise of manifold regulations and rules. The basic conditions in the prison remained unchanged.

The prison system of California, and the nation, faces a crucial decision in the years to come. The object lesson of Soledad prison in 1970–1971 can lead in two directions. Prison administrators may decide that prisoners must be even more tightly controlled in order to prevent the recurrence of violence. Plans are already in the offing for two small supermaximum-security prisons to replace San Quentin. These prisons would be equipped with all of the most modern devices of electronic surveillance and would create a setting for almost total physical control of the prisoner's life. Although much of the press, building upon the statements of the Department of Corrections, heralds the closing of San Quentin as a step in the direction of reform, these new facilities will, if built, be far more repressive and dehumanizing than even San Quentin and Soledad. Other proposals are to handle the problem of prisoner violence through brain surgery or by building a maximum-security psychiatric prison where violent prisoners could be confined and drugged. All of these responses to prison violence deal with the problem by increasing the lawlessness and oppressiveness of the prison.

The other choice is for legislatures, the courts, and the people to realize that prisons must be brought under the rule of law. Prison administrators must be placed under reasoned restraint. Prisoners must be given channels for the *effective* redress of grievances. The civil rights of prisoners as well as defendants must be rigorously protected. And the courts must be willing to intervene systematically in the internal operation of prisons to guarantee that protection. It is the absence of law, not "outside agitators," which is responsible for the violence, death, and suffering in the prisons. Not "law and order," but law and restraint upon administrators and guards, will relieve it.

A political analysis of the possibility of achieving such an objective—the true rule of law—in our society is beyond the scope of this chapter. The outlook is not bright, but the profound human and political crisis in the prisons is compelling.

PART IV

Challenges to the System

CHAPTER 12

From Riot to Revolution

by John Pallas and Robert Barber

The deaths of forty-one persons at Attica and six at San Quentin in 1971 brought home to America the fact that social revolution has come to the prisons. This discovery was surprising and shocking to most Americans, yet it need not have been. The social history of the country can be as well understood by examining the prison as by examining any other American institution.

Prisons are society's ultimate means of control over people who are actually or potentially disruptive of the social order. Thus, any resistance which poses a serious threat to the prison threatens the entire society as well. The prison's capacity to achieve this goal of control rests largely on its ability to reduce prisoners to active accomplices or passive recipients of their own oppression.

The ideology and composition of prisoner resistance has changed dramatically over the past twenty years. In order to best understand these changes it is necessary to examine not only the evolution of the prison movement itself but also the wider struggle within American society.

Three types of prison struggle occurred during the period 1950–1971: the traditional prison riot such as those which were widespread during the 1950s; the organizing of black prisoners by the Nation of Islam; and the revolutionary upheavals of the late 1960s and early 1970s. This is not to say that the progression from one type to another was inevitable, or that other important things have not been happening in prisons during this period. Earlier forms of prison struggle still exist, and many prisoners continue to be apolitical. Nevertheless, the events at Attica and elsewhere suggest a radically new dimension in prison resistance, a dimension which has implications for the wider revolutionary movement and for state repression.

On the one hand, participants in the prison movement such as Malcolm X and George Jackson have provided models of leadership for the movement as a whole. Their writings have illuminated for millions of people the nature of American society and its legal system. On the other hand, the repression of political rebellion in prisons is connected to the repression of other rebellious domestic groups (such as the Black Panthers) and of people's movements in Latin America and Southeast Asia. There are, therefore, practical and analytical insights to be gained from an examination of rebellion by prisoners.

Any discussion of prison riots and strikes must be conducted in the framework of a political analysis. If "political" events are those dealing with the existing arrangements of power, then clearly acts that stem from the powerlessness of prisoners are political. Such powerlessness is rooted in the social and economic structure of the society. The lack of a political articulation of prisoners' grievances by no means negates their political nature. Even acts rooted in psychological despair, such as self-mutilation, are expressions of an unarticulated political revolt.[1]

RIOTS IN THE EARLY 1950s

More than 50 major riots occurred in American prisons between 1950 and 1953; until the disturbances of the 1970s, the

1. See Franz Fanon's *The Wretched of the Earth* (New York: Grove Press, 1963), especially the chapter entitled "Colonial War and Mental Disorders."

early fifties were characterized as the worst period ever for American prison administration.[2] These riots and strikes were largely spontaneous uprisings against intolerable living conditions. Such uprisings have often occurred in prisons and continue to occur today. Yet the increase in their intensity in the early fifties presaged the current period of organized political rebellion, for the inability of the system to respond to their demands created the conditions in which more radical ideas could take root.

The riot of April, 1952, at Jackson state prison in Michigan was typical of these upheavals. Two prisoners overpowered a guard, took his keys, and released the other prisoners in the maximum-security wing. They smashed up several wings of the prison and liberated the canteen to provide food. For five days they held hostages at knifepoint, refusing to release them until officials agreed to hear their grievances and publish them in the local newspaper. The demands, quickly formulated after the riot began, were as follows:

1. 15-block (the maximum-security wing) be remodeled to provide for adequate lighting and treatment facilities.
2. Counselors have free access to the disciplinary cells in the 15-block.
3. Segregation (solitary confinement) policies be revised, and a member of the individual treatment staff be given a position on the segregation board.
4. Only guards who would not be inhumane in their treatment be picked for duty in the 12-block (reserved for epileptic, semimentally disturbed, blind, handicapped, and senile cases).
5. The carrying of dangerous hand weapons and inhumane restrainment equipment by guards be prohibited.

2. Richard McCleary, "Correctional Administration and Political Change," in Lawrence Hazlerigg (ed.), *Prison Within Society* (Garden City, N.Y.: Doubleday, 1968), p. 130.

6. Adequate and competent personnel for handling mental cases, and more adequate screening of such cases.
7. A letter on prison stationery be sent to the parole board asking for a revision of procedures to give equal treatment to all parolees.
8. Postoperative care be given under the direction of the medical director (instead of by prisoner technicians).
9. Equal opportunities for dental care for all prisoners, with special regard to the elimination of special buying preferences.
10. Creation of a permanent council elected by prisoners, to confer periodically with prison officials.
11. No reprisals against any leader or participant in the revolt.

The uprising ended when officials agreed to publish the demands, allow an outside group to inspect the prison, and not take action against the participants. But eventually the leaders were indicted for conspiracy and almost none of the demands were met. Things continued at Jackson much as before.

A number of generalizations can be drawn from the Jackson revolt. It was unplanned and uncoordinated. The demands put forward reflected the day-to-day needs of the prisoners. They dealt with internal conditions and problems of survival, and their accomplishment would have materially improved the prisoners' lives. Despite their narrow focus, these demands were in fact political, because they were demands for social justice.

The pattern of leadership at Jackson is indicative of the level of organization in this type of riot. A white prisoner named Earl Ward imposed his leadership upon the group when it became clear that internal fighting and disorganization needed to be controlled. He prevented prisoners from attacking the hostages and supervised the formulation of the demands. He decided when the group should surrender, although a number of his fellow prisoners clearly disagreed with his decision.

In general, the leadership of such revolts was white, although blacks, Puerto Ricans, and Chicanos participated. The leaders were generally prisoners feared or respected for their toughness; power accrued to them by default. Rarely, however, would they use their position to their own personal advantage. The apparent unity of the moment usually concealed intense personal or racial hatreds, which the leaders, through force or personal persuasion, had to control in order to prevent the revolt from disintegrating.

Once such outbreaks were under way, the prisoners would often willingly negotiate with certain members of the prison staff whom they regarded as sympathetic to their cause. Such individuals were usually members of the "treatment" staff, such as psychiatrists and counselors. These trusted individuals had great influence over the leaders. At Jackson, prison psychiatrist Vernon Fox convinced the prisoners to modify some of their demands. He also convinced them that the officials were sincere in their promises of change. After the revolt was over, Fox wrote an article in *Collier's* entitled "How I Crushed the Prison Riot."

State and prison officials faced conflicting pressures during such disruptions, but the question was a tactical one: whether to crush the revolt with force or to bring it to an end through empty negotiations. Whichever method was chosen, the results were the same, and the prisoners accomplished little or nothing. The lessons of such experiences were not lost on them, however.

The tenor of the demands and political thrust of these riots and strikes was consistent with the general forms of challenge to American society which occurred in the 1950s and early 1960s, especially the civil rights movement. Likewise, officials of the state used essentially the same means of containing and suppressing prison revolts as they did for the larger civil rights movement.

During the period between 1950 and 1960 the mechanisms of social control in American society appeared to be working fairly well, and few significant political groups disputed the legitimacy of the social order. Those groups who had not yet shared in the general wealth were seeking to be included. The accompanying political style was "pluralism": various political groups attempted to bring pressure on the authorities to fulfill their obligations as defined by the prevailing system. In this sense, both the prison movement of the time and the civil rights movement were expressions of the same impulse. They were aimed at eliminating explicit practices and customs which were seen as antithetical to American democracy. They challenged the abuse of power rather than its nature.

The goal of the civil rights movement was the integration of black people into the mainstream of American life. In prisons, at this time, the notion of "rehabilitation" was gaining credence. This notion implied that prisoners were "deviant" and in need of treatment which would enable them to "adjust properly" to the existing society. The demands for an increase in the role of treatment officials in prison life and the trust shown those officials by prisoners during their uprisings indicate that prisoners tended to place hope in the idea of rehabilitation. In this sense, rehabilitation and integration were identical—they both posit the adaptation of individuals to the social structure which opens up to receive them.

Although the civil rights movement attempted to bring change through established channels such as the courts and the legislature, its cutting edge was the use of direct action, undertaken with the faith that the federal government would back it up. Effectively closed off from the legal channels of change outside prisons, prisoners also turned to direct action to influence their institutions. Their faith in at least part of that institutional structure (the treatment staff) indicates that they still granted some legitimacy to the power exercised over them.

Both movements met with similar response from the state. Violence was used routinely to break up civil rights actions and prison revolts. The civil rights movement, able to enlist the support of various segments of the population, achieved limited progress through the legal system. With no outside constituency at this time, prisoners were unable to prevent prison officials from revoking promised reforms after a rebellion was over. In the short run, both civil rights and prison dissent were crushed or coopted. Such responses by the state, however, only laid the groundwork for more radical challenges to the society and its prisons.

BLACK MUSLIMS

During the time that these essentially reformist efforts were being made, political activity was being carried out in another way among black people by the Nation of Islam. A high degree of organization and discipline enabled this group to reach large numbers of blacks on both sides of the walls. Although their organizational talents were important in gaining recruits, the most significant element in their success was the fact that their philosophy spoke to the anger and frustration of poor blacks, and especially black prisoners.

This philosophy stood in sharp contrast to that of the mainstream of the civil rights movement, which was essentially geared to integrating middle-class and professional blacks into the existing society and to bringing poor southern blacks into minimal participation in the political system. Little attention was paid to the cities of the North, where racism seemed less naked than in the South.

The Black Muslims, however, concentrated their organizing in the northern urban ghettos and in the prisons. Instead of attempting to obliterate race consciousness, they taught that black people should be aware of their group identity and collective oppression. Their ultimate objective was the creation of a separate black nation. They viewed prisons as a place of recruitment for new members of this nation, rather than as a point of political struggle in its own right. Their demands focused on the requirements of the religion, not on general prison conditions.

Central to their philosophy was the notion that blacks as a group were victims of white society, that the miseries they faced were not the result of their own personal deficiencies. Muslim organizers within prison always stressed this point: "The black prisoner, he [Elijah Muhammad, the Muslim leader] said, symbolized white society's crime of keeping black men oppressed and deprived and ignorant, and unable to get decent jobs, turning them into criminals."[3]

Muslims generally came from the same class background as most black prisoners: the unemployed or irregularly employed working class. Their philosophy appealed to this class, the class that had the least hope of benefiting from the assimilationist approach of the civil rights movement. The Muslims spoke more realistically about the nature of prisons for blacks than did the (white) leaders of the spontaneous uprisings of the time. Thus, the Muslims recruited large numbers of black prisoners to their movement, and fewer and fewer participated in the general riots and strikes.

Their chief mode of organizing was through personal contact. Because of their class background, many Muslims were at one time or another in prison. Once in prison they devoted their full time to contacting and organizing other blacks. Muslims on the outside wrote continuously to prisoners, espousing the Muslim philosophy. Prisoners were encouraged to write to Elijah Muhammad; they always received a personal reply and literature. Malcolm X became a Muslim while in prison through continued correspondence with his family and Elijah Muhammad.[4]

Throughout the early part of the 1950s, the Muslims remained more or less "underground" in prisons, educating new

3. Malcolm X, *The Autobiography of Malcolm X* (New York: Grove Press, 1966), p. 169.
4. *Ibid.*, especially the chapters entitled "Satan" and "Saved."

recruits and building an organization. By the late fifties, they had the allegiance or sympathy of most black prisoners, and began pushing their demands. The demands were few: the right to hold religious meetings, the right to purchase the Koran, the right to build a mosque, and the right to receive visits from Muslims outside.

The organization, discipline, and unity which backed those demands presented a threat to the prison's goal of isolating prisoners from one another. The organization was based on complete loyalty to the philosophy and way of life of the Nation. Each prison mosque was rigidly structured along the lines of the mosques outside, with clearly delineated channels of authority. The prisoner-minister was recognized both by his followers in the prison and by the Muslim hierarchy outside as the leader of the Muslims in prison.

These ministers were trained to prevent violence on the part of Muslims. No acts of violence or retaliation against white guards or inmates were permitted. Eldridge Cleaver relates,

> After the death of Brother Booker T. X., who was shot dead by a San Quentin guard, and who at the time had been my cell partner and the inmate Minister of the Muslims at San Quentin, my leadership had been publicly endorsed by Elijah Muhammad's west coast representative, Minister John Shabazz of Muhammad's Los Angeles Mosque. This was done because of the explosive conditions in San Quentin at the time. Muslim officials wanted to avert any Muslim-initiated violence, which had become a distinct possibility in the aftermath of Brother Booker's death. I was instructed to impose iron discipline upon the San Quentin Mosque. . . .[5]

The offiical policy of refraining from violence despite provocation was in part imposed because violence was seen as suicidal: the Muslims were afraid of creating a situation which could be used as an excuse for the mass killing of their number by guards.

5. Eldridge Cleaver, *Soul on Ice* (New York: McGraw-Hill, 1968), p. 57.

More importantly, however, this decision grew from Muslim attitudes toward the prisons. They wanted as many new recruits as possible to be active in their communities; the goal was to get them out on the streets safely.

Two essential tactics, strikes and lawsuits, were used by the Muslims to achieve their demands within the prison. Strikes were usually called in the aftermath of a particular incident. After the killing of a Muslim by a San Quentin guard in 1967, the Muslims called a work strike and demanded the prosecution of the guard. They also reiterated their central demands for religious freedom. Their primary tactic, however, was the use of lawsuits to force the prisons to grant them this freedom. They invariably lost the suits, but turned the losses to political advantage by pointing to the biased nature of the court system.

In dealing with the Muslims, the goal of prison officials was primarily to break up the Muslim organization. Meetings were disrupted, ministers continually transferred from prison to prison, Muslims routinely placed in isolation, and communication with the outside cut off. State and prison officials publicly portrayed the Muslims as violent fanatics who posed the gravest threat not only to the prison system but to the society as a whole.

Although the Muslims declined in influence in the mid-1960s, a positive legacy of their work remained. They helped destroy the barriers to political consciousness which have impeded prisoners in previous attempts to struggle against their oppression. The Muslims introduced disciplined organization among prisoners, the idea that collective action could be taken to achieve desired goals. They also introduced the notion of collective oppression to black prisoners, which counteracted the prison ideology of individual pathology. Although they located the source of that oppression in the "white devil" and his institutions rather than in specific class-related institutions, their insistence upon the collective nature of that oppression marked an important step in the transformation of black consciousness. In addition, the Muslims brought with them the notion that out-side support for a movement inside could strengthen that movement. Finally, the Muslims brought with them models of successful anticolonial struggles in Africa. They could point to the newly independent African nations as examples of self-determination for black people in struggle against white op-pression. This development was crucial for the continuing growth among black prisoners of their self-conception as people involved in a worldwide struggle, and it placed them firmly in the vanguard of the new prisoners' movement. As Malcolm X once pointed out, "The first thing the American power struc-ture doesn't want any Negroes to start is thinking *internation-ally.*"[6]

The immediate causes of the Muslims' decline in influence in the mid-1960s lay in the nature of the Muslim religion and movement itself. The split between Malcolm X and Elijah Muhammad in 1963 led to an uncertainty about the future of the Muslims. Furthermore, the Muslims had promised that Al-lah was coming to deliver blacks from the white devils; Allah's failure to appear caused a great deal of disillusionment with the theological analysis of the Nation of Islam. And finally, the Mus-lims' refusal to define prisons as a point of struggle alienated many new converts who needed legal support and wanted ac-tion in prison. As prisoners grew in political sophistication, they became increasingly aware that the Muslim philosophy of na-tionalism with its religious emphasis was reactionary and inap-propriate for the prison struggle. The Muslim preoccupation with separatism and black racial superiority played right into the hands of the administrators who wanted nothing more than to keep black and white prisoners divided. What the black and white inmates needed, in fact, was to unite with one another in opposition to the prison administration. Malcolm's changed analysis of racism after his 1965 trip to Mecca forced many

6. *The Autobiography of Malcolm X,* p. 347.

Muslims to reexamine their own attitudes toward this issue. Malcolm wrote of his changed perceptions, "The white man is *not* inherently evil, but America's racist society influences him to act evilly. The society has produced and nourishes a psychology which brings out the lowest, most base part of human beings."[7]Malcom's special appeal to black prisoners gave his change of mind a special impact. Cleaver later wrote:

> Many of us were shocked and outraged by these words from Malcolm X, who had been a major influence upon us all and the main factor in many of our conversions to the black Muslims, but there were those of us who were glad to be liberated from a doctrine of hate and racial supremacy. The onus of teaching racial supremacy and hate, which is the white man's burden, is pretty hard to bear.[8]

THE REVOLUTIONARY PRISON MOVEMENT

In the wake of the decline of the Muslims between 1964 and 1967, the prisoners' movement underwent fundamental changes in its political thrust. The bitter lessons of the fruitless riots of the 1950s and the inability of the Muslims to relate to specific prison struggles left the prisoners open to new influences and new forms of struggle more consistent with the state of society and the movement of opposition to it. Changing conditions in the United States and around the world during this period laid the groundwork for the rise of a revolutionary movement in prisons.

During this period the contradictions within American society had become increasingly clear. Unable to respond to the rising pressure for reform, the system turned increasingly to the repression of its challengers, the advocates of Black Power and the antiwar movement. The war in Vietnam and the intervention in the Dominican Republic revealed the roots of American

7. *Ibid.*, p. 371.
8. *Soul on Ice*, pp. 56–57.

foreign policy in imperialism and its concomitant racism. In this context, opposition to the state grew more radical and militant, and was met with increasing repression.

In the spiral of challenge and retrenchment, of revolution and repression, new political movements in the U.S. and around the world appeared: a Black Power movement expressed in ghetto riots and the growth of the Black Panther party; an anti-imperialist movement among white students and intellectuals manifested in campus revolt; Third World liberation groups rooted in local communities; and revolutionary movements in Indochina, Latin America, and Africa. These groups articulated an understanding of the interrelationships of domestic and foreign repression, of the role of racism as an ideology used to divide people of different races in the interest of economic exploitation, and of the necessity for international solidarity among the victims of imperialism. They proceeded to act upon these analyses, thus providing models of revolutionary theory and practice, and a general atmosphere of confrontation for prisoners.

The impact upon prisoners of these developments in the outside world cannot be overestimated. Nonwhite prisoners especially made quick connections between their struggles inside and the struggles of oppressed peoples around the world. These prisoners were joined by an influx of new prisoners, imprisoned for radical activities. Black, Puerto Rican, Chicano, and other nonwhite men and women active in radical movements, and an increasing number of whites arrested for offenses stemming from their opposition to the Indochina war, brought their politics and organizing talent to prisons.

Since 1964, then, the prison struggle has consciously become a part of an international struggle. Among the political leadership inside prisons, the need for interracial unity and political education and organizing has become accepted. Putting the new precepts into practice, however, has been more difficult, for prison and state officials have not stood by to let these developments happen of their own accord. Prisoners have had to overcome their own backgrounds of hate and mistrust. This attempt is paralleled on the outside by the increasing number of street gangs of white and Third World youth who have buried their former conflicts and turned to political activity in their communities.

Prison authorities have never hesitated to exploit racism as a divisive element to further their control of prisoners. Interracial violence continues, often encouraged or ignored from above. Such conflict, however, has been increasingly repudiated by a growing united front of black, brown, and white prisoners.

The situation at San Quentin prison in California provides a model for the changing nature of revolt during this period. A massive race riot in January, 1967, involving nearly half of the 4,000 prisoners, resulted in cautious attempts at reconciliation by prisoner leaders. The self-defeating nature of such violence was acknowledged by the inmates, and truces were arranged between various black and white groups. An underground newspaper called the *Outlaw* began publication. It attacked the prison system and called for unity among the prisoners.

Within a year, open racial hostility had nearly ended, and a united general strike in early 1968 caused the shutdown of nearly all of the prison industries. At this point, officials moved to break up the incipient organizing by transferring suspected leaders to other prisons and increasing the general harassment of everyone. (The facilities of the *Outlaw* were discovered, although the paper continued to be occasionally published outside and smuggled in.)

The degree of prisoner participation and outside support of a second strike on Unity Day in August, 1968, brought an investigation of grievances by a legislative committee, as well as further repression by the prison administration. Guards began passing out weapons and manufacturing threats among antagonistic racial groups. They clamped down on all prison activities, and again transferred the leaders. Within months unity had dissolved into racial killings and polarization.[9] But the precedent of unity had been set.

Three more recent prison revolts indicate a greater ability on the part of prisoners to deal with the problem of racism, and provide insights into the nature of the new prison movement. Each new revolt draws upon the experience of previous revolts and invokes the memory of earlier struggles; each revolt provides an inspiration for the next.

In early October, 1970, prisoners took over the Long Island branch of the Queens House of Detention, immediately touching off similar revolts in other city jails around New York. At Long Island a number of hostages were taken and a list of demands issued. The central demands concerned bail and speedier trials. Members of the prisoners' negotiating committee which presented the demands identified themselves only as "revolutionaries." The committee included four blacks, one Puerto Rican, and one white. They demanded immediate bail hearings on forty-seven cases they had selected as examples of the racism involved in the granting of bail. A group of individuals with whom the inmates had asked to meet attempted to persuade them to give up this demand and release the hostages.[10] In addition, Mayor John Lindsay attempted to assure them that such a demand was unnecessary because a complete review of the bail system was to be undertaken in the courts "within a week." He also suggested that force would be used immediately if the prisoners did not capitulate. The prisoners refused to be persuaded or intimidated. Victor Martinez of the negotiating committee told newsmen, "Unless that pig judge

9. See Robert Minton and Stephen Rice, "Race War at San Quentin," *Ramparts,* vol. 18, no. 7, Jan., 1970.

10. Herman Badillo, a former Bronx borough president, Representative Shirley Chisolm of Brooklyn, Manuel Caseano, former executive director of the office of the Commonwealth of Puerto Rico, Louis Farakham, a Black Muslim minister, and George McGrath, New York Corrections Commissioner.

appears here you will never see those hostages alive."[11] Subsequently, three state supreme court judges held hearings inside the jail on thirteen cases; nine paroles and four reductions in bail were granted.

Several of the demands related to the Panther 21, then in jail on conspiracy charges and unable to pay the high bail.[12] A number of these Panthers were involved in the revolt. After the bail hearings, the hostages were released, but some prisoners continued to hold out for the demand of a "jury of peers" for the Panthers and for bail for one of the defendants. The issues of bail and lengthy pretrial detention had been chosen not only to assist the Panthers but also to dramatize to the public the interrelationships among political repression, racism, and the refusal to grant reasonable bail. At this point, officials ordered the police to storm the jail with tear gas and clubs, and the revolt was crushed.

Within a month, in November of 1970, a work stoppage began in Folsom prison. It grew into the longest and most nonviolent prison strike in the history of this country. Nearly all 2,400 prisoners held out in their own cells for 19 days in the face of constant hunger, discomfort, and continued psychological and physical intimidation.

They issued a 31-point "Manifesto of Demands and Anti-Oppression Platform," labeling prisons the "Fascist Concentration Camps of Modern America," and calling for "an end to the injustice suffered by all prisoners, regardless of race, creed, or color." The demands focused on the denial of political and legal rights to prisoners and the exploitative nature of work programs inside the prison.

11. *New York Times*, Oct. 3, 1970, p. 58.

12. In 1969 twenty-one black men and women were arrested on 156 counts of "conspiracy to commit murder," "arson," and various other charges. The Panther 21 trial, perhaps the longest criminal trial in the history of the United States, ended when the jury acquitted all the defendants of all 156 charges after deliberating for only 90 minutes.

In the months prior to the strike, interracial cooperation had been building among the prisoners. The Muslim group offered their help to Chicanos in holding a memorial service for a Chicano journalist killed by police in Los Angeles. After the service a number of the participants were attacked by prison guards and the Muslim minister was officially rebuked for having conducted the service.

After the strike began, the prisoners designated certain members of the radical community outside the prison to represent them in negotiations with authorities.[13] Prison officials refused to meet with these negotiators and even refused to admit that a united strike was occurring.

After nineteen days the strike was finally broken through a combination of force and deception. One prisoner described the collapse this way:

> The strike was broken *not* because the prisoners had become disenchanted. The Collective Spirit and optimism were too real to make me believe that the prisoners went to work as a result of disillusionment. Two thousand men don't strike for 19 days and then suddenly become disenchanted. Only the most naïve fools would believe that such a thing could happen. Therefore it is only logical that devious means were employed to break the strike.
>
> It is clear as crystal that Craven [the warden at Folsom] used political deception and brute force to get the prisoners to go back to work. On the 23rd of November [Monday morning, the day the strike was broken] the prison pigs, armed with rifles and wooden clubs, stopped in front of each man's cell and ordered each man back to work. Of course the order was weighted down with the threat of violence. Not wanting to be shot or clubbed to death, the prisoner naturally complied with the pigs' vicious method of brute force.
>
> In Building One, one of Craven's inmate agents drew up

13. Sal Candelaria (Brown Berets), Huey P. Newton (Black Panther party), Charles Garry (Third World Legal Defense Counsel), and a representative from the California Prisoners' Union.

several reactionary leaflets and circulated them throughout the building [Building One is where "Kitchen Row" is
located]. The leaflets, which were passed from cell to cell
by the inmates, said that the kitchen workers were supposed to go back to work so that the prisoners could start
eating hot meals. Because so many legitimate leaflets and
notes were being circulated throughout Building One, the
inmates in that building naturally assumed that those reactionary leaflets were the real thing. This was the method
used to get the kitchen workers back to work.[14]

After the suppression of the strike, four prisoners were singled
out for a brutal 14-hour ride to another prison, shackled and
naked on the floor of a van. Another 52 were thrown into the
hole. In spite of all this, many prisoners felt that the strike was
a success. One prisoner wrote:

The strike may have fallen short of our goal, but it was
not a failure. We accomplished something that has never
been accomplished before. Not just the record length, but
more important is that the spirit of awareness has grown,
and our people begin to look around and see what's happening. The seed has been planted and grows. If we have
accomplished nothing else, we have accomplished this. Let
this knowledge at least console you from the disheartening
news you received that the strike was broke.[15]

The demands of the Folsom strike became the model (sometimes on a word-for-word basis) for the demands of the striking
prisoners at Attica state prison in Attica, New York. The Attica
Liberation Front had been formed in May, 1971, around 29
demands centering on prisoners' rights to organize politically
and economically, and on living and working conditions. Included was a demand that the warden be fired. A negotiating
committee met with officials several times, but the officials did
nothing about the prisoners' grievances.

14. Eve Pell (ed.), *Maximum Security* (New York: Dutton, 1972), pp. 206–207.
15. From a letter to an Oakland, California, attorney.

On September 9 several hundred prisoners captured the prison yard and seized numerous guards as hostages. Their numbers swelled immediately to 1,500, and two demands were added to the original list: transportation to a nonimperialist country for those who wished it (later dropped), and total amnesty for participants in the action. Discipline and an operating support system were quickly organized in the yard. Leadership was chosen from the Panthers, Young Lords, Muslims, radical whites, and other groups.

Negotiations around the demands soon came down to the issues of amnesty and the resignation of the warden. These demands put into focus the political nature of the revolt. If granted, they would have established the precedents that prisoners have a right to participate in (if not control) the process of choosing who rules them, and that they have a right to rebel without fear of punishment. Both prisoners and officials knew that these issues were at stake and that the implications went far beyond the walls of Attica.

The demand for amnesty in particular indicates the political progression of prisoner revolts from twenty years earlier. Increasingly, the demand for a guarantee against reprisal is being replaced by a demand for amnesty. The term "amnesty" denotes a relationship between political actors; the term "reprisal" implies a power relationship independent of specific political conditions. More important than the semantics is the fact that amnesty is becoming one of the central demands in prisoner revolts. It was over this demand that the Attica negotiations broke down. Inmates and administrators alike are coming to realize the political significance of this demand. Prisoners are no longer looking only for personal protection; they are seeking the legitimization of a political tool.

The prisoners at Attica had no trust in the officials they were dealing with. From past experience they knew that whatever promises were made by the warden would later be revoked;

hence the demands for his removal had implications beyond his personality. The prisoners' only hope lay with whatever power the Observers Committee may have had to win concessions for them and to follow them up. In the end it was shown that the committee had no power; it was not even informed of the impending attack by state troopers.

In the short period of its heyday, the Attica Liberation Front exemplified several aspects of the new prison revolution. The overcoming of mistrust and hatred between black and white prisoners was the crucial development which allowed the Attica prisoners to live by their slogan, "The Solution Is Unity." All reports indicate that there was complete racial harmony in the yard. Journalist Tom Wicker, a member of the Observers Committee, noted: "The racial harmony that prevailed among the prisoners—it was absolutely astonishing. . . . That prison yard was the first place I have ever seen where there was no racism."[16]

Following the crushing of the rebellion, forty prisoners were thrown into segregation and charged with numerous "crimes." One of them told a lawyer:

> They don't realize how they're helping us. They think they're slick, but we get tighter and stronger every day. Hell, we don't even want to go back to the general population. Up here we're all together, we can keep our eyes out for each other so they don't rip us off one at a time. I never thought whites could really get it on. . . . But I can't tell you what the yard was like. I actually cried it was so close, everyone so together. Now we're more united than ever, and the longer we stay together, the tighter we get. Everything they do, they're helping us.[17]

16. Tom Wicker wrote a number of articles for the *New York Times* about the Attica uprising in which he stressed the racial solidarity that prevailed. One of the most interesting was " 'Unity': A Haunting Echo from Attica," *New York Times,* Sept. 15, 1971, p. 1.

17. Cited by Gus Reichbach, in "Attica: War Behind Walls," *University Review,* no. 22 (1972), p. 5.

A week after the massacre, prisoners at Attica smuggled out a statement discussing the revolt and placing it in the context of a revolutionary struggle against American capitalism. The statement concluded, "These brothers whose lives were taken by Rockefeller and his agents did not die in vain. Why? Because the uprising at Attica did not begin here nor will it end here."[18]

The revolutionary prison movement, still in its infancy, has several characteristics, then, which set it apart from earlier movements. To the traditional and still unwon demands for decent food, shelter, and health care have been added demands that challenge both the ideology and the structure of the prison system and larger society. Prisoners are collectively articulating what was once expressed in a less eloquent way by loosely knit groups of individuals. The leadership of these collective groups is based on mutual consent and an apportioning of responsibilities among various racial and political groups, as an indication not only of the strategy of unity but also as a concrete manifestation of its practicality. Organizing inside the prison is around education: education involving the acquisition of simple tools such as reading and writing, and education involving the sophisticated political writings of past and present revolutionaries. The new movement addresses its demands to the people of the world, calling on them to assist in their own liberation through support for prisoners. The movement operates in conjunction with outside support groups and groups of ex-prisoners who see their task as bringing support to the prisoners in whatever way possible. As George Jackson concluded: "Only the prison movement has shown any promise of cutting across the ideological, racial, and cultural barricades that have blocked the natural coalition of left-wing forces at all times in the past. So this movement must

18. *Berkeley Tribe*, vol. 6, no. 8 (Oct. 1–7, 1971), p. 10.

be used to provide an example for the partisans engaged at other levels of struggle."[19] In addition, these outside groups focus independent attacks on the prison system, the court system, the legal and medical professions, and the corporate system, all of which contribute to and benefit from the exploitation of prisoners. For example, the Medical Committee for Human Rights is investigating the use of drugs to tranquilize and torture militant prisoners and the use of prisoners for testing new drugs by the multibillion-dollar drug industry.

The crucial measure of the advancement represented by the current movement in prisons is its level of political articulation. The rioters of the 1950s were not conscious of the similarities between their protest and protest in the larger society. Today's revolutionaries are not only conscious of that connection, but strive to make it more complete. The current movement offers a class analysis of American society which sees prisons not only as an institution for class control in the United States but also as part of the global system of class control called imperialism. The movement grounds its activity in this analysis and is based on interracial and international solidarity. It represents the development of the revolutionary potential of the most exploited part of the working class, the wretched of the earth, with that forsaken class providing both leadership and analysis for the larger movement. To the degree that these things are true, even in the face of incredible repression, the prisoners' struggle today is in the forefront of the revolutionary movement in America.

As prisoners have moved from riot toward revolution, the state has responded with intensified repression. At this point, the direction that this repression will take is not completely clear, although it is clear that it is linked with the intensified repression in the society in general: the death of George Jackson in San

19. George Jackson, *Blood in My Eye* (New York: Random House, 1972), p. 109.

Quentin, for example, immediately brings to mind the murders of Fred Hampton and Mark Clark in Chicago.[20]

The indications are that the basic technique of preventing rebellion will continue to be the pitting of prisoners against each other, particularly along racial lines. Promises of early parole and good treatment and threats of torture or denial of parole will be used against prisoners to prevent them from participating in political activity. When such tactics fail and a revolt does occur, the prison will continue to turn to intense repression to deal with the situation: transfers, torture, assassination, officially sponsored racial violence, and other forms of crisis management.

The use of differential rewards and punishments to prevent prisoners from cooperating with militants may still work, since all prisoners are at the mercy of the system and not all are strong enough to resist completely. But an increasing number of prisoners are turning their backs on bribes and threats. And because of increased public consciousness and alertness about prisons, especially after the murders at Attica and San Quentin, it is becoming more difficult for prison officials to hide or defend the practice of mass murder and torture behind the walls.

Because of these developments, the prison system is looking for new techniques of dealing with disturbances. A dim outline of the "prison of the future" is emerging. It is based on the application of sophisticated techniques of medicine and social

20. On December 4, 1970, fourteen special police, acting on the orders of State's Attorney Edward Hanrahan, raided the Illinois Chapter of the Black Panther party. Deputy Chairman Fred Hampton was murdered by the police while he slept, and Mark Clark, also a Black Panther, was critically wounded and died shortly thereafter. Hanrahan described the incident as a shoot-out, and said police fired only after the Black Panthers had fired several volleys at the police. However, subsequent investigations revealed that the police had fired approximately 99 shots, and that the Panthers *might* have fired one shot. As other evidence was uncovered, it became clear that Hanrahan had lied and that Hampton and Clark had not been killed in a "shoot-out" but rather had been deliberately murdered. Despite the efforts of a number of government officials to prevent any action from being taken against Hanrahan, he and 13 law officers were indicted on August 24, 1971 for "conspiring to obstruct justice."

science to solve the "problem" of prisons. These techniques include mind-altering drugs and brain surgery designed to eliminate violent, "antisocial" characteristics, and electric shock and pain-inducing drugs designed to "negatively condition" prisoners. These techniques may be clothed in the respectability of psychiatry, but they represent the same basic effort to control the lives of recalcitrant prisoners.[21]

Along with these new techniques, we are beginning to see the rise of a new breed of penologist: liberal, academically trained, and sophisticated enough to understand the revolutionary movement and its appeal to prisoners. He will attempt to undercut that revolution through "far-reaching reforms" aimed at removing the boredom and frustration from daily prison life. He will understand and sympathize with the drive for cultural and racial identity by members of Third World nationalities. He will talk about opening "lines of communication" and "sharing power with responsible inmates." Yet, all this time he will be ready and willing to use whatever force is necessary to deal with prisoners who do not cooperate with the system, and his ultimate goal will be the maintenance of a prison system whose primary purpose is the integration of prisoners into the existing social order; for him, rehabilitation will still mean conformity. With these new techniques and new prison administrators, the "liberal totalitarianism" of American prisons will become an even more pervasive reality.

The construction of such liberal horror chambers has implications for society as a whole. Just as drugs are used on rebellious prisoners, so too are tranquilizers being used to control "troublesome and overactive" children in schools. Just as prison officials have proposed the increased use of electronic technology to maintain constant surveillance of prisoners (closed-circuit television, electronic sensing devices, etc.), so too the FBI, local

21. See Chapter 15 for a more detailed discussion of the new methods of control.

police, and corporate establishments have stepped up the use of electronic surveillance of citizens at large. More and more people are coming to see that they are not free, but merely prisoners in a "minimum-security" wing of the same prison in which prisoners are held. The rise of a revolutionary movement among prisoners is inseparable from the rise of a larger revolutionary movement in America and around the world; so too is its fate.

CHAPTER 13

Prison Reform Through the Legislature

by James F. Smith

Virtually all legal protections for those accused of crimes have been the result of judicial construction of the federal Constitution rather than of legislative action. Federal judges, who are appointed for life, are considerably less susceptible than elected officials to pressure from public outcry against "coddling criminals" or "permissiveness." Consequently, they have been decidedly more protective of civil liberties than state judges, U.S. Congressmen, and state legislators who must stand for reelection. To a large extent the conservatism of elected officials concerning crime and punishment stems from the economic base of campaign funding. Both Democratic and Republican parties are dependent upon funding from the very rich, who tend strongly to see their interests served by a repressive criminal justice system. Many politicians have built their careers on condemning "softness on communism" or "coddling of criminals." In addition, the conservative policies of public officials on these issues are to an important extent the result of the political effectiveness of the police and prison establishment (police associations, district attorneys, associations of prison officials). These groups are well organized throughout the country. They maintain pressure on politicians to retain or increase harsh penalties, and they are quick to condemn judicial leniency.[1]

This kind of political pressure has not been challenged by a countervailing political force. Teachers, consumers, ecology groups, and labor unions have established themselves as viable political influences in many statehouses. Prison reform groups have not.[2] A myriad of community groups, friends and relatives of prisoners, prison lawyers, convict unions, and radical prison movement groups exists. These groups, however, have not yet allied to launch a concerted political challenge to the conservative influence of the police establishment. These groups are the most knowledgeable about, and dedicated to, prison reform, but they remain unwilling or unable to concentrate their energies and resources on legislative bodies.

Given the enormous frustrations of trying to influence a state legislature, it is easy to understand why prison reform groups have not actively tried to work through this body. It is nonetheless true that fundamental change in the prison system on a state or federal level necessarily involves legislative reversal of previous enactments. The courts simply cannot do it alone. In response to the high level of publicity in the press and elsewhere about the problems of American prisons, legislatures are likely to enact some kind of change in the prison system. But unless prison reform groups are actively involved in the politics of those legislative bodies, these changes will probably be more in line with the wishes and interests of the police and prison establishment than with the wishes and interests of prisoners.

This chapter presents a detailed discussion of the attempts at

1. For an excellent analysis of the political sophistication of the law enforcement lobby, see William W. Turner, *The Police Establishment* (New York: Putnam, 1968).

2. The word "reform" is not meant to exclude the abolition of prisons, but merely to characterize any changes or modifications (including abolition itself) of the penal system.

prison reform in the 1971 session of the California legislature. Although California has certain special problems, the fate of prison reform legislation is illustrative of similar reform attempts throughout the country.

PRISON REFORM BILLS IN THE 1971 CALIFORNIA LEGISLATURE

In the 1971 California legislative session, more than 150 bills were introduced on the subject of prison reform. This had become a popular legislative issue, seen by politicians as favorable to their image. Most of the bills were hastily prepared without benefit of research or understanding of the problems faced by prisoners, and most were totally irrelevant to the convicts' powerlessness vis-à-vis the Department of Corrections and state parole boards. The majority were not seriously pushed by their authors but were allowed to die in the initial policy committee. At most, 20 of the bills dealt with significant reform issues: the indeterminate sentence, parole granting and revocation procedures, the extensive use of solitary confinement or adjustment center cells, civil rights and First Amendment protections, and attempts to set up a prison ombudsman or other machinery for resolving prisoner grievances.

The Adult Authority

The bill that received the most publicity during the session was one which was widely heralded as a measure that would end the abuses of the Adult Authority. It was originally introduced in the 1970 session (designated AB 1511) by a bipartisan coalition of assemblymen and senators. As drafted, the measure provided that the Adult Authority must "determine the length of time a person shall be imprisoned" within 12 months of the end of such person's minimum sentence if five years or less, or within 30 months if his minimum sentence is higher. Furthermore, the Adult Authority would be required to set forth in writing the grounds for denial of a parole. The bill attempted to establish a standard that every prisoner should be paroled at his minimum term unless "his offense was substantially more serious than usual"; "he has a history of excessive criminality"; "there was a substantial danger that he would inflict serious bodily injury on others if released"; "he was previously granted parole"; or another provision of the law required that he be imprisoned for a longer term. Finally, the bill provided that the Adult Authority should consist of the director of the Department of Corrections as chairman, one attorney experienced in criminal justice, a social or behavioral scientist experienced in deviant behavior, an educator experienced with disadvantaged or handicapped pupils, and a law enforcement agent.

Even in its original form, it is questionable whether AB 1511 would have significantly limited the discretionary power of the Adult Authority. The existence of an all-powerful parole board authorized to decide when, if ever, a prisoner would be paroled was maintained. There was nothing in the bill that precluded the Adult Authority from setting a prisoner's term at the maximum until such time as it decided to do otherwise. The refusal to grant parole could be justified under the terms of the bill, merely because the prisoner had previously been paroled. This, in fact, would involve a very high percentage of those serving long terms. Moreover, the parole board could easily assert that any given prisoner's crime was "more serious than usual," or that he had a "history of excessive criminality" whenever it wished to keep the man in prison. The bill set forth no requirement that the Adult Authority show meaningful evidence in making these determinations or that the prisoner be protected by due process in the parole hearings.

AB 1511 was essentially "window dressing"—the kind of reform that politicians always propose when a system is under attack and the politics of the problem necessitate the appearance of reform. The most important substantive issue in reforming the Adult Authority—the abolition of the indeterminate sentence—was not even considered. As the bill meandered through the legislature in the 1970 session, it was repeatedly watered down. When it finally reached the senate, it was amended, just before it was killed, to emphasize what was already evident: nothing in the proposed law shall be construed (in the words of the amendment) "to create any right for the prisoner to be released on parole not later than a minimum term prescribed by law." The Adult Authority's unbridled discretion was not touched.

In the 1971 session the amended version of AB 1511 was reintroduced, with virtually no changes, as AB 483. With considerable fanfare, AB 483 was touted as the most significant prison reform measure to be introduced in the 1971 session.[3] The bill passed the assembly, but its author let it die quietly in the senate after the alleged escape attempt by George Jackson from San Quentin prison in August, 1971. It seemed that even a mild reform was too controversial.

The Adult Authority reacted to all of this by proposing its own ostensible reform measure. In October, 1971, the parole board announced the passage of a resolution that would abolish the indeterminancy of the Indeterminate Sentence Law, "alleviate the tension in the correction system and take away the main gripes that the inmates have."[4] On closer examination the resolution simply provided that inmates were to be given "contingency parole dates" within one month of their minimum sentence if they had no substantial disciplinary write-ups; but the date could be taken away for any disciplinary between the contingency parole board hearing and the parole date. The hypocrisy of the Adult Authority's reform measure is transpar-

3. Newspapers carried the story that Assemblyman Leo Ryan, the author of AB 483, had conceived of the provisions of his prison bill while spending a few (very well publicized) days inside Folsom prison in the spring of 1970. In fact, Mr. Ryan's bill was virtually identical to the previous year's bill.

4. Memorandum to Adult Authority Chairman Henry Kerr from Adult Authority member Curtis Lynum, dated August 30, 1971.

ent when one considers that most disciplinaries are totally subject to the discretion of the individual guards and that the most typical disciplinary is for violation of Director's Rule 1201 ("Inmate Behavior"), which states: "Always conduct yourself in an orderly manner. Do not fight or take part in horseplay or physical encounters except as part of the regular athletic program. Do not agitate, unduly complain, magnify grievances, or behave in any way which might lead to violence."

Of almost equal importance to the question of due process during parole hearings is the question of due process during parole revocation hearings. AB 1180 was an attempt to provide minimal procedural safeguards for parolees in revocation hearings. Although the bill still made it possible for parolees to be ordered into custody without notice for alleged violation of their parole, it required a formal hearing within 10 days after the prisoner had been taken into custody. The bill further provided that the parolee was entitled to a notice setting forth the alleged violation, and that at the hearing before the Adult Authority the parolee had the right to have counsel present to represent him and present evidence in his behalf. The Adult Authority was instructed not to base its disposition upon any alleged violation other than those found to be true. This bill was the most limited possible implementation of due process. It hardly reduced the discretionary power of the Adult Authority to abruptly terminate a paroled prisoner's freedom.

The issue of due process in parole revocation hearings was one problem which seemed ripe for reform by 1971. The U.S. Supreme Court, in the case of *Mempha* v. *Rhay* (389 U.S. 128, 1967), had ruled that the defendant, who had been placed on probation for two years under the Deferred Sentencing Law of the state of Washington, was entitled to counsel at a hearing where his probation was revoked and the deferred sentence imposed. Several lower court decisions had followed suit, requiring counsel or counsel substitute at parole revocation hearings.

AB 1180 easily passed the state assembly, but failed to clear the Senate Judiciary Committee. Even though the bill was extremely moderate, and even though the courts had set the stage for reform, the committee saw it as politically risky, and so they stopped it.

The Prison Ombudsman

The most significant success of the 1971 legislative session was the passage by the state assembly and senate of a bill to establish a correctional ombudsman for the state of California (AB 1181).

Despite California's reputation as having one of the most advanced penal systems, its institutions, in fact, contain thousands of prisoners who seethe with resentment. Channels for communication and resolution of grievances are essential to avoid the hopelessness and despair that preceded the tragedies of Attica and San Quentin. When such channels are blocked, or nonexistent, prisoners have utilized riots and the taking of hostages in order to inform the free world of their grievances. Most of the major penal reforms that have occurred have been, at least in part, the result of riots or scandals.[5]

The California Department of Corrections receives more than 300 letters per month from prisoners under its jurisdiction. The Adult Authority also reports a large volume of monthly correspondence, including: 100 formal appeals of Adult Authority actions, 200 prisoner complaints or requests for information, and 300 additional letters from prisoners' families. According to the CDC's estimate, at least one-third of the prisoner correspondence concerns matters which do not come under its jurisdiction (for example: criminal convictions, legal issues). Most prisoners' grievances receive a routine reply from the Department's grievance coordinator, or are sent back to the institution

---

5. Perhaps the best example of how reform follows scandal is the Arkansas prison system. See T. Murton and Joe Hyams, *Accomplices to the Crime* (New York: Grove Press, 1970).

where the individual is confined. The practice of referring a complaint back down the chain of command often results in an investigation by the very staff against whom the complaint is lodged. The prisoner accurately perceives that his grievances are not treated seriously, and he is powerless against the injustices and deprivation he suffers.

In December, 1970, the California Assembly Interim Committee on Criminal Procedures conducted a hearing on the desirability of a correctional ombudsman. From their extensive investigation, a committee report was filed and the correctional ombudsman bill, AB 1181, was introduced into the assembly. Under the terms of the bill, the correctional ombudsman was to be supervised by a joint legislative committee consisting of four state senators and four state assemblymen. The ombudsman was to be appointed by the joint committee for a term of four years. The committee was authorized to appoint a maximum of 13 investigative deputies (one for each of the state prisons). The ombudsman and his staff were to include a minimum of one person schooled and experienced in law, one person schooled and experienced in investigative technique, and one person schooled and experienced in criminology and corrections. The ombudsman was to have the power and duty to establish procedures for receiving and processing complaints, for investigating the administrative acts of the Department and state parole boards, for reporting his findings, and for suggesting appropriate remedies.

Although the bill provided that no person has a right to be heard by the ombudsman, the ombudsman was required to inform the complainant of the reason for refusing to investigate a complaint. In the course of his investigations, the ombudsman could make inquiries, obtain information, enter the prisons without notice, and hold hearings in public or in private. He was required to maintain secrecy with respect to the identities of the complainants, except as disclosure might have been necessary to enable him to carry out his duties and to support his recommendations. He was authorized to bring suit in an appropriate state court to enforce these powers and to present his opinions and recommendations to the governor, the legislature, or the public.

From the very beginning, it was clear that state funds would not be available for the correctional ombudsman. Accordingly, the Law Enforcement Assistance Administration in Washington, D.C., assured the bill's supporters of full financial support under the Federal Omnibus Crime Control Act.

Despite the fact that the author of the ombudsman bill was the minority whip leader in the assembly, the bill faced severe opposition, particularly from supporters of the Reagan administration. The major confrontation came in the senate. Instead of the usual procedure of sending the bill to the Senate Judiciary Committee, the correctional ombudsman bill was sent to the Senate Governmental Organizations Committee for almost certain death. The bill received strong opposition on the first hearing. Many of the committee members hesitated to support the bill because of their apprehension concerning legislative interference in administrative matters. Others felt that they could not support the bill because the California Correctional Officers' Association, owing to recent prison disorders, had not yet decided what position to take on the issue. In spite of these objections, the bill did in fact pass the committee, largely because of the energy exerted by the author of the bill in personally lobbying the individual members of the committee. After considerable debate on the senate floor, the bill was passed and sent to the governor. Many observers thought that the Republican credentials and the untarnished moderate reputation of its author would assure the governor's approval of the bill. It was vetoed.

Exactly why the governor vetoed this measure is difficult to determine, but the influence of the police establishment was certainly very important. Reagan's legal affairs secretary,

Herbert E. Ellingwood, advised the governor on criminal justice issues. As the former lobbyist for the Peace Officers' and
District Attorneys' Associations of California, Mr. Ellingwood
was well qualified to act as the political spokesman for the police
establishment. Whether or not Mr. Ellingwood delivered the
coup de grace to the correctional ombudsman legislation,
unquestionably the political sophistication and power of the
police lobby was a major factor in its ultimate defeat.[6]

Conjugal Visits

The prison system has historically disengaged itself from the
community. In 1950 attention was finally directed toward outside communication when the American Prison Association established the basic principle that outside social relationships are
a crucial stimulant for the prisoner's successful adjustment. The
association's conclusions denounced prison administrators' continued restriction on visiting programs and their use of visitation as a privilege, to be applied as reward or punishment for
conforming behavior.

> The Administration of prison must regard it as a duty to
> establish adequate conditions, pleasant settings . . . to re-
> store to the inmate some of the more normal feelings of
> social living and to prevent institutionalization with its re-
> sultant deterioration and spoilage of attitudes and behav-
> ior. . . . Visits from friends and relatives are a human right,
> although not a legal one. It would be very unfortunate,

6. Ellingwood expressed the importance of the police lobby this way: "It is
not possible to list the many notable achievements of law enforcement legislative activity. We can look with pride to such things as the Commission on Peace
Officer Standards and Training, the state teletype system, the State Department of Justice, the laws on conspiracy, the narcotic penalty and rehabilitation
program, and many others as our work product. In addition, we have been able
to retain the death penalty, stop unworkable changes in criminal responsibility,
and indicate to the legislature many proposals which would have a detrimental
effect on the citizenry . . . law enforcement's role in legislative matters must
be one of aggressive leadership. . . . " Cited in Turner, *The Police Establishment*,
p. 236.

however, if the idea prevailed that because visits are a privilege that they are permitted merely as a generosity on the part of the prison officials. On the contrary, visits rank with food or medicine as meeting basic needs of inmates and as leading toward their reformations.[7]

In the past, California prisons have attempted various temporary projects which focused on the prisoner's outside contacts, but such programs have been relatively few and far between.[8] Finally, in 1968 the California Correctional Institution at Tehachapi began an experimental program in extended family visiting for selected prisoners. Even though family-conjugal visiting as a correctional technique has existed for more than fifty years, the Department spent two years testing and recording the results of the family visiting program.[9] With all indications being positive, the California correctional system began in 1971 to slowly institute a limited form of special family visitation.

In response to the interest surrounding visitation, a bill was introduced (AB 2063) which provided for the majority of state prisoners to have private visits up to 48 hours (minimum of 24 hours). Prisoners would be eligible three times a year for this special visitation with families and friends. The legislation was designed to establish visiting as a right and to allow more prisoners to receive outside contact, thus furthering the possibilities of successful parole. Unfortunately, the legislative proponents of conjugal visiting seemed more interested in utilizing the bill as a publicity mechanism than pushing it seriously. The visitation bill ("sex bill") quickly developed into a highly controversial issue which barely received passage in the assembly's policy and fiscal committees, even though both committees are "lib-

7. American Prison Association, *Handbook on the Inmate Relationship with Persons from Outside the Adult Correctional Institution*, 1953, p. 26.

8. Norman Fenton, *The Prisoner's Family* (Palo Alto: Pacific Books, 1959).

9. D. F. Miller, "Inmate Attitudes and Views of Two Experimental Programs," *Australian and New Zealand Journal of Criminology*, vol. 14, no. 1 (March, 1971).

eral." It was evident that it was doomed unless further amendments were accepted. The author consented to take a less radical approach. However, he was, unwilling to expend further energies on behalf of the bill. It was soundly defeated after a jocular barroom session on the sexual implications of family visiting.

Adjustment Centers

Legislative reaction to the issue of the Adult Authority's administration of the indeterminate sentence was artificial and contrived, dealing with the politics, rather than the substance of prison reform. Community groups, the United Prisoners' Union, and prison lawyers were, however, able to persuade sympathetic legislators to introduce more substantive legislation to deal with the extremely important issue of the abuses of prison disciplinary procedures and the "adjustment center."

The use of solitary confinement cells almost invariably means that the prisoner is sentenced to additional months and often years of confinement. The Adult Authority is very unlikely to parole men so confined because it considers such confinement evidence of their failure to be "rehabilitated." Psychological studies have indicated that the monotony of prolonged solitary confinement and the concomitant extreme sensory deprivation cause mental deterioration in most subjects. In November, 1971, a Department representative testified that some 850 prisoners were confined in these small cages. However, an extensive report commissioned by the state disclosed that 1,224 men were so confined on January 7, 1971, which, according to the report, is a higher percentage than other states.[10]

Many California prisoners are sentenced to life imprisonment under the indeterminate sentence law. Those in the adjustment

10. Robert E. Keldgord (program director), *Coordinated California Corrections,* vol. 1, "Institutions," (Sacramento: Board of Corrections, Human Relations Agency, 1971).

center for indefinite periods are sentenced to an indeterminate sentence within an indeterminate sentence, as well as to a prison within a prison; they never know when, if ever, they will be released from the cage.

A coalition of the Prisoners' Union, prison attorneys, and community groups convinced several state legislators to introduce in their respective houses a bill to require procedural due process for inmates whose alleged disciplinary violations could cause them to be sentenced to the adjustment center. These protections included the right to advance notice of the disciplinary charges, the right to call witnesses and to cross-examine accusers, the right to be represented by staff or fellow prisoners, the right to have guilt determined on the preponderance of evidence, and the right of appeal. The bills also required a superior court finding that a prisoner was "incorrigibly violent" before long-term adjustment center confinements could be approved (more than 60 days in any six-month period).

The senate bill died quickly in the Senate Finance Committee. The assembly bill passed the assembly and was sent to the senate. In order to become state law, it had to pass the Senate Finance Committee and the senate floor, be returned to the assembly for concurrence on amendments, and then be sent to the governor for his approval.

Like most legislative bodies in the United States, California has a "graveyard committee" where progressive or reform bills are weeded out. In the California State Legislature it is the Senate Finance Committee. This committee must pass on any legislation having a fiscal impact on the state. Its members have a remarkable record for stopping reform legislation.

The committee is ruled with an iron hand by its chairman, a rural conservative Democrat who has been a member of the state senate since 1938. At first he refused even to schedule a hearing for the assembly bill. Subsequently, a former Catholic chaplain at Soledad prison made a special trip to Sacramento to speak to the chairman and ask him to hold a hearing. The chairman agreed; it is hard to turn down a priest.

Four days before the adjournment of the 1971 session, the assembly adjustment center bill was finally heard before the committee. The chairman reflected the general atmosphere of the hearings when he remarked, after a witness testified that one man had been held in solitary confinement for as long as five years, that prisoners like that "must be hard nuts to crack." To make matters worse, the ostensibly neutral and expert legislative accountant also testified against the "policy" of both bills. He argued, along with the Department of Corrections, that the bills would unnecessarily tie the hands of the Department as well as cost the state some $700,000 for the hearings required. (This position fails to take into account the fact that adjustment center confinement is more than twice as expensive as general population confinement.) Throughout the hearing the Department of Corrections grossly misrepresented the nature of the adjustment center, characterizing long-term solitary confinement as merely a "part of our classification program." Seven votes were needed for passage. One Republican voted for the bill, along with three Democrats, but three other Democratic senators, who had previously indicated their support for the measure, were "absent," and the bill thus failed to pass.[11]

The assembly adjustment center bill went further in the legislative process than any significant prison reform legislation other than the ombudsman bill. This relative success was attributable to the author's personal commitment to the bill, as well as to the tenacious efforts of its supporters.

11. Being "absent" is often a politically tactful way of withdrawing support for a bill or of abstaining from support. It is one device by which a legislator can get credit for having verbally supported a bill, without really taking the political risks of working for a measure which might be controversial.

THE APPEARANCE OF REFORM

Legislators are often much more concerned with their public image than with their substantive legislative accomplishments. With a hot political issue like prison reform, the legislature, like most political bodies, is skillful at appearing concerned and dedicated to resolving the problem, while at the same time endlessly delaying any meaningful change that might be controversial.

Many techniques are used to create this illusion of reform. First of all, politicians are good at introducing legislation which they loudly proclaim will solve the problems of prisons, but which, in reality, is "window dressing." And if a bill does in fact deal with some of the real problems of prisons, it is likely to be amended into window dressing as it struggles through the legislative committees. In the 1971 legislative session, the various bills designed to reform the Adult Authority were this kind of empty reform.

A second technique of appearing concerned with reform is to introduce high-sounding, "relevant" legislation at the beginning of the legislative session, and then to ignore it, allowing it to die quietly in the course of the session. The legislator thus gets good publicity for being concerned about the issue in question, without having to face the political consequences of really doing something about it. Most of the bills introduced in the 1971 session represented this kind of tactical political show of concern without any commitment to the issue.

A third approach to creating the appearance of reform is the "exhaustive study." This is an attractive technique because it has the advantage of taking a great deal of time, of indicating a rational, cool-headed, yet concerned approach to the problem, while still not involving any actual changes in the system itself. The California legislature has conducted five major studies of the California prison system in the period 1968–1971.

These studies have painstakingly documented, among other things, the failure of California prisons to rehabilitate, the arbitrariness and irrationality of the parole boards' practices, the excessive length of California prison sentences, and the dismal failure of the correctional industries program. Many of the suggestions for prison reform that have been derived from these studies have been made before in federal studies and criminology reports, or are simply conventional wisdom among penologists. Despite the redundancy, the California legislature continues to pass resolutions calling for additional research, and the well-heeled federal Law Enforcement Assistance Agency has been most generous in granting hundreds of thousands of dollars to fund these studies on state as well as federal levels.

Not to be outdone, in 1970 Governor Reagan commissioned yet another exhaustive study of the California criminal justice system. He announced that no prison bills would be signed by him until the completion of the study. The California Council of Criminal Justice (the state planning agency for the Omnibus Crime Control and Safe Streets Act) granted the state $250,000 to fund the study. Fifty-seven expert penologists were hired as consultants. The study was conducted under the leadership of Robert E. Keldgord (the California director of the National Council on Crime and Delinquency, 1962–1968, and author of numerous studies on American criminal and correctional systems). The goal of the study was to compare present practices with the conventional wisdom of academic penologists and criminologists, and to develop a model system of corrections aimed at "protection of society by minimizing the probability of illegal conduct." Although the Keldgord Study had been reviewed prior to George Jackson's alleged escape attempt at San Quentin, the governor commissioned yet another study on September 8, 1971, directing the Board of Corrections to conduct "a thorough review of security procedures in our prisons." The report was promptly issued, placing the blame for any and all prison violence or discontent on amorphous and sinister outside agitators, "revolutionary attorneys," the underground press, and other misguided individuals.

Through these techniques the California legislature has managed to confront the violence and oppression of California prisons and do absolutely nothing about it. Until concerted political pressure is brought to bear on the legislature to act rather than merely talk, this is likely to continue. Those few legislators who are sincerely committed to prison reform will be unable to push through significant legislation until they are strongly backed by a well-organized, vocal political organization.

LEGISLATIVE POLITICS AND PRISON REFORM

The 1971 session of the California legislature is both encouraging and hopeless. It is encouraging to know that a Republican legislator was able to secure legislative passage of the correctional ombudsman bill, even though it was eventually vetoed; and it is slightly encouraging that the assembly adjustment center bill went as far as it did. Nevertheless, the essential elements for achieving major prison reform through the legislature seem hopelessly unattainable. Above all, the obstacle of an extremely conservative governor on the one hand and the absence of a well-organized coalition of prison reform groups on the other make the prospects for meaningful reform very slim.

The governor's office in California, as in other states, has immense influence over the legislative process, whether in prison reform or any other area. The governor can exercise his veto over any legislation of which he disapproves, thus negating in a moment the enormous energy necessary to get progressive prison legislation through the legislature.[12] In addition to the power of the veto, the governor has at his disposal the vast lobbying power of the Department of Corrections (which in

12. A veto can be overruled by a two-thirds majority, but this almost never happens in state politics.

1971 had a budget exceeding $130 million) and of the state's parole boards. In the 1971 session, the governor used both the threat of veto and the lobbying influence of the Department of Corrections and the Adult Authority to discourage and defeat every constructive prison reform bill introduced in the session.

Without the pressure from a politically sophisticated prison reform movement, even relatively liberal governors and state legislatures are unlikely to enact major revisions of the prison system. In order for prison reformers to become effective in applying this pressure, they must involve themselves in the mundane chicanery of partisan politics (this is not meant to exclude the creation of new political parties). Since they lack the wealth to become important sources of funds for political candidates, they must build their influence with people's time and energy in day-to-day political activity. They must become involved in party platform conventions and registration of young and minority voters. And very importantly, they must participate fully in political campaigns and work to exact pledges from candidates prior to their election.

Most leftist groups in America have been unwilling or unable to participate this way in establishment politics. They express outrage at the inhumanity and repression of the criminal justice system, but refuse to become involved in conventional politics as a way of dealing with these problems. Instead they engage in armchair discussions of revolution and "increasing political consciousness." For many it is a matter of ideology, a firm belief that the system cannot reform itself. For others it is a matter of life style, an unwillingness to make the personal compromises in dress, language, and personal activity that are necessary to deal with the "straight" world. For some it is a matter of inertia. The impotence of the American left is not so much a matter of its intrinsic weakness as rather its pervasive unwillingness to unite and gain political power through established channels.

It is perhaps unfortunate, from a moral and pragmatic point of view, that the United States is not on the verge of revolution.

But until a revolutionary situation exists in the United States, conventional politics has the undeniable advantage over *armchair* revolution in that it can accomplish some positive changes.[13] If prison reform groups are to have any real hope of modifying the prison system in the foreseeable future, they must begin to focus their energies on established political institutions, for in the foreseeable future it is through these institutions that change must come.

13. Participation in conventional politics should not be considered inconsistent with the long-run possibilities of revolutionary change. Every modern revolution has been preceded by a period of halting social reform which appears to have whetted, rather than satisfied, the appetite of the oppressed for liberation.

CHAPTER 14:

Change Through the Courts

by Brian Glick

Courts and lawyers have always been very important to the prisoner. They put him behind bars and yet, at the same time, offer one of his few hopes for early freedom. Since the 1960s courts and lawyers have also begun to deal with the internal operation of prisons. Lawyers have filed suits to protect prisoners' legal rights and improve prison conditions and they have won some major courtroom victories. Some of this increasing legal activity on behalf of prisoners has strengthened the political struggle to change both prisons and the class and race relations which determine how prisons are used. It has not, however, had significant direct impact on prison life. Its limits are rooted deep in the American legal system and revealed throughout prisoners' experiences with the law.

PRISONERS AND THE LAW

Prisoners know, better than most people, the sham and corruption, and the class and race bias, of criminal law enforcement in the United States. They know the assembly-line processing that passes for representation by public defenders. They know that judges and prosecutors are political appointees who, in many cases, have literally bought their positions.[1] They know that these well-paid, professionally privileged men, almost all of them white, fear and look down on the poor men and women, very disproportionately nonwhite, whom they send to prison. Prisoners know also that "white-collar" criminals generally do not serve time because their crimes are not considered a serious threat to the social order, they have money for bail and private counsel, and prosecutors and judges treat them more as equals.[2]

Most prisoners are behind bars as the result of a "plea bargain," a deal between the public defender, the prosecutor, and, more often than not, the judge. More than 90 percent of the people convicted of crimes in the United States plead guilty. Typically, a poor defendant is charged with a more serious crime than can be proved in court. He is threatened with certain conviction and maximum sentence if he stands trial, but promised leniency if he pleads guilty to a lesser offense. Frightened, intimidated, confused by court procedures, held for weeks or months in a degrading detention cell, under pressure from police, prosecutors, and his own attorney, even the totally innocent poor defendant usually "cops a plea." Frequently the authorities do not keep their end of the bargain and the defendant serves many more years in prison that he was led to expect.[3]

The process which put him behind bars is, to the prisoner, one face of the law. The other face is legal action to release him

1. The going rate for a New York City judgeship in the late 1950s was a contribution to the local Democratic party reportedly ranging from a minimum of $20,000 to as much as two years' salary as a judge, or approximately $60,000. Wallace Sayre and Herbert Kaufman, *Governing New York* (Russell Sage Foundation, 1960), p. 542.

2. Data for rate of conviction and time served by class, race, and type of offense can be found in tables 1, 2, 4, 5, 9, and 10 in this book.

3. Sometimes the prosecutor and judge double-cross a defendant and give him a heavier sentence than they promised. More often they deceive him by not explaining how much time he can serve for the crime to which he pleads guilty, especially in states which use the indeterminate sentence. For a general description and analysis of the "plea-bargaining" process, see Abraham Blumberg, *Criminal Justice* (Chicago: Quadrangle, 1967).

from prison and protect his rights while he is there. This positive side of the law is limited in its capacity to help the prisoner by the same biases and bureaucratic mentality that helped put him in prison in the first place.

Judges generally consider themselves too busy to take seriously the writs of habeas corpus by which prisoners seek release from prison. Every year thousands of prisoners submit such writs to have their criminal convictions declared invalid. Although decisions of higher courts have cast doubt on the constitutionality of procedures by which many of them have been convicted, only a handful are allowed to appear in court to argue the merits of their cases, and still fewer ultimately win their freedom. In many places the prisoner simply receives a form postcard indicating that his writ has been denied and giving no further explanation.[4]

The courts even dispose casually of legal papers which have been carefully prepared by competent "jailhouse lawyers" who specialize in writing writs for fellow prisoners. Several courts have ignored writs prepared by one of California's most skilled jailhouse lawyers when they were submitted in the prisoner's name, only to grant relief when the identical documents were resubmitted under attorneys' names.[5]

For most of the country's history, lawsuits that challenged the

4. Habeas corpus is the only procedure by which a prisoner can challenge his conviction if he has lost his appeal, failed to file a notice of appeal within the brief period of time allowed by law, or waived his right to appeal by entering a plea of guilty. Most prisoners file in the state courts, where their writs are treated in the manner described here. A prisoner who believes his conviction violates the U.S. Constitution or statutes can submit a writ of habeas corpus to a federal court, which generally will treat his case more responsibly.

The writ of habeas corpus is also the form prisoners generally use to attack prison conditions in the state courts. Prisoners' experience using habeas corpus for this latter purpose is included in the general discussion below of legal action to change the internal operation of prisons.

5. John van Geldern, the jailhouse lawyer who had these experiences described them in letters to me. Since prisoners are authorized by law to submit writs of habeas corpus on their own behalf, there is no legal reason why a writ submitted by a prisoner should receive less attention than an identical document submitted on his behalf by an attorney. That an attorney's signature makes a difference to many judges reveals their biases against prisoners.

internal operation of prisons did not receive even the cursory consideration generally given to writs seeking release from prison. Until the 1960s the courts openly refused to determine the merits of such litigation. Following a "hands-off policy," they let prison staff do as they pleased, free from judicial interference.[6]

The courts gave three reasons for this policy, all of which reveal the political biases of the judiciary. Two of the reasons, "separation of powers" and "lack of judicial expertise," had not stopped the same courts from restricting government agencies that regulate business activity: for years the courts have carefully examined and significantly limited the work of the Securities Exchange Commission, the Interstate Commerce Commission, and numerous other administrative agencies.[7] The third reason the courts gave for refusing to decide prison cases, "fear of undermining prison discipline," indicates the real ideological basis of the hands-off doctrine. Where poor people are concerned, especially poor blacks and Latinos, the courts have been willing to sacrifice constitutional rights in order to strengthen social control.

The hands-off policy prevailed until mass movements in the 1960s began to resist the oppression of blacks, Latinos, and poor whites, who together make up the bulk of the prison population. In this new political climate, the courts could no longer openly ignore the widespread violation of prisoners' constitutional rights. So judges began to rule on cases concerning the internal operation of prisons—although, as we shall see, they did not give up the ideology underlying the hands-off doctrine but instead found new ways to achieve its objectives.

In the sixties the U.S. political and economic system came under widespread attack. Through the civil rights movement, ghetto rebellions, the Black Panther party, and local commu-

6. "Beyond the Ken of the Courts: A Critique of Judicial Refusal to Review the Complaints of Convicts," in *Yale Law Journal*, 72 (1963), p. 506.
7. L.L. Jaffe, *Judicial Control of Administrative Action* (Little, Brown, 1965).

nity groups, black people were at the cutting edge of mass action for basic change. Black prisoners, and others who learned from them, came to understand prison as one part of an unjust system in which power is based on class and race. They no longer accepted their treatment in prison as proper or inevitable, and began working to change it.[8]

The political developments which led prisoners to challenge prison conditions in the sixties also affected judges and lawyers. The U.S. Supreme Court, influenced by the new political climate, expanded the constitutional rights of poor and minority people and imposed new constitutional constraints on public officials. Lawyers mobilized by the civil rights movement and the "war on poverty" began to represent poor people in constitutional test cases in federal court.

Central to the new litigation was the revival of the Federal Civil Rights Act of 1871. This law had been enacted during Reconstruction to enable black people to by-pass the state courts and sue in the more responsive federal courts to enforce their newly won constitutional rights against racist state and local officials. As the southern white aristocracy regained its power after Reconstruction, federal court rulings effectively nullified the Civil Rights Act. The U.S. Supreme Court did not fully overturn these rulings until 1961, early in the nation's second period of mass struggle for the liberation of black people.[9]

8. Chapter 12 of this book reviews the political history of the prison movement.

9. The Civil Rights Act is codified as section 1983 of Title 42 of the United States Code and known colloquially among lawyers as "section 1983." The key U.S. Supreme Court decision resurrecting the Act was *Monroe* v. *Pape*, 365 U.S. 167 (1961). For a general history of the Act and the court cases which interpret it, see Thomas Emerson, et al., *Political and Civil Rights in the United States*, 3rd ed. (Boston: Little, Brown, 1967), II, ch. 15, and sources cited there. In this instance, as in many others, although one cannot *prove* causal connection between political developments and court decisions, their coincidence in time and connection in content make it reasonable to assume that the political events substantially influenced the direction of court rulings which could, in terms of legal doctrine, have been quite different.

In 1964 the Supreme Court confirmed that the Civil Rights Act entitles prisoners to sue state officials in federal court,[10] and federal judges began issuing rulings to protect the legal rights of prisoners. The most far-reaching court decisions came in the early 1970s, as the interconnected political and legal developments of the sixties came together around prisons. Strikes and rebellions inside prison grew more radical and more frequent by 1970, and political movements outside began to pay more attention to prisons.[11] Many lawyers responded to and aided these developments. Prison law became a new specialty. Judges —as always both contributing to new political struggles and deflecting them—began to decide more and more cases in favor of prisoners.

Although the new court decisions made a practical difference for a few prisoners and were sometimes useful in political efforts to change prisons, they had little direct significant effect on prison life. It is necessary to examine these decisions in order to understand their practical limitations. The following summary of the law of prisoners' rights is intended to provide a descriptive basis for the critical analysis which makes up the bulk of this chapter.

THE LAW OF PRISONERS' RIGHTS

The decisions prisoners won between 1964 and 1972 prohibit prison authorities from impeding prisoners' efforts to obtain judicial relief or from discriminating against prisoners on the basis of their religion, race, or sex. They also outlaw the worst conditions and forms of punishment in prison, require that prison officials provide some procedural safeguards when they discipline a prisoner, and protect some forms of political expression by prisoners.

10. *Cooper* v. *Pate*, 378 U.S. 546 (1964).
11. See chapter 12 of this book.

Administrative Interference
with Prisoners' Access to Court

In its first prison decision the U.S. Supreme Court held in 1941 that prison authorities may not screen writs of habeas corpus to determine which will be submitted to court.[12] Soon afterward the court ruled that official interference with a prisoner's efforts to appeal his conviction would similarly deny him the due process of law guaranteed by the Fourteenth Amendment to the U.S. Constitution.[13] These decisions established for prisoners a general right of unimpeded access to court, which federal courts defined in more detail during the 1960s. It is now illegal for a prison official to confiscate, censor, delay, or otherwise interfere with legal papers or correspondence addressed to a court. Nor, according to the courts, may a prisoner be punished for suing the prison administration or criticizing it in court.[14]

Recognizing that a prisoner cannot effectively prepare legal papers without access to expert assistance and legal research materials, the courts have provided some protection in these areas as well. Although prison authorities do not need to provide lawyers for prisoners they must let prisoners consult with their own lawyers. Prisoners are supposed to be allowed private meetings with their lawyers, free from human or electronic surveillance. It is also illegal for prison officials to confiscate or

12. *Ex Parte Hull,* 312 U.S. 546 (1941).
13. *Cochran* v. *Kansas,* 316 U.S. 255 (1942); *Dowd* v. *U.S. ex rel. Cook,* 340 U.S. 206 (1951).
14. Citations to most of the court decisions summarized in this chapter can be found in two comprehensive articles which review prison law decisions through 1970. William Bennett Turner, "Establishing the Rule of Law in Prisons: A Manual for Prisoners' Rights Litigation," *Stanford Law Review,* 23 (1971), pp. 473–518, and Ronald Goldfarb and Linda Singer, "Redressing Prisoners' Grievances," *The George Washington Law Review,* 39 (1970), pp. 175–320. I will provide references only for especially important decisions and for cases decided since 1970. Important decisions about prisons since October 1971 are reprinted in *The Prison Law Reporter,* available in law libraries and by subscription, 1st Floor, Hoge Building, Seattle, Washington 93104.

delay correspondence between prisoners and their lawyers. Whether prison officials may read such mail and delete nonlegal matter, however, remains unsettled. Some courts accept such inspection while others limit or prohibit it.[15]

Since most prisoners cannot afford to retain private counsel and few states provide free legal aid for prisoners, the courts have had to protect prisoners' ability to represent themselves. In 1969 the U.S. Supreme Court ruled that prison authorities who do not provide lawyers for prisoners may not stop prisoners from helping each other with legal work.[16] In 1971 the Court upheld a ruling that prisons must maintain minimally adequate law libraries for prisoners.[17] Lower courts, however, have let prison authorities make jailhouse lawyers obtain permission to practice, work only for free, and comply with reasonable restrictions as to when, where, and how they help other prisoners. Prison authorities may also prohibit a writ writer from keeping lawbooks or completed legal papers in his cell and sharing them with other prisoners, on the pretext that he might extract compensation for the use of these resources.

Religious, Racial, and Sexual Discrimination

The revival of the Federal Civil Rights Act led to a raft of federal lawsuits in the mid-sixties, asserting a prisoner's right to practice his or her religion. These suits were mainly initiated by the Black Muslims who were, at that time, the group most

15. In addition to the cases cited in the law review articles listed in note 14, see *Smith* v. *Robinson*, 328 F. Supp 162 (D. Ma. 1971), which entitles a prisoner to be present when prison staff open letters from his attorney to check for contraband.

16. *Johnson* v. *Avery*, 393 U.S. 483 (1969). In *Novak* v. *Beto*, no. 31116 (5th Cir., Dec. 9, 1971), 1 Pris. Law Rptr. 85, a federal appellate court held that two lawyers and three law students do not provide an adequate alternative in Texas. The court indicated, however, that Texas needs only to make available enough lawyers for habeas petitions and does not need to concern itself with assistance to prisoners filing civil rights suits against prison conditions.

17. *Gilmore* v. *Lynch*, 319 F. Supp. 105 (N.D. Cal. 1970), affirmed sub nom. *Younger* v. *Gilmore*, 404 U.S. 15 (1971).

actively organizing among prisoners.[18] Prisoners now have the legal right, within "reasonable restrictions," to hold religious services, consult and correspond with a minister of their faith, possess religious books, subscribe to religious literature, and wear religious medals and other symbols. The courts are split as to whether prison officials must prepare separate food for prisoners whose religion requires a special diet.

Judges have agreed, after some initial conflict, that racial segregation of prisoners is unconstitutional, under the principle of the Supreme Court's school desegregation decision (Brown v. Board of Education).[19] The courts have also banned racial discrimination. Prison officials may not, for instance, let prisoners subscribe to white-oriented publications but prohibit literature directed to blacks. The courts are split over whether a prisoner has a legal standing to challenge racial discrimination in prison hiring practices.

Responding to the resurgent movement for women's liberation, the Supreme Court held in 1971 that unreasonable discrimination based on sex denies women equal protection of the law.[20] A federal judge has applied this principle to require that women prisoners be included in work furlough programs, previously open only to men.[21] As of mid-1972, however, the courts had not applied the equal protection clause to ban discrimination against homosexual prisoners.

Conditions and Treatment

The Eighth Amendment to the U.S. Constitution prohibits cruel and unusual punishment. In a string of decisions begin-

18. See chapter 12 of this book.

19. The Brown decision is reported in 347 U.S. 483 (1954). A recent, well-reasoned decision that prohibits racial segregation in prisons is McClelland v. Sigler, 327 F. Supp. 829 (1971).

20. Reed v. Reed, 92 S. Ct. 25, 35 L. Ed. 2d 225 (1971). See also Sailor v. Kirby, 5 Cal 3d 1 (1972).

21. Dawson v. Carberry, Civil No. C-71–1916 (N.D. Calif. Nov. 19, 1971).

ning in 1966 federal judges interpreted this provision to prohibit both corporal punishment of prisoners—flogging, tear gassing, chaining or handcuffing them within a cell—and exceptionally degrading conditions of solitary confinement.[22] Opinions in the solitary confinement cases examined conditions in the disciplinary sections of a particular prison—inhuman food, cold, darkness, bad sanitation, poor clothing, no beds or mats—and found that taken together these conditions amount to cruel and unusual punishment. But the courts have not specified minimum standards which prisoners and their lawyers could then invoke to challenge conditions in other prisons. Nor have judges been willing to rule that prolonged isolation is unconstitutional regardless of conditions.[23]

Only one state, Arkansas, has been ordered to improve conditions in the mainline as well as the maximum-security sections of its prisons.[24] And this was only to make Arkansas prisons more like prisons elsewhere by providing some form of rehabilitation program and ending the state's unique system of substituting inmate "trustees" for outside staff in most guard and low-level administrative positions. Federal judges have ordered local officials to overhaul general conditions in a number of county jails, but these decisions have been mainly to protect people awaiting trial, who are not supposed to be punished until after they have been convicted.

The courts have not been able to prohibit forced labor in

22. The latest and most sweeping of these decisions, *Landman* v. *Royster,* 333, F. Supp. 621 (E.D. Va. 1971), prohibits use of bread and water diet, chains, handcuffs, tape, or tear gas for purposes of punishment, keeping a prisoner nude, and placing more than one prisoner in a solitary cell. But *Novak* v. *Beto* (note 16) allows a starvation diet (two pieces of bread per day) so long as hygiene is adequate.

23. In *Sostre* v. *Rockefeller,* 312 F. Supp. 863 (S.D.N.Y. 1970), Constance Baker Motley held that confinement in punitive segregation for more than 15 days constitutes cruel and unusual punishment. That part of her decision was reversed, however, in *Sostre* v. *McGinnis* 442 F. 2d 178 (2nd Cir. 1971).

24. *Holt* v. *Sarver,* 309 F. Supp. 362 (E.D. Ark. 1970), affirmed 442 F. 2d 304 (8th Cir. 1971).

prison because the U.S. Constitution (in the Thirteenth Amendment) explicitly authorizes the involuntary servitude and enslavement of prisoners. Courts have held, however, that it is cruel and unusual punishment to make a prisoner work when he is seriously ill.

They have also imposed on prisons a general duty to provide medical care for prisoners. Complete denial of medical treatment to a prisoner who needs it violates the Eighth Amendment. As long as some care is provided, however, the courts will not evaluate its adequacy. Even widespread systematic medical malpractice had not been held unconstitutional as of mid-1972. Nor had judges recognized the right of a prisoner to refuse potentially harmful medical treatment as long as it is not explicitly punitive. They have even upheld the forced injection of Anectine to deter aggression by inducing general paralysis and drowning sensations.[25]

Several federal court decisions in 1970 and 1971 (most of them pending appeal in 1972) require that prison officials meet constitutional standards of due process of law before they severely punish a prisoner.[26] Severe punishment, under these decisions, includes any loss of good-time credits or prolonged confinement in an isolation cell, adjustment center, or segregation area, even when officials claim that such confinement is merely "administrative," "for the good of the institution," or for the convict's protection. Before they impose such punishment,

25. This use of Anectine (technically succinylcholine chloride) is known as "aversive conditioning." One recent court decision upholding such conditioning is *Mackay* v. *Procunier*, Civ. No. S-1983 (E.D. Cal., Nov. 2, 1971). Judges have also let prison staff forcibly inject heavy doses of Thorazine, Prolixin, and other strong tranquilizers, despite medical knowledge of the possibility of serious adverse effects. Prolixin is allowed in *Smith* v. *Baker*, 326 F. Supp. 787 (W.D. Mo. 1970), Thorazine in *Peek* v. *Ciccone*, 288 F. Supp. 667 (W.D. Mo. 1969).

26. *Clutchette* v. *Procunier*, 328 F. Supp. 767 (N.D. Cal. 1971); *Bundy* v. *Cannon*, 328 F. Supp. 165 (D. Md. 1971); *Urbano* v. *McCorkle*, 334 F. Supp. 161 (D. N.J. 1971); *Sostre* v. *Rockefeller* (note 23); *Landman* v. *Royster* (note 22). Other decisions are cited in the articles by Turner and Goldfarb and Singer (note 14).

officials are supposed to give the prisoner written notice of the charges against him (so he can prepare his defense) and an opportunity for a "fair hearing" on those charges. One court has required that prison authorities make known in advance "reasonably definite" written rules specifying standards of conduct and punishment for various offenses.[27]

These court rulings do not entitle a prisoner to all the safeguards of a criminal trial. Nor do they guarantee a right of appeal outside the prison system. The prisoner is entitled, however, to call witnesses on his behalf, confront and cross-examine adverse witnesses, and have the assistance of private counsel or a "counsel-substitute" (a prisoner or prison staff member). Although the officials who conduct the hearing may work for the prison system, they cannot have been previously involved in the incident at issue, and their decision is supposed to be based only on evidence introduced at the hearing.

A very few decisions have also required notice and a rudimentary hearing in cases of "minor" punishment, such as a fine or the loss of commissary, recreation, or other privileges.[28] The prisoner may present his side of the story, but he cannot bring outside counsel or confront and cross-examine witnesses who testify against him. One court has required this minimal procedure whenever a prisoner's security classification is downgraded.[29] Other decisions, however, uphold the transfer of a prisoner from a minimum-security prison to the mainline of a maximum-security facility as purely adminstrative and therefore requiring no procedural safeguards.[30]

Prison officials have appealed most of the decisions that require fair disciplinary and parole procedures. In the one appeal

27. *Landman* (note 22), pp. 654–656. Although the decision strikes down "agitation" and "misbehavior" as insufficiently definite, it allows such vague offenses an "insolence," "harrassment," and "insubordination."

28. *Landman, Bundy, Clutchette.*

29. *Morris v. Travisono,* 310 F. Supp. 857 (D.R.I. 1970). This decision merely ratified new rules issued by prison officials.

30. See *Bundy,* for example.

decided as of mid-1972, the appellate court upheld prisoners' right of due process in cases of severe punishment, but refused to specify minimum procedures—leaving that up to prison officials (who have done nothing pending a Supreme Court decision on whether to review the case).[31] The other appeals are expected to fare as poorly or worse.

Political Expression

Most of the disciplinary procedure suits were brought by political activists within the prisons—Martin Sostre in New York, John Clutchette and George Jackson in California, Maryland prisoners accused of leading work stoppages and forming an "unauthorized inmate association," jailhouse lawyers and an alleged strike leader in Virginia. While the courts have been willing, in these and some other cases, to specify the forms officials must follow to punish prisoners, they have done little to protect the substance of the activities for which prisoners are punished. The courts have been especially hesitant to recognize prisoners' First Amendment rights in relation to correspondence, literature, and speech within prison.

Some courts have invalidated punishment based on the content of a prisoner's letters and severely limited official censorship of prisoners' correspondence. One court recently ordered prison officials to let prisoners send news media letters critical of prison administration.[32] Yet, other courts have held that censorship does not abridge prisoners' right to free speech, and no court has stopped prison authorities from reading a prisoner's mail or deciding with whom he can correspond.[33]

31. *Sostre* v. *McGinnis* (note 23).
32. *Nolan* v. *Fitzpatrick*, 326 F. Supp. 209 (D. Mass. 1971), affirmed 451 F. 2d 545 (1st Cir. 1971).
33. The ocassional exception, noted above, involves correspondence with attorneys and courts, which some courts have protected from all inspection. In *Palmigiano* v. *Travisono*, 317 F. Supp. 776 (D. R.I. 1970), a federal court severely limited official inspection of mail to and from prisoners awaiting trial, on the basis of reasoning which may also help convicted prisoners.

New York officials have been told they cannot punish a prisoner for possessing black nationalist and revolutionary literature, but that they can confiscate the literature if there is reason to fear the prisoner might subvert prison discipline by letting other prisoners read this material.[34]. The courts also ordered New York officials to let any prisoner receive the newsletter of an ex-convict organization moderately critical of prisons, but they allowed the same officials to restrict the Black Panther paper to party members, control its dissemination to other prisoners, and decide "when and how" Panthers may read it.[35] Other courts have let prison authorities screen out "reasonably objectionable," "inflammatory," or "subversive" articles or publications.

The courts have held that prisoners' speech within prison can be limited only if there is a "clear and present danger" to prison security. They have, however, generally accepted official judgments as to when such a danger exists. As recently as 1966, for instance, a U.S. Court of Appeals upheld punishment of a prisoner for "agitating" by circulating and posting on the prison bulletin board copies of a letter he had sent to the governor suggesting prison reform and urging prisoners to make their grievances known.[36] No court has upheld for prisoners the right, constitutionally protected outside, to freely assemble and organize for political purposes. Officials are free to disband prisoners' organizations, stop them from distributing political literature within prison, and transfer organizers to other parts of the state.

34. *Sostre* v. *McGinnis* (note 23).

35. *Fortune Society* v. *McGinnis*, 319 F. Supp. 901 (S.D.N.Y. 1970); *Shakur* v. *McGrath*, an unreported opinion in civil case #4493, S.D.N.Y., Dec. 31, 1969.

36. *Landman* v. *Peyton*, 370 F. 2nd 135 (4th Cir. 1966).

THE LIMITS OF JUDICIAL ACTION: A CASE STUDY by John van Geldern

[Although many of the decisions prisoners won in the sixties and seventies marked a radical departure from earlier legal reasoning, they have had little direct effect on the day-to-day operation of prisons. For the most part, prison officials have simply ignored court rulings or made insignificant superficial adjustments. Inhuman cell conditions, vicious brutality, arbitrary punishment, and racial discrimination continue unabated. John van Geldern, a leading California jailhouse lawyer, shows in the following report how prison officials have circumvented even the decisions protecting prisoners' access to the courts.]

For many years now, courts throughout the land have consistently held that prisoners have a right of access to the courts. This right represented a breach in the wall of silence surrounding prisons. It meant that prison practices could be revealed to the world outside through the courts. And it gave the prisoner an avenue through which to seek judicial redress.

Threatened by the prospect of lawsuits and publicity, prison authorities circumvented every decision which expanded the prisoners' right of access to the courts. For example, when the courts held that a prisoner cannot be denied parole for unsuccessfully petitioning for habeas corpus, prison authorities took a new semantic tack. They thereafter denied parole so long as the prisoner had any action *pending* in the courts.

When the volume of prisoner-authored petitions for judicial relief grew to a flood in the mid-1960s (as a result of court decisions and other factors), prison authorities took more overt action to stop the erosion of their previously unrestrained power. They made each prisoner fill out a form for everything he did in seeking access to court, from requesting to use the law library to mailing a petition to a court or receiving visits from court-appointed attorneys. Each form was clearly marked in the lower left-hand corner: "copy to central file." The prisoner's counselor or other prison officials would remind the prisoner that the Adult Authority, which reads the central file to decide whether to grant or deny parole, frowns on "writ writers."

In 1967 the director of the California Department of Corrections ordered all lawbooks then in California prisons destroyed, except for seven approved books which were all but useless in preparing habeas petitions and totally useless in presenting Federal Civil Rights action. Even the approved books could be read only with the warden's special permission. At the same time, prisoners were prohibited from purchasing or possessing their own lawbooks and from helping each other prepare legal papers.

Guards began to harass jailhouse lawyers. They took away and destroyed legal materials. Some writ writers were thrown into the hole and brutalized. Disciplinary infractions were manufactured against us and used as a basis for denying parole. The most successful writ writers were arbitrarily designated strike agitators and transferred to lockup sections of other institutions. We were moved from prison to prison, never left in any one place long enough for a local court to rule on our legal actions to stop this harassment. Meanwhile all of a prisoner's accumulated legal material would be conveniently "lost in transit."

Finally we were able to get a lawsuit out of Folsom prison to the U.S. District Court, together with a motion for a temporary restraining order. The court ordered the Corrections Department to stop destroying books and stop implementing the rest of its directive until a final decision in the case.

This, however, did not stop the attorney general from issuing surreptitious orders to the State Law Library and to prison wardens listing the books which prisoners were not to check out or read. Particular volumes were allowed into prison only when ordered by an official for his own use. On May 28, 1970, three years after the director's order had been issued, a federal court finally upheld prisoners' rights to unrestricted access to law books in the case of *Gilmore, van Geldern* v. *Lynch.*[37] Before the ruling could have any effect, however, the attorney general appealed to the U.S. Supreme Court, which did not affirm the lower court decision until November 6, 1971.[38]

In the meantime the Supreme Court had ruled in *Johnson* v. *Avery*[39] that a state must let prisoners help each other with legal papers unless it provides a reasonable and effective alternative. Though the mandate of that ruling was quite clear, California prison administrators devised numerous ways to circumvent it.

New rules made it a prison infraction to have in one's possession anyone else's legal materials or transcripts. Other rules authorized prison wardens to designate when and where prisoners could assist each other with legal work. The place designated usually would accommodate no more than 15 or 20 prisoners (out of 2,000 to 3,000), and the location and times would be all but impossible for many prisoners.

In 1970, in the case of *In re Harrell*, the supreme court of California firmly reiterated the doctrine of *Johnson* v. *Avery*, but this ruling also went all but unheeded.[40] Prison camp centers and such places as Tehachapi, Chino, and California Men's Colony at San Luis Obispo continued to implement the overruled and repealed director's rules of pre-*Gilmore*, pre-*Johnson*, and pre-*Harrell*.

At California Men's Colony, anyone who became known as a writ writer was immediately charged with one or another offense and shipped to the segregation units of Folsom, San Quentin, or Soledad prison. The prison librarian at CMC still

37. *Gilmore* v. *Lynch*, 319 F. Supp. 105 (N.D. Cal. 1970).
38. *Younger* v. *Gilmore*, 404 U.S. 15 (1971).
39. *Johnson* v. *Avery* 393 U.S. 483 (1969).
40. 2 Cal. 3rd 675 (1970).

discourages the use of the law library by requiring that a man get a pass from the captain's office before he can use lawbooks. Only 20 to 30 such passes are issued per day.

Donations of lawbooks from outside groups or lawyers are not permitted. The Inmate Welfare Fund, which pays for the operation and book purchases of prison libraries, still cannot be spent on lawbooks. And two weeks after the Supreme Court affirmed the *Gilmore* decision, the CMC librarian stated he would not change his policy since the U.S. Supreme Court does not run "his" library. So the fight goes on.

THE LIMITS OF JUDICIAL ACTION: A GENERAL ANALYSIS

Van Geldern shows what little effect judicial decisions have had in protecting prisoners' rights of access to court. His conclusions are not unique to this one area of prison law. Prison administrators have been even more brazen in their disregard for legal rulings about areas of prison life less directly involving the judiciary; and judges have been more hesitant to press for change in those areas. Prisoners' legal rights to minimally decent living conditions, freedom from brutality, fair disciplinary procedures, and racial equality have been even less honored in practice than their right of access to court.

This failure of judicial decisions to significantly alter prison life does not stem only from the recalcitrance of prison officials. Nor can it be fully explained by the difficulty prisoners have found in obtaining effective legal representation. The limits of judicial action to change prisons are also rooted deep in the American legal system.

One source of these limits lies in the internal structure of the legal system. Some of the apparently farthest-reaching prison decisions—almost all of those requiring fair disciplinary procedure—have come from U.S. district courts. The losing party is entitled to appeal a district court decision to a U.S. circuit court of appeals, and the loser there may petition the U.S. Supreme Court to review the appellate decision.[41] Each level of review can easily take a year or more. Higher courts were expected to narrow or reverse many prison decisions pending appeal early in 1972, especially because Nixon's judicial appointments have made these courts very conservative in matters of criminal law enforcement. District judges, fearing their rulings will not survive appeal, generally have not exercised their power to enforce their orders pending appeal. As a result, illegal practices continue unrestrained and a number of apparently significant prison decisions have had little direct effect on prison life.

Even after it is final and theoretically in force, a court order binds only the parties named in a particular lawsuit. The typical suit covers a single prison. No suit can cover more than one state's prison system. New lawsuits have to be organized in every jurisdiction, despite similarity in prison conditions and procedures. Before a decision can affect the great majority of prisoners, the expensive and time-consuming process of preparing a suit, litigating, and defending appeals must be repeated in place after place. Even after this long process, a favorable decision in one part of the country does not guarantee similar decisions elsewhere, for not every judicial precedent is legally binding. The only decisions a court must respect are those rendered by a higher court having jurisdiction over it. Traditionally, a court also follows its own prior decisions. Precedents outside these two categories are merely advisory; they show one judge how another judge interpreted the law. Thus, the U.S. Supreme Court decision is the "law of the land" binding on all federal and

41. A suit which challenges a statewide law, regulation or administrative practice is heard by a special three-judge district court from whose decision the losing party can appeal directly to the U.S. Supreme Court. Prisoners' lawyers generally have tried to avoid this route, however, because it can take months for judges to determine whether a particular case is appropriate for a three-judge court and because it is easier to find one sympathetic judge than two out of three (especially when one of the three must come from the Court of Appeals, which generally is more conservative than the district courts).

state courts. But a decision of a federal court of appeals binds only the U.S. District Courts in one appellate region; state courts, and federal courts in other circuits, are free to render contradictory decisions. A district judge's opinion does not bind even other judges in the same district. A decision of a state supreme court is binding in that state, but is only a basis for analogy in other states.

While this judicial autonomy enables exceptionally liberal federal judges like Constance Baker Motley in New York and Alfonso Joseph Zirpoli in California to make new law for prisoners, it simultaneously limits the impact of their rulings.

It also helps judges in the lower-level state courts—which still receive the bulk of suits against prisons—to circumvent the prisoner-rights decisions of federal and higher state courts. These judges have developed ingenious methods implementing the spirit of the hands-off doctrine. When a complaining prisoner is transferred to another part of the state, the local judge typically dismisses the prisoner's suit as "moot," despite higher-court rulings that a suit should not be dismissed under these circumstances if a favorable ruling would affect other people or clarify a significant legal question. When a local judge cannot avoid ruling on a suit against a prison administration, he often denies relief after perfunctory procedures like those used to dispose of prisoners' writs for release. A judge in one California county with a large prison regularly refers prison suits to the local district attorney or court clerk. This official "investigates" by way of conversation or correspondence with prison officials. He then routinely prepares an order, which the judge signs, denying relief without a hearing—solely on the basis of the institution's version of the facts.[42]

42. This procedure is described in *Reaves* v. *Superior Court,* 99 Cal. Rptr. 156 (1971). The decision in the Reaves case prohibits use of the local district attorney as the "investigator" upon whose report the prisoner's writ is denied, but the decision allows the court to use the very same procedure if the court clerk serves as "investigator." The California Supreme Court has refused to review the decision. A very rare exception to the general practice of lower state

Judges in the federal and higher state courts who have been willing to decide cases in favor of prisoners have resurrected the hands-off doctrine when it comes to the enforcement of their own rulings. As van Geldern has shown, judicial rulings are far from self-enforcing—especially against prison officials who, like the California Men's Colony librarian, consider the prisons "their" property to be run as they choose. Yet the courts have been reluctant to take the measures needed to ensure that their decisions are obeyed. They either refuse to define specifically what must be done, or they let prison authorities ignore orders which do spell out specific changes.

Some prison decisions merely set forth general principles of law, such as due process, and rely for compliance on the good faith of the very officials whose rampant disregard for the law forced the prisoners to seek judicial relief. Other decisions are narrowly based on a detailed description of a complex of conditions and practices in a particular prison at a specific time. Since the decision prohibits only that one combination of factors, authorities can claim compliance after making insignificant adjustments. After a much-heralded 1966 federal court decision outlawed the use of "strip cells" to discipline prisoners at Soledad, prison officials merely changed the name to "quiet cells" and replaced toilets which only guards could flush and so-called oriental toilets (holes in the floor) with automatic flush toilets. Six years later cells identical in almost all other respects were still in use throughout the state.[43]

Even when the court order is specific and comprehensive, rarely is a specific time limitation imposed on prison officials. The judge who in May, 1971, required specific changes in San

courts in prison cases is the broad, strong decision of the circuit court for Montgomery County, Maryland in *McCray* v. *Maryland,* Misc. Pet. 4363 (Nov. 11, 1971), 1 Pris. L. Rptr. 92, regarding procedures for disciplining or transferring prisoners, conditions in disciplinary areas, and mail censorship.

43. *Jordan* v. *Fitzharris,* 257 F. Supp. 674 (N.D.Cal. 1966).

Quentin disciplinary procedures still was overseeing negotiations between prisoners' lawyers and prison authorities in mid-1972. Only in a very few cases have the courts been willing to assess damages to compensate prisoners for injuries suffered as a result of deprivation of their constitutional rights.[44] Despite frequent flagrant violations of judicial edicts, no judge has held a prison official in contempt of court, and fined or jailed that official, for failing to comply with a court order.[45]

If all prison decisions to date were enforced as effectively as possible, they still would not seriously limit the power of prison officials. The new court rulings generally allow prison officials to determine, without procedural safeguards, where each prisoner lives within the prison system, when and where he is transferred, and what privileges he receives. Prison staff retain significant influence over when a prisoner is released. They handle all incoming and outgoing mail. They are allowed to decide who can correspond or visit with a prisoner and the circumstances of each visit. They control, within broad limits, what each prisoner eats, where he sleeps, what reading material he receives, what he can have in his cell, his sanitation facilities, exercise periods, education and work programs, and medical care. Officials can confiscate reading material, stop prisoners from sharing literature, and punish organizers and "agitators."

Since visiting, correspondence, and literature remain restricted, prisoners have trouble learning of new legal decisions and outsiders cannot easily determine when a court ruling has been disobeyed. Official control over prison life means that a prisoner who tries to assert his legal rights, or complains when other prisoners are abused, can find his privileges lost, his mail misplaced, his food and cell a mess, visiting obstructed, a program he needs for parole suddenly closed, a complaint filed

44. In the Jordan case, for instance, the court denied damages without comment. The major exception is *Sostre* v. *Rockefeller* (note 23), in which a prisoner was awarded $25 for each of 374 days of illegal solitary confinement.
45. Goldfarb and Singer, "Redressing Prisoners' Grievances," p. 281.

against him for a mysterious prison stabbing—and on and on and on.

The courts cannot effectively impose a "rule of law" in the form of due process administrative procedure. It would be totally impracticable for prison officials to hold even a rudimentary hearing over each of innumerable daily administrative decisions which affect a prisoner's life. While court decisions may force officials to provide minimal due process before they withdraw privileges available to the general prison population, the courts cannot possibly require a hearing for every prisoner who applies for a job-training program, a new pair of glasses, special medication, honor block, work furlough, or a conjugal visit. Nor can the courts force officials to hold a hearing each time they relocate a prisoner separating him from his friends, cutting short his education and training programs, and forcing him to adjust to a new community. Finally, due process cannot provide protection against unauthorized, informal punishment by the guards who control food, mail, access to medical care, and the prisoner's general living conditions.

Where due process *can* reasonably be required without making a prison administratively inoperable, it will ultimately make little real difference in how the prisoner is treated. An occasional prisoner may escape the most serious punishment if prison officials decide he does not merit the time and expense of a full hearing. When the officials consider a disciplinary case worth the effort, however, they will be able to use the new procedure to impose the same punishments.

For even the most progressive court decisions, dealing with the most severe forms of punishment, give the prisoner far fewer rights than he was afforded at his original trial. His will be a closed trial, from which officials may exclude family, friends, and news media. He is not entitled to appointed counsel and will have difficulty obtaining free legal aid. He has no right to trial by a jury or even by a judge who does not work for the prison, and no right of appeal outside the prison system. The officials who conduct his hearing will be free to doubt the credibility of the prisoner's witnesses and accept only the testimony of witnesses against him. Since witnesses will not have to testify under oath, and therefore will not be liable to charges of perjury, prison staff will find it easy, whenever necessary, to bribe and coerce other prisoners to testify falsely against the prisoner. We have seen how the full panoply of constitutional safeguards does not protect poor people from being sent to prison without regard to the evidence against them. Should prison officials ever be forced to hold due process disciplinary hearings, they will be in an even better position to manipulate constitutionally required procedures to ratify almost any action they choose to take.

If prison officials remain free in practice to punish whomever they please, they can continue to use adjustment centers and solitary confinement to force prisoners to abandon their legal rights and submit to administrative totalitarianism. In a setting of such total staff control, judicial rulings against racial discrimination cannot stop white guards—taught racial superiority and hatred since childhood and allowed little other real power— from promoting interracial strife and taking out their personal problems on black and brown prisoners. (Integration of prison staff, were the courts to order it, still would leave whites in charge at the top—able to pick, train, and direct the nonwhites they hired.) Nor, in a society in which male identity is so deeply rooted in the illusion of sexual superiority, can judicial rulings stop all-powerful prison staff from using their control of prison life to extract sexual privileges from both men and women prisoners, and from treating women and homosexual men differently from heterosexual male prisoners.[46]

The enormity of official power and the weakness of judicial

46. The point is not that women prisoners and gay men are generally treated more harshly, but that women are offered very different rehabilitation programs and models, based on sexist notions of the proper role of women, and that gay men frequently are segregated from other prisoners and specially mistreated.

control over prisons becomes graphically clear in times of crisis. Events following the murder of George Jackson at San Quentin prison in August, 1971, illustrate the limits of legal action to protect prisoners' rights. Guards stripped Jackson's adjustment center tier mates, forced them to crawl naked on gravel, threatened and beat them, and shot one prisoner in the leg. For days the authorities kept out press, lawyers, legislators, doctors, and family. Political periodicals and underground papers were banned from San Quentin and most other prisons. Ethnic culture associations were shut down and their leaders transferred to other prisons. Hundreds of prisoners were locked up throughout the state as "potential troublemakers," even though they were not charged with violation of any prison rules. Many of these prisoners were transferred from minimum-security prisons to the adjustment centers of Folsom and San Quentin. Some were kept in isolation for several months. They received no hearings, or only sham hearings without clear charges or procedural safeguards.

Judicial precedents prohibit most of these measures. Corporal punishment, discipline without a hearing, racial discrimination, denial of access to attorneys, punishment for political beliefs, censorship of newspapers, denial of medical care, inhuman conditions in lockup cells—all have been held unconstitutional. Lawyers filed a flurry of suits late in August and throughout the fall. But no court would act until February, 1972, and then only to help a single prisoner locked up for radical politics for more than five months starting the day after Jackson was shot.[47]

The judges who failed California prisoners after the San Quentin incident were not unusually reactionary. The U.S. dis-

---

47. *In re Hutchinson*, 100 Cal. Rptr. 124 (1972). Court action following Attica was similarly late and inadequate. See 1 Pris. L. Rptr. 16, 65; *Inmates of Attica* v. *Rockefeller*, Nos. 284, 334 (2nd Cir. Dec. 1, 1971).

trict judge who stalled a suit challenging the mass lockup at San Quentin had earlier required overhaul of local jail conditions and due process in disciplinary hearings.[48] He is generally regarded as one of the country's most liberal and socially conscious jurists. Nor are the judges who have failed to enforce their prison decisions especially conservative. That they have decided cases in favor of prisoners indicates, in fact, that they are more liberal than most.

The problem does not lie in the morality or courage of individual judges. The limits of judicial action to change prisons are rooted in the very nature of courts and law. For real reform to occur, judges would have to transfer authority over prisons to prisoners themselves or to black, brown, and poor white communities, since only people with the same cultural background and class interests as prisoners can be counted on to respect prisoners' rights. Such a substantial change in power relationships is obviously beyond the legal or political capacity of a court, however.

The function of a judge is to enforce laws which establish and maintain a particular economic system and social order. The constitutional provisions he applies—due process, equal protection, free speech, no cruel and unusual punishment—are standards for regulating how state power is exercised, not for determining what groups or classes exercise that power. A judge does not have the means to enforce his decisions by himself. He depends on moral authority derived from his role within the established order and on the threat of violence from the police and other armed forces of the state. His decisions become mere rhetoric if he steps outside his assigned role and orders actions which the state will not back up.

Nor is a judge at all likely to want to transfer government power from prison authorities to prisoners or poor communities. Judges are beneficiaries of the current social order. It is in

48. The lockup suit is *Bly* v. *Procunier,* C-712019 AJZ (N.D. Cal. 1971).

their interest to support the structures of power which maintain that order. A judge's public position, educational background, class, race, and professional status lead him to identify with prison administrators and to fear and misunderstand convicts. It is the judge, after all, who initially incarcerates blacks, Latinos, and poor whites while releasing their "white-collar" counterparts. He cannot be expected, once those same people are in prison, to move to enhance their political power at the expense of public officials who share his basic outlook and interests.

Although many judges probably wish that prisoners were better treated, and would try to be more humane if they had direct responsibility for prison administration, the U.S. political and legal system gives them neither the power nor the inclination to enforce basic changes in the internal power structure of prisons. As a result, court rulings can have little significant impact on prison life.

THE POLITICAL USES OF LEGAL ACTION

Direct impact on official behavior is not the only measure of legal action. For many years after the Supreme Court's landmark school desegregation decision, more black students attended racially segregated classes than had before the decision. Yet *Brown* v. *Board of Education* helped launch the black liberation struggles of the sixties, which won some concrete gains for black people and set in motion other popular movements for radical change.

Legal action to change prisons can be similarly evaluated. Prisons cannot change significantly without a restructuring of the class and race relations which determine which persons are in prison and who controls the legal system which puts and keeps them there. Prisoners' struggles are an important part of efforts to alter these fundamental power relationships. Courtroom victories and legal representation of prisoners can help prisoners' struggles to grow, though they may also be misused in ways which hinder those struggles.

Favorable judicial rulings encourage prisoners, providing them with another small weapon with which to fight. Van Geldern and other jailhouse lawyers would be even less able to defend themselves without the decisions in *Johnson, Harrell,* and *Gilmore.* The overall impact these and other decisions have on immediate conditions in prison and on the growth of collective struggle depends on how the rulings are used to promote organization and confrontation—on how courtroom victories are integrated into political strategy. It is on the basis of this understanding of legal action as one method of struggle "by any means necessary" that revolutionaries like Martin Sostre and Ruchell Magee have trained themselves to be effective jailhouse lawyers.

Aggressive litigation and favorable court rulings can also help to build an outside political movement to support prisoners and expose prison conditions. The process of litigation is an important source of publicity and pressure, regardless of the final outcome. Newspapers, radio, and TV describe the conditions and treatment which a lawsuit challenges. Prison authorities are interviewed and asked to explain their actions. State officials must expend time and resources defending themselves in court and in the media. They may decide to lay off a prisoner because of the public attention focused on his situation.

Courtroom victories can, however, lead to serious long-range political errors. We have been taught that law is separate from politics, that judges are disinterested and objective, that whatever is legal is proper and everything illegal is wrong. As a result, court rulings against prison practices legitimize the prison movement for large numbers of people. More people will believe a judge who says that prison conditions are desperately bad than would accept the word of a convict or a radical lawyer. It is tempting for a movement to try to exploit this popular view of the law by framing its objectives in terms of prisoners' legal rights and an end to official lawlessness. This tactic obscures the basic class and race issues of prisons. In fact, law is a tool of whoever exercises political power, and judges protect the established order, including the present prison system, by making that order appear legitimate and moral. A radical movement's efforts to educate people about this conservative political function of law are undermined when the movement opportunistically uses the mystique of the law, and thereby reinforces that mystique, in pursuit of short-term gains in public support.

Another potential political pitfall in trying to change prisons through legal action lies in exaggeration of the significance of a court order. Prisoners and their supporters can easily gain the impression that an issue has been settled when in fact they have won only a very limited victory, useful mainly as a weapon for further struggle. When the newspapers carried front-page stories in the fall of 1971 announcing a new judicial "Bill of Rights" for Virginia prisoners they did not inform their readers that it could be two or three years before the decision takes effect, that narrowing or reversal is quite possible on appeal, that the decision pertains mainly to the disciplinary process and jailhouse lawyers, that it affords prisoners only a watered-down version of a few of the protections guaranteed in the real Bill of Rights, and that court rulings generally have had little effect on the internal operation of prisons.[49] Many earnest supporters of prison reform have stopped demanding change in California's disciplinary procedures because they assume California prisoners have been receiving due process hearings since the *Clutchette* decision was announced in May 1971.[50] In fact, as of mid-1972 no California prison had significantly changed its disciplinary procedure.

49. *Landman* v. *Royster* (see note 22). A typical news account appeared in the *San Francisco Chronicle*, Nov. 1, 1971, p. 1.
50. *Clutchette* v. *Procunier* (see note 26).

A good lawyer does not represent his clients only in court. Through informal pressure lawyers can sometimes ease the situation of individual prisoners, such as by arranging for treatment by a private physician or for a transfer to a prison closer to home. Because of the prisoner's unique isolation, his lawyer serves as an important link to the world outside prison. The lawyer can be an important source of moral support and friendship to a prisoner allowed few other correspondents and visitors. The lawyer also provides badly needed information about events outside prison and a means for the prisoner to communicate to the outside world about developments inside. During the period when California allowed sealed correspondence between prisoners and their lawyers, letters from prisoners provided the first detailed public information about the horrors of prison conditions. These letters have been important in developing public awareness of prisons and political motion for change.[51]

The prisoner's lawyer can also play a harmful role. Since lawyers can visit prisoners and correspond with them more easily than most people, they exercise substantial control over the information which the public and the prison movement receive about conditions and struggles within prison. They are often looked to by the media and legislators as spokesmen for the prison movement. In these roles, as in the planning and carrying out of litigation, lawyers are under no economic pressure to accept political direction from prisoners since they almost always work without fee. Since their livelihoods do not depend on their clients' satisfaction with their work, they are free to act in whatever manner they consider most effective. In this context, lawyers' professional elitism and the racial and class differences between them and their clients often lead law-

51. Many of these letters have been collected by Eve Pell in *Maximum Security* (New York: Dutton, 1972).

yers to subordinate the needs and desires of prisoners to their own notions of political strategy.

Lawyers have been known to censor prisoners' letters politically before releasing them and to downplay the militance of revolutionary prisoners. Speaking for the prison movement, they have focused on lawlessness and atrocities, obscuring the basic questions of class and race and reinforcing conservative myths about law.

Lawyers understandably evaluate strategic and tactical options, especially regarding litigation, in a framework of change through the courts. They may refuse to file a politically useful suit for fear it will establish a harmful precedent for future cases, or they may reject politically important trial tactics on the grounds that they detract from the chances of winning the particular suit. Many lawyers for prisoners overlook the broader political effects of their choices or regard those effects as secondary. As a result, they make decisions which contradict the interests of the prisoners they represent and undercut the prisoners' political struggle.

The law is thus an ambiguous weapon for the prisoner. The class and race biases which helped put the prisoner behind bars also limit the aid judges and lawyers will give him once he's there. The internal structure of the legal system and the judges' lack of independent political power further limit the impact of judicial rulings on the practices of prison staff. Court rulings and legal representation can be misused so that they hinder prisoners' political struggles more than they help them.

Still, prisoners have at least won judicial recognition of their constitutional rights of unimpeded access to court, religious, racial, and sexual equality, minimally decent living conditions, freedom from brutality, fair disciplinary procedures, and a limited degree of political expression. These legal victories have done much to expose prison conditions and to encourage and assist political struggle in and outside prison. Prisoners, lawyers, and political activists who understand the limits and pitfalls of legal action have learned to use lawsuits and legal representation as one weapon in the struggle for the social and political revolution which alone can change U.S. prisons.

CHAPTER 15

Prison Reform and Radical Change

By Erik Olin Wright

PERSPECTIVES ON REFORM

The basic premise of most efforts to reform the prison system is that this can be done without any fundamental transformation of the structure of society as a whole. When prisons are viewed as autonomous institutions, separate and isolated from society, the solution to their oppressiveness becomes quite simple: those aspects of prison life that are oppressive simply need to be exposed and laws need to be passed to change them. Such a view does not imply that change will necessarily be easy, but that all that needs to be altered is the defective elements in the institution, not the society as a whole.

This perspective is certainly appealing. It enables the reformer to focus his energies on a narrow problem without having to worry a great deal about larger social and political issues. Many liberal reformers see the fundamental task of prison reform as simply convincing those in power of the soundness of particular changes in the prison system, rather than struggling against that power structure for political control.

In contrast, radicals see prisons as intimately bound up with the class and power structure of the society as a whole. Stated simply, the liberal perspective on reform is that fundamental changes in the prison system are possible without fundamental changes in the rest of the society, while the radical perspective is that fundamental change in prisons can come about only through radical change in the society itself.

Each of these perspectives has something to offer. In order to see what kinds of reforms are possible in the present society and what kinds are contingent upon radical social change, it will be useful to look at four general issues involved in prison reform: the social ends of punishment; the power relationships within prison; prisoners' rights; and prison conditions. The basic proposition of this chapter is that reforms involving the fundamental social ends of punishment are impossible without radical change in the society itself, but reforms limited to concrete prison conditions are achievable without fundamental social change. Reforms which mainly involve power and prisoners' rights fall into a somewhat ambiguous category: they are not entirely impossible within the present society, but they face very serious obstacles. When a proposed reform of the internal operation of prisons impinges on the social ends of punishment, these obstacles may become virtually insurmountable. We will first examine the question of reforming the ends of punishment and then turn to the question of reforming the internal operation of prisons.

PUNISHMENT, CLASS, AND THE STATE

The warden of San Quentin expressed an important truth about prisons when he said they "exist to protect society." What he failed to say was that they exist to protect a *particular* society, a particular pattern of social institutions. In the United States the society is a liberal-capitalist system; prisons and other forms of punishment are a repressive means of protecting this particular society, including its structure of power and distribution of wealth.

Punishment achieves this end in three interrelated ways: (1)

by being a deterrent to certain kinds of crime; (2) by making the victims of crime politically dependent upon the state; (3) by *not* punishing certain acts and punishing others.

The question of deterrence has been extensively discussed in Chapter 2, so only a brief review of some of the arguments will be presented here. When an individual decides to commit a crime, especially a property crime, one factor that he considers at least cursorily is the possibility of punishment. Although this consideration may not deter him from committing a criminal act per se, it certainly influences the target he chooses for his crime and the manner in which he executes it. Punishment protects a particular society by determining what are high-risk and low-risk crimes, and in this way directing criminal activity toward low-risk crimes.

To say that prisons protect a liberal-capitalist social order by deterrence does not mean that prisons punish only crimes committed against the "capitalist class." On the contrary, most crimes that result in imprisonment are committed against the poor by the poor. The protection of the social order is reflected not in the intrinsic characteristics of those acts which are punished, but rather in the social and political consequences of punishment. One of these consequences in American society is that by defining high-risk and low-risk crimes in a particular way, punishment has the effect of channeling crime against poor people. This has two main results. First, it means that the property of the wealthy is protected. Second, it means that crime is robbed of much of its latent political content. The image of a Robin Hood who takes from the rich and gives to the poor is a potent symbol of social protest, adding a certain legitimacy to crime. Because it lacks this element of social justice, crime committed against the poor by the poor is much less threatening to the established social order.

There is a second general consequence of the system of punishment which may be as important as the question of deterrence. Punishment not only directs most crime against the poor as victims, but at the same time it makes the poor dependent upon the state for protection against crime. However ineffective the police may be in apprehending burglars or robbers, however ineffective they may be in preventing violence, they are the only agency available to most people for dealing with these problems.

This is especially important to the working-class poor, the poor who are not destitute. Because they have something, albeit little, to lose, the rigorous enforcement of the law and an expansion of the power of the police seems in their interests. The system of punishment, then, channels crime against the poor, while at the same time it becomes their only source of protection. The poor, while being the victims of the social order protected by punishment, become fervent supporters of the system of punishment itself.[1]

In certain situations this pattern of dependence breaks down. The most notable example in American society is the relationship of poor blacks to the police. Knowing how totally ineffective the police are at apprehending thieves and retrieving stolen property in the ghetto, poor blacks feel it is futile to call on the police when a crime occurs. Even more importantly, poor blacks are so frequently the victims of the police as well as the victims of crime that strong norms have developed against calling them.

1. This may be one source of what is referred to as the "hard hat" mentality of many working-class people in the United States: they are strong supporters of law and order because they are among the primary victims of crime. Some workers thus support very conservative, even quasi-fascist, political orientations which cry for obedience to the law and protection of the social order through coercion.

A study conducted by the University of Michigan Survey Research Center on American attitudes toward violence supports this general interpretation of the relationship of the poor to law and police. It was found that the working class was much more likely than the middle class to take a hard line on the use of the police in riots, on the need to increase police strength, on the acceptability of police violence, etc. Monica D. Blumenthal, Robert L. Kahn, Frank M. Andrews, and Kendra Head, *Justifying Violence* (Ann Arbor: Institute for Social Research, 1972).

Finally, in addition to acting as a deterrent and creating political dependence, punishment sustains the social order as much by what is *not* punished as by what is. In a capitalist society, for example, the law protects the right of a businessman to ruin a competitor economically. This may result in the laying off of many workers and in the economic destitution of the ruined businessman and his family; but as long as it is done according to the rules of the game, it is legal. It would, however, be illegal for the workers in a firm to take over and physically expropriate the enterprise. In both cases economic harm is intended toward the victim, but one of these acts is protected by law, the other proscribed. This pattern of protection and proscription defines the range of action that is possible "within the system." This is especially important in terms of political action. Radical groups are acutely aware that if they go beyond this range they risk confrontation with the police, the courts, and, ultimately, with the prisons. In a pervasive way, it is through this pattern of protection and proscription that the criminal justice system sustains the social order.

While it is easy to show that prisons in the United States support a capitalist social order, it is more difficult to demonstrate that they are a *necessary* tool in sustaining that social order. Many people argue that the stability of society rests on internalized values and ideology. Some liberal reformers maintain that probation programs can replace prisons entirely if they are combined with constructive job training programs and other forms of social action. They point to the failure of prisons to rehabilitate and argue that such rehabilitation could be accomplished much more effectively, much more humanely, and much less expensively in other settings.

These arguments neglect crucial aspects of the relationship of punishment to other forms of social control, and to the problem of crime itself. While it is true that values and ideology are significant, in many cases their effectiveness rests heavily upon the extent to which they are backed up by coercive forms of control. The relationship of values and ideology to behavior is not simply "values cause behavior." Values are only one element in action decisions. As discussed in Chapter 1, values and priorities compete in many situations. Which value will be stronger in a particular individual is not simply a question of his socialization or his personality. It also is very much a function of the problems he faces, the options available to him, and the personal consequences of acting on one value or another. Punishment is an essential factor in this action situation.[2]

The system of punishment is thus necessary for sustaining the effectiveness of values as social control mechanisms. But why are prisons in particular necessary? Why aren't such punishments as probation or fines sufficient? In California, only about 10 percent of all felons convicted in 1971 were sent to state prisons; 65 were put on probation. But the threat of imprisonment hung imminently over the heads of those felons placed on probation. Prisons are necessary because they put teeth into the system of social control, backing up other, milder forms of punishment.

The system of social control can be seen, on the one hand, as a *hierarchy of escalating punishments* and, on the other, as a *hierarchy of inducements.* The effectiveness of any given punishment is dependent upon the harsher punishments in the hierarchy and upon the available inducements for compliance. At the most basic level, conformity to the laws of society depends upon the entire hierarchy of punishment. Conformity to

2. A second sense in which punishments back up values was discussed by Emile Durkheim in his writings on law and morality. He argued that punishment is itself an affirmation of certain values—or what he called the "collective conscience"—and serves a vital educational and socializing role in society. Punishment becomes a public ritual by which these values are affirmed and a declaration that their violation will not be treated lightly. See Durkheim's *Division of Labor in Society* and his essay "Moral Education." For a general discussion by Durkheim of the relationship of prisons to social structure and values, see his essay "Deux Lois de L'Evolution Penal" (*L'Anée Sociologique,* 1900), pp. 65–95.

the restrictions of probation or parole depends upon the threat of imprisonment; conformity to the rules of prison depends upon the threat of being held in prison longer or being confined in the adjustment center. Similarly, at each level of the system, there are bribes for compliance: prisoners in the adjustment center are promised privileges and the "freedom" of being in the mainline population if they comply with the demands of prison officials; prisoners in the general population are offered the inducement of special privileges and parole; people on parole are offered the freedom to move about and to conduct their lives as they wish if they conform to the conditions of parole.[3] Some threatened punishments are simultaneously inducements: the threat of being denied a parole for resistance is also the inducement of being released for conformity. These escalated threats and inducements provide answers at every level of the system to the questions: What have I got to lose by resisting? What have I got to gain by conforming?[4]

3. These two hierarchies are, in a sense, inversely related. As one moves toward the top levels of the hierarchy of punishments the system has fewer and fewer threats at its disposal. For a prisoner in an adjustment center with a life sentence and no immediate prospect for a parole, the only viable threat the prison authorities have left is the threat of death (either by a guard or by a fellow prisoner). But although the arsenal of threats becomes more limited, in a sense the arsenal of inducements becomes greater. A person in the adjustment center is denied virtually all freedoms, even the freedom to have a conversation. If he yields totally to the demands of the prison for conformity, he is offered the "freedoms" of the mainline population—recreation, education, conversation—and eventually the possibility of a parole. As you move down the hierarchy of punishments, the scope of such inducements necessarily narrows. Finally, at the very bottom of the hierarchy—a "free" individual on the streets—the inducements for conformity can become fairly marginal. A poor black may feel that he has very little to gain from compliance. In such a situation, the basis for control switches to the hierarchy of punishments—what the individual stands to lose by defying the laws—rather than the hierarchy of inducements.

4. This description is in some ways an overrational view of the hierarchy of punishments and inducements. People do not necessarily make entirely rational assessments of the losses and gains in resisting or conforming to authority. Their actions grow out of fears and irrational expectations, as well as personalities which dispose them toward conformity or rebellion. Similarly, state authorities do not administer the hierarchy of punishments and inducements in an entirely dispassionate, rational way. They can respond arbitrarily out of per-

Prisons constitute the essential institution at the top level of this coercive apparatus; without them, the lower levels would lose much of their potency. It is because of this structural importance of prisons in the hierarchy of punishment, and the importance of the hierarchy of punishment for the protection of the social order, that the social ends of imprisonment cannot be changed without radical change in the society at large.

This rules out certain broad categories of prison reform in the present society. It rules out the reform of using prisons in America consistently to punish the crimes of the rich—price fixing, income tax evasion, pollution, false advertising—rather than merely the crimes of the poor. It rules out the reform of abolishing prisons completely. And, of course, it rules out reforms which would define private profit, speculation, and the accumulation of vast wealth as crimes and punish them by imprisonment. Such reforms would themselves constitute a radical change in the basic organization of the society. As long as American society remains unchanged, prisons will be filled with the poor.

LIBERAL REFORM: OBSTACLES AND OPPORTUNITIES

Reforms which focus on prison conditions, prisoners' rights, or the power relationships within prison are not structurally impossible in the same way as reforms that undermine the social ends of punishment. Any discussion of reform within prisons must confront four related issues: *resource allocation,* the *deterrent function* of punishment, the notion of *rehabilitation,* and *internal control* within prisons. We shall discuss each of these in terms of the obstacles and opportunities which they

---

sonal dislike, paranoia, confusion between different levels of the bureaucracy. Such arbitrariness makes it very difficult for prisoners to know what they should do to avoid punishment or gain privileges, and consequently undermines the effectiveness of the system of social control within prison.

pose for constructive reform of prison conditions, prisoners' rights, and the power structure within prisons in the United States.

Resource Allocation

The issue of resource allocation poses an important obstacle to prison reform. Legislatures have been unwilling to appropriate adequate funds to prisons for a variety of reasons. Prisoners lack real political leverage in legislatures. Not only do they face the usual political problems of the poor and of minorities, but they are disenfranchised, are prevented from communicating with the outside, and have historically lacked the support of any organized political force on the outside. But perhaps even more basically, legislatures have always been reluctant to appropriate adequate money for programs to help the poor, especially when they are nonwhite. The racism that pervades legislative activity in areas such as public housing, welfare, and education also pervades legislative involvement in the prisons. Politicians frequently feel that any money spent on prisons beyond the bare minimum necessary for secure custody is money wasted.

Yet, of the various obstacles to prison reform which we shall discuss, the problem of resource allocation is probably less difficult to overcome than the others. With the growth of political organizations working for prison reform, and with increased pressure from prisoners, it is likely that at least some of the financial obstacles to improving prison conditions will be reduced in the future.

Paradoxically, there is a sense in which the financial obstacles can become an *opportunity* for change, rather than just an impediment. In California, to imprison someone for a year costs around $3,000 but to supervise him on parole or probation costs only about $500. This has been one of the important reasons for the dramatic increase in the use of parole and probation in the state. Likewise, fiscal considerations provide at least one pressure on the prison system to reduce the length of terms.

A variety of other possible reforms in the prison system are facilitated by fiscal problems. Prison officials have generally opposed the extensive use of volunteers in prison. They argue, with some cogency, that volunteers will tend to support the prisoners against the "professional" paid staff. In many ways, however, volunteers can offer more constructive help to prisoners than the staff can, precisely because they are less integrated into the prison power structure. The economic squeeze makes it easier to pressure the administration into allowing volunteers to participate in education and job training programs.

One reform which prisoners have been demanding for many years is a minimum wage in prison industries. Prison officials have responded to this demand by saying that they simply cannot afford to pay prisoners more than a few cents an hour. It has been proposed that outside private industry be allowed to open up businesses within prison walls and that they pay prisoners the going wage. Out of this wage a certain proportion would be subtracted to cover part of the costs of imprisonment. Although there are serious drawbacks to this reform, it is one of several ways in which the economic difficulties of the prison system provide an opportunity for reform.[5]

The Deterrent Function of Prisons

For prisons to deter they must, obviously, be a negative alternative to the life situation of the potential criminal. It has often been argued that the essential deterrent effect of imprisonment

---

5. I have serious reservations about the desirability of introducing private industry into prisons. It could easily develop into a situation where private industry was getting the use of "slave labor" for the purpose of making high profits. Because of the constant interruptions prisoners are subjected to during their work day, the tensions within the prison, and the low commitment to work in the context of imprisonment, prisoners would probably work somewhat less efficiently than "free" labor. Lower efficiency could be used as a pretext for paying prisoners substantially less than the going wage on the outside, and this could easily lead to heavy exploitation of penal labor. Aside from this, the general principle of employment at well-paying jobs within prison is certainly a good one.

stems from the deprivation of liberty rather than from the conditions within prison. It is an open question whether or not this is the case.

Imagine for the moment a prison which offered prisoners a good standard of living and provided rich educational and job training opportunities that held out the promise of interesting, well-paying jobs after release. Imagine a prison which rigorously protected the civil rights of prisoners and which guaranteed them the freedom to read and to study and to organize politically. It is obviously questionable how effective a deterrent such a prison would be to a poor, unemployed worker. (It is not uncommon, after all, for the poor to join the army voluntarily, seeing it as an opportunity for social mobility, job training, and security. The prison fantasy we have just painted is not so different from the army.)[6]

Thus the real question is not whether prisons have to be unpleasant but rather how wretched prison conditions have to be in order for prisons to present a real threat. Whatever is the "correct" answer to that question, the strength of the view that truly decent prison conditions would destroy the deterrent value of prisons is a serious obstacle to reform.

The Notion of Rehabilitation

In many ways, the idea of rehabilitation is a wolf in sheep's clothing, creating serious obstacles to constructive prison reform. These obstacles stem from two problems inherent in the "rehabilitation model": a confusion of the notions of punishment and treatment; and the image of what a "rehabilitated" prisoner is like. It is a small step from "curing" criminals to the

6. It is frequently argued that one of the main sources of deterrence by prisons is *stigma*. To the extent that this is true, our fantasy prison would be worse than the army for most people. However, it is questionable whether much stigma is attached to imprisonment among the poor, especially among blacks in the ghetto where a very high proportion of men have "done time." In certain instances, serving time in a state penitentiary may even be a source of status.

notion that prisoners should be kept in prison until they are rehabilitated.[7] This is the basic logic behind the indeterminate sentence. The result is that the length of time a prisoner spends behind bars bears less relationship to the criminal act which sent him there than to his behavior within prison. If a prisoner resists the conditions of prison life, he may be kept in prison indefinitely. This, of course, is done in the name of "rehabilitation." Any attempt at reforming the prison system has to cope with the confusion and deception which calls punishment "treatment."

An equally serious obstacle to reform created by the rehabilitation ideology is the definition of a "rehabilitated" criminal. Successful rehabilitation is epitomized by the young black who enters prison angry and rebellious after a series of armed robberies and leaves a dutiful worker, on his way to a steady job in a factory. He enters prison contemptuous of established authority; he leaves prison with his head bowed, obedient and respectful of the law. The rehabilitation failure is the angry rebellious young black who enters prison after a series of armed robberies and leaves prison a dedicated revolutionary. The rehabilitation efforts of the prison must try somehow to create the responsible worker rather than the dedicated revolutionary.[8]

Basically, two tacks can be adopted to accomplish this goal of rehabilitation. On the one hand, prisons can offer a range of education and job training programs which might expand the

7. For a good discussion of the confusion of the notions of punishment and treatment, see *Struggle for Justice*, prepared for the American Friends Service Committee (New York: Hill and Wang, 1971), especially Chapter 6.

8. From the perspective of the prison establishment and society as a whole, the revolutionary is far more dangerous than the criminal. A prison system which becomes a "school for revolution" would be politically unacceptable. This is one focus of right-wing criticism of prisons in America today. It is argued that prisons must become even more repressive in order to control political activity within the prison walls. Many liberals argue that tighter repression would only increase radicalism and militancy among prisoners. The significant point is that although they disagree on the appropriate way of coping with the problem, both liberals and conservatives agree that prisons must be kept from becoming hotbeds of revolution.

prisoners' options upon release. On the other hand, the prison can try to destroy the rebellious spirit of prisoners, to break them into conformity. Both approaches are used in American prisons. In theory, the emphasis is on programs; in practice, it is on coercion.

It is questionable how successful even the best rehabilitation programs, abundantly funded, could be. Necessarily, none of the programs within prison deals with the fundamental causes of crime—the social conditions and lack of opportunities on the outside—and thus they cannot hope to have other than limited success.[9]

In their efforts to "cure" criminals, prisons have, therefore, resorted to the second tack: the attempt to coerce the prisoner to conform to established authority. This has become, in practice, the central approach in most prisons, and conformity to authority has become the basic criterion for the release of prisoners on parole. The resulting pattern is the "liberal totalitarianism" described in Chapter 8.[10]

9. One of the basic fallacies in prison rehabilitation programs as well as in many other government programs in a welfare-capitalist system is the notion that there are *individualistic* solutions to *structural* problems. The problem of crime is not a question of individual pathology or simply the lack of job skills in individuals, but rather of the social conditions facing a collectivity—in the case of America, the poor, and especially the black. The view that rehabilitation programs can in any way solve the problem is similar to the notion that unemployment can be solved by high school dropouts' going back to school and getting better training. The result of such a solution is simply that unemployment shifts from high school dropouts to high school graduates. Unemployment is a structural problem, not a result of individual failings. The high levels of unemployment among college graduates in the early 1970s reflect this same issue.

10. It has often been argued, especially by liberal reformers, that this approach to changing prisoners—i.e., the systematic destruction of the prisoner's autonomy and individuality, and the insistence on strict conformity to authority—is extremely ineffective. A high proportion of prisoners return to criminal activity when they leave prison, and so, it is argued, the oppression of prison life has obviously failed to change them. While I feel that such oppression is profoundly wrong, I think it is an open question whether or not it is effective. Nationally, somewhere between 40 and 60 percent of ex-prisoners are not convicted of a new felony within five years of release. This could easily be interpreted as a sign of considerable "success" by the prisons. The outside world

As long as the rehabilitated prisoner is defined as obedient and conforming, it will be difficult to change the authoritarian aspects of prisons which are directed precisely at ensuring those qualities. As long as prisons are seen as places to "cure" criminality, it will be difficult to challenge the enormous discretionary power of parole boards and prison administrations over the length and type of punishment to which a prisoner can be subjected. This is not to deny the opportunities for prison reform which have been created by the rehabilitation ideology; but the new obstacles which have been created should not be underestimated.

The Problem of Internal Control

Of all the obstacles to prison reform, the problem of internal control is probably the most serious. Prisons confine people against their will; this creates serious problems. Sheldon Messinger put it this way:

> Whatever the ultimate aims of imprisonment—punishment, deterrence, reformation or simply safekeeping—the proximate aim and daily task of prison administration is to maintain the security of the institutions for which they are responsible. The physical safety of staff and inmates demands security. Further, administrators say, without security nothing is possible; even "treatment" depends upon it. And it is hardly cynicism to add that the tenure of administrators depends upon the maintenance of security as well. . . .[11]

has not changed significantly for the ex-convict. It still poses most of the same economic and social problems, and he still has the same limited options for dealing with those problems. Furthermore, he has the added liability of a prison record. It might well be expected that under such conditions virtually all ex-prisoners would return to crime. The fact that about half do not could indicate that oppression is a relatively effective technique for breaking resistance to authority.

11. Sheldon L. Messinger, "Strategies of Control" (unpublished doctoral dissertation, University of California, Berkeley), p. 190.

To achieve internal order, three interconnected strategies of control are particularly important: (1) the maintenance of divisions and antagonisms within the prisoner population; (2) the concentration of all formal power in the hands of prison officials; and (3) the use of the hierarchy of punishments and inducements.[12] Any reforms which undermine the effectiveness of these strategies of control would be resisted with the utmost energy by prison officials.

1. Many tactics are used to break down unity among prisoners. The explicit and implicit encouragement of racism within the prison, the use of honor blocks and other privileges to create a group of prisoners supportive of the prison administration, and the constant transfers of prisoners from one institution to another to prevent organizing are all important techniques of keeping the inmate population divided. This "divide and conquer" strategy creates a significant obstacle to reforms which would facilitate the ability of prisoners to organize within the prison.

2. Many totalitarian features of the prison system are justified on the grounds that they are necessary to maintain the internal order of the prison. Since the prison is incapable of creating any sense of *obligation to obey* on the part of prisoners, it tries to maintain internal control by destroying the prisoner's *will to resist*. Total power is crucial in demonstrating the futility of resistance.[13] Reforms which would infringe on the power of prison officials—such as establishing the right of due process in disciplinary and parole hearings—have to surmount the enormous obstacles created by the totalitarianism of the prison power structure.

3. Both prisons and prisoners are graded from minimum to

12. The term "strategies of control" has been borrowed from Messinger, *ibid.*
13. For a discussion of the problems of authority and legitimacy within prison, see Gresham Sykes, *The Society of Captives* (Princeton, N.J.: Princeton, University Press, 1958), Chapter 3, "The Defects of Total Power."

maximum security status. At each level of the system, privileges can be withdrawn, and restrictions can be added. A prisoner knows that any sign of noncooperation, and especially any open resistance to the officials' orders, can jeopardize whatever privileges he might have. The threat of being transferred to a "tougher joint," of being reclassified with a tighter security status, or of being placed in disciplinary cells pervades prison life. What is even more important, because of the indeterminate sentence procedure, prisoners know that any resistance on their part may result in much longer prison sentences.

As one moves up the hierarchy of punishment, it becomes increasingly difficult to control prisoners. At the top levels of the system, the threat of harsher punishment becomes a much less potent force of social control because fewer and fewer punishments are available to the prison. Inducements may also become less effective, for many of the prisoners at the top levels of the hierachy have rejected the inducements at the lower levels. In this situation, the prison system relies less and less on the deterrent effects of harsher punishments, and more and more on immediate *physical* control of the prisoner. In the most extreme cases, the prisoner is completely controlled by solitary confinement in the adjustment center. The hierarchy of punishment and inducements creates real obstacles to any reform which would blunt the potency of the top levels of the hierarchy or reduce the discretion of the prison officials to grant and withdraw privileges at will.[14]

14. There is another important obstacle to reform which is closely bound up with the question of the internal power structure of prisons. Any efforts at modifying the totalitarianism within prison have to contend not only with the importance of absolute power for internal control, but also with the psychological importance of absolute power to the custodians. For a good discussion of these issues, see especially an article by Philip G. Zimbardo, "Pathology of Imprisonment," *Transaction*, April, 1972, pp. 4–8. Also see Erving Goffman, *Asylums*, (New York: Anchor Books, 1961), Chapter 1, and Sykes, *The Society of Captives*, especially Chapter 2.

If prisoners passively accepted the prison regime, if all prisoners felt guilty about their crimes and felt that their imprisonment was just and proper, and if prisoners felt that the prison administration had their best interests at heart, then there would be little problem about guaranteeing prisoners rights and even giving them some measure of power. Prisoners in the "super-honor" block at San Quentin, after all, have keys to their own cells, and since they have been given the "power" to elect a prisoner committee to supervise the tiers, they are largely free from the close surveillance of prison guards. For a hand-picked selection of compliant prisoners, the totalitarianism of the prison power structure can be significantly mitigated.

However, the vast majority of prisoners, at least in the maximum-security prisons, are unwilling or unable to play the game according to these rules. Especially in the case of black prisoners, the fact of imprisonment itself is often seen as unjust and oppressive. Many prisoners *are* disrespectful of authority, because the authorities they have encountered all their lives have not seemed worthy of respect. As a result, they are unwilling to conform passively to the demands placed upon them by the prison regime.

Still, it might be expected that with such an elaborate system of social control, prisons should be relatively tranquil places. As we have seen, quite the opposite is actually the case, especially in maximum-security prisons. Much of the violence within prisons grows out of the contradictions within the prison's system of internal control. As argued in Chapter 11, the lawlessness of the totalitarian prison generates considerable violence. More indirectly, the hierarchy of punishments tends to concentrate in the maximum-security prisons those prisoners who resist the prison regime.

Prisoners who refuse to accept passively the rules and treatment of the minimum-security prisons, whether out of ideological principle, personal pride, or simply an inability to accept any authority, get transferred to tighter institutions. The maximum-security facilities—Soledad Central, San Quentin, and Folsom in the California system—thus tend to have a higher concentration of prisoners who are not easily intimidated by threats of harsher punishment and who are willing to resist— at times violently—the control of their lives by the prison administration.

The prison system has for a long time been trying to find effective ways of coping with prisoner violence without modifying its system of controls. A number of solutions have been proposed by the Department of Corrections. One is to create one or two super-maximum-security prisons that would house the most violent and troublesome prisoners in the state. Such a prison would constitute a new final stage in the hierarchy of punishment. Another proposal, which by late 1971 had reached the stage of serious intent, is to try to develop techniques of "neurosurgical treatment of violent inmates." A letter from the director of the Department of Corrections to the executive officer of the California Council on Criminal Justice discusses this proposal:

> Subject: Letter of Intent—Proposal for the Neurosurgical Treatment of Violent Inmates
> Dear Mr. Lawson:
> The problem of treating the aggressive, destructive inmate has long been a problem in all correctional systems. During recent years this problem has become particularly acute in the California Department of Corrections institutions. To date, no satisfactory method of treatment of these individuals has been developed.
> This letter of intent is to alert you to the development of a proposal to seek funding for a program involving a complex neurosurgical evaluation and treatment program for the violent inmate. The program would involve the neurosurgery staff of the University of California at San Francisco Medical Center. Initially, following a screening at the California Medical Facility at Vacaville, a period of acute hospitalization would be involved at the UCSF Hospital for a period of 5 to 7 days. After this, during a period

of two or three weeks, the patient would undergo diagnostic studies, probably on an outpatient basis, being transported as necessary from either California Medical Facility
at Vacaville or San Quentin. During this time, surgical and
diagnostic procedures would be performed to locate centers in the brain which may have been previously damaged
and which could serve as the focus for episodes of violent
behavior. If these areas were located and verified that they
were indeed the source of aggressive behavior, neurosurgery would be performed, directed at the previously found
cerebral foci. Finally, if it were found that surgery was
indicated the patient would be rehospitalized at the UCSF
Medical Center for its performance.

It is estimated that the total effort, including the necessary screening by physicians, the hospitalizations, pay and
transportation for correctional officers would amount to
$48,000; grant funds required would be $36,000 with the
Department of Corrections providing the 25% in kind
match.

Very sincerely,   R. K. PROCUNIER

Milder forms of the same solution are already in effect through
the use of psychiatric facilities and drugs to control "violent"
prisoners. Such proposals are a natural extension of the
totalitarianism of the power relationships within prison and the
problems of control in the hierarchy of punishments. Not only
does the prison reform movement have to contend with the
considerable obstacles presented by the totalitarianism of the
prison system, but with the prospect of increasingly sophisticated techniques of control in the future.[15]

15. The relationship of the totalitarianism of the prison power structure to the
problems of internal order is reflected dramatically in the massacre at Attica
prison in August, 1971. A great deal of debate has arisen since then as to the
wisdom of the decision to storm the prison with state troopers. *From the stand-
point of preserving the existing power relationships within prison,* the decision
may well have been a correct one. The internal order of prisons is grounded
in the use of force and the exercise of total power by the prison administration.
The credibility of that force and power was at stake at Attica. The rebellion was
not merely a threat to certain concrete conditions within the prison; it was a
basic challenge to the structure of power itself. The attempt was made by
officials to buy off the rebellion with strategic concessions. But the prisoners

In spite of the fact that the problem of internal control creates serious obstacles to reform, in a rather perverse sense it has opened up important reform opportunities. The hierarchy of punishment has two basic implications: on the one hand it tends to support the existence of harsh, totalitarian prisons; on the other hand, it facilitates the development of milder, more humane forms of punishment. Probation and parole are both possible, under present social conditions, because of the harsher punishments which back them up. The development of minimum-security prisons is possible because of the existence of maximum-security prisons. The experiments in minimum-security living units—such as the honor blocks at San Quentin—are possible because of the maximum-security housing units and adjustment centers in the same prisons. Awareness of this ironic reality, however, should not be taken in any way as an ethical endorsement of the conditions at the top of the hierarchy.

would not capitulate peacefully on terms acceptable to the state. Of course, given more time, more patience, and more pressure, the prisoners might have yielded. But since they could not be bought off, the resort to violence by the state was probably necessary to protect the status quo within the prison. This does not mean that the massacre was in any sense morally justified, but rather that it was politically necessary. If one regards the system itself as immoral, then the attack on Attica prison becomes a moral outrage. But to say this does not mean that the attack was irrational or ineffective.

It is often argued that political violence never accomplishes anything. This implies a naïve faith that sheer force is ineffective as an instrument of social control. Political violence like the attack on Attica raises the stakes. Prisoners in future rebellions will know that prison authorities and the state will not hesitate to use extreme force to defend the system, even if it means killing the state's own agents. Before prisoners again undertake a sustained rebellion, they will have to have a higher level of commitment than before. Force *does* intimidate people, especially when it is severe and certain, and this is one of the reasons police states survive. The question is: What are the social and human costs of such violent intimidation? Is it worth it? Is a capitalist social order worth defending at this price? Do the ends justify the means, and if not, what are the social and political alternatives which would make this level of repression unnecessary?

LIBERAL REFORM:
PITFALLS AND STRATEGIES

Reform can often prove dangerous. What looks like a progressive move may ultimately be coopted by the prison regime and turned into a weapon against prisoners. A good example of this is the indeterminate sentence. Originally conceived as a humanitarian reform which would change prisons from custodial dungeons into hospital-like centers for rehabilitation and training, in practice it has become one of the most potent weapons of control available in prison.

It is important, therefore, that proposed reforms be examined not only in terms of their apparent humanitarian quality, but also in terms of their practical consequences. Several reforms which have frequently been discussed in California appear constructive on the surface, but in reality may turn out to be harmful. In early 1972 it was announced that San Quentin prison would be closed by 1974 and replaced by two 400-man super-maximum-security facilities. It is argued that such smaller centers would allow for more flexible, personal treatment programs, for closer personal relationships between counselors and inmates, for better living conditions, and for prisoners to be placed closer to their families. At least some of these changes are unquestionably positive. But small prisons also pose certain dangers. Four hundred men would be much easier to control than 2,500. Emergent political organizations among prisoners would be even more fragmented, and it would be even easier for the prison officials to break them up by administrative transfers. It would be much easier in such small prisons quickly to identify and isolate prison radicals and send them to special centers for "incorrigibles." The anonymity of a large prison offers the prisoner a certain protection. These new centers could easily become more oppressive than the archaic fortress they are replacing.

Another reform which poses some of the same dilemmas is the proposal to build a modern psychiatric prison. There is no doubt that the psychiatric facilities at Vacaville prison are outdated and inadequate and that some prisoners are certainly in need of psychiatric treatment. However, the new, greatly expanded facility could very easily become a substitute for the adjustment centers in the maximum-security prisons. The adjustment centers have come under considerable criticism in recent years, and one way of dealing with the criticism is to send "troublemakers," especially political troublemakers, to a psychiatric prison-hospital. By defining them as violent psychopaths, the prison regime can deal with inmates who refuse to conform by drugging them in the name of psychiatric therapy or even, as has been proposed, by neurosurgery.

A prison reform movement thus has to deal not only with the serious obstacles to reform, but also with the negative consequences of the reforms themselves. These problems can easily make reform seem a hopeless task. As we saw in Chapters 12–14, various attempts at prison reform have not been very successful in the past. The prison regime has reacted with extreme repression to attempts by prisoners to force changes in the system. Legislatures have balked at any significant reform efforts. And the courts have taken only a few, marginal steps toward correcting some of the abuses within prison. Nevertheless, in spite of the frustrations of reform activity, reform struggles can still be useful and important.

Reform can be approached in two ways. First of all, it can be seen as a specific program which political organizations try to get accepted through legislative lobbying, court cases, and so on. This is the traditional liberal ethic of reform, and it has been the thrust of most efforts in the past.

Second, instead of viewing reform efforts as an activity which results in "a reform" and then stops, such efforts can be viewed as part of an *ongoing struggle* against the prison system. In this approach, the effectiveness of the reform movement is less a question of accomplishing a formal, structural change in the system than of the impact on the prison of the process of struggle itself. In these terms, the reform efforts of the late 1960s and early 1970s may have begun to have a significant effect on the prisons. The administrations of many American prisons (especially those in California and New York) cannot go quietly and efficiently about their business when they face organized opposition to their policies. Prison atrocities are less apt to be automatically swept under the carpet. In much the same way that the state uses punishment to deter crime, reform struggles can use the threat of bad publicity, demonstrations, "public outcry," and so forth to deter the most flagrant oppression.

One of the possible consequences of this new political reality within prison is that the Department of Corrections in California made the decision in 1970 to reduce the number of inmates in the California state prisons. The number decreased from a high of around 29,000 to just over 20,000 in early 1972. Some 8,000 to 9,000 fewer people are locked up in California prisons. This would seem largely the result of the pressure generated by the struggle of prisoners within the prison system. Even though the conditions of the remaining prisoners have not significantly improved, the reduction in the number of human beings imprisoned in the state is a real victory for the prison movement.[16]

Reformist groups whose activities center on the courts can have this same kind of impact, but in a slightly different way. In the past, for example, if a prisoner was denied adequate medical care, there was very little he could do about it unless he could afford a lawyer. However, with the emergence of a number of lawyers' groups which are willing to handle cases on behalf of inmates, this situation has slowly begun to change.

16. It is interesting in this regard that the reduction in the total number of inmates was never an explicit demand of the California prison strikes and revolts. It represents a response to the struggle rather than part of a "reform program" accomplished by the struggle.

Now if the prison refuses to give a prisoner adequate medical care, he can write to such a lawyers' group and ask for help. The prison will frequently yield the specific point simply to avoid a court fight. Such lawyers' groups are still very limited in size and resources, and the demand for legal help by prisoners is vastly greater than they can handle. Yet, they are slowly becoming a viable force in the struggle between prisoners and prison officials.

Intervention by lawyers in cases like that of the Soledad Seven (see Chapter 10) is becoming progressively more important. Until the early 1970s, it was extremely rare for prisoners accused of acts of violence within prison to be effectively defended by lawyers in court. The prisons had almost unlimited discretion to charge an inmate with an offense and to have him convicted in court. Legal action on behalf of prisoners has begun to change this. Such intervention has not "reformed" the structures of the prison, but the threat of suits and strong court defenses can act as a constraint on the officials' freedom of action.

Reformist activity focusing on legislatures is necessarily the least "struggle-oriented." Unlike action within prisons and in courts, legislative activity significantly impinges on prisons only when a reform is actually passed into law. This is not to say that the publicity surrounding legislative activity does not create pressure on prison administrators, but it is less focused than that from prisoners' direct action or from court battles.

The notion that reform organizations should see themselves as part of an ongoing struggle is alien to the logic of much liberal reform. Reformist activity as a means to reformist ends has some possibilities of success, especially in terms of the opportunities for reform discussed earlier. But in terms of dealing with the most serious sources of oppression within prisons, reform struggles which are part of a process of challenging the wider social order as a whole will probably have a more profound impact.

HUMANIZING PUNISHMENT
AND SOCIALIZING SOCIETY

The basic radical criticism of prisons in a capitalist society is that they protect an exploitative, unjust social order. It is not so much that prisons are intrinsically unjustified, but rather that they are unjustified when they serve the interests of a small portion of the population. From this central criticism comes one basic conclusion: society needs to be radically transformed so that the institutions of the state (including prisons) serve the interests of the people rather than of an elite. Socialism is the context in which this transformation can occur.

Before discussing the nature of punishment in a socialist society, it is important to clarify what I mean by the word "socialism": it will be used to refer to a dynamic process rather than a static structure; a socialist society is one which is in the process of becoming *radically democratic* and *radically egalitarian*. By "radically democratic" I mean that political power is firmly in the hands of the people rather than some power elite, whether that be a bureaucratic elite, a party elite, or an economic-class elite. By "radically egalitarian" I mean that distinctions of class, race, and sex have progressively less relevance for questions of the allocation of resources, the exercise of power, and the patterns of life opportunities. Taking the two concepts together, control over the economy and the state in such a society is exercised by the people, not on the basis of an inherited stratification, but on the basis of cooperative participation toward the realization of collective goals.[17]

17. No society at the present time embodies these principles, and it is not clear whether any society is really in the "process of becoming radically democratic and radically egalitarian." At various times socialist experiments in Cuba, China, and the Soviet Union seemed to be moving toward these goals. These countries have certainly made enormous strides toward equality. Their progress toward these goals, however, has not been unfaltering, and they should not be taken as consistent models of a socialist society.

This definition of socialism, needless to say, raises many questions. How can power ever be firmly in the hands of the people? Is not a technocratic elite essential for a smooth-running modern industrial society? Won't there always be ambitious people who will try to dominate others? These are all issues which have proved to be extremely problematical during the attempts at building socialism in such countries as the Soviet Union, Cuba, and China. I cannot pretend to have the answers to these questions; the answers will come as more attempts to create socialist societies occur. For the moment, it can only be said that these are problems with which any socialist society will have to struggle. My assumption is that the difficulties can be resolved in the direction of constructing a radically democratic socialist society. On the basis of this understanding of socialism, let us examine some of the implications of a socialist society for punishment.

Socialism will not eliminate the political need for prisons of some form or another. For the foreseeable future, even the most progressive of socialist societies will face serious problems of social conflict and social control; and in all probability, prisons will be part of the political strategy for coping with those conflicts. However, while prisons will continue to exist, the system of punishment will operate under very different general principles from those in a capitalist society.

Principles of Punishment in a Socialist Society

Punishment is an instrument of social justice. In a socialist society punishment, especially imprisonment, would be used to deter acts which undermine social equality and social justice. Acts which are physically dangerous to individuals would fall into this category, but also important are acts which undermine the central institutions of socialism. Crimes which involve the abuse of positions of public trust for personal gain would be especially serious. Punishment—the coercive arm of the state— would be a positive tool in creating and sustaining a socialist society.

There is a danger in this principle. Since priority would be placed on social justice and collective interests, there is a real danger of erosion of the concept of individual rights. The ultimate ideal of socialism is to create the social conditions in which individual needs and interests and collective needs and interests are basically harmonious. Before that harmony emerges, there will be a tension between individuals and collectivities, and there will be pressure to disregard the individual in favor of the community.

Since the social organization of bourgeois society is being rejected, ideological pressure would exist to reject totally all elements of "bourgeois" justice. This means that many of the values of classical liberalism, including those focusing on the question of civil liberties and due process of law, might be rejected along with the values that are more closely connected to the class structure of a capitalist society.

The rejection *in toto* of liberal values reflects an inadequate analysis of the nature of "bourgeois" justice and of social justice in a socialist society. The central fault with bourgeois liberalism is not the principles of civil liberty, but rather the way in which those principles have been institutionalized and the social conditions in which they operate. Due process of law is a sound principle; but in a society in which many people are desperately poor, it loses much of its significance. This is the meaning of Anatole France's remark: "The Law, in its majestic equality, punishes the rich and the poor alike for sleeping under bridges, begging in the streets and stealing bread." The fact that a poor person accused of stealing bread—or of burglarizing a home— is tried under "due process of law" does not reduce the oppressiveness of the system; it merely systematizes that oppression. The fault in the legal system lies not in the concept of due process, but in the social context in which due process operates.

The core values of liberal justice (due process, confrontation of accusers, trial by jury, habeas corpus) and the associated values of civil liberties (freedom of speech, freedom of assembly, and so on) can be fully realized only where there is under-lying *social* justice. Or to put it another way, socialism becomes the social context in which classical liberal values can operate. But it is also true that social justice must ultimately rest on a rigorous defense of individual justice. In the trial procedures of a socialist society it would be important that the rights of the defendant be protected and that the trial be just: to serve the ends of social justice, punishment must be applied justly to individuals.

Punishment is explicitly political. In all societies, imprison-ment and other forms of punishment by the state are intrinsi-cally political acts. But their political meaning is usually dis-guised. In American society, prisons are portrayed as institutions for protecting "society," for "rehabilitating" violent individuals, and so on. The class interests which the criminal justice system serves are never made explicit. One of the core principles of a socialist society is that the structures of society are "demystified." People must be educated about the political role of the repressive apparatus of the state in general, and of prisons in particular. The social ends which punishment would serve and the political criteria for the use of prisons must be made explicit.

The individual offender does not bear total responsibility for his offense. Part of the socialist demystification process is the awareness that individuals are part of collectivities, and that the collectivity bears some of the responsibility for individual offenses. Crime would be considered a collective problem, not just a "failure" by the individual, and the community would have the responsibility to deal with that collective problem as well as to punish the misdeeds of its members. What this means in practice is that punishing a member of a community must be accompanied by an examination of the problems within the community that are bound up with the offense. The practice of "criticism/self-criticism" meetings in the People's Republic of China, for instance, represents, among other things, an attempt to establish some level of collective self-examination in response to individual offenses.[18] A crime is taken as an occasion for education by the whole community as well as by the individual offender. When such collective self-examination is a continual process, rather than merely the response to crisis situations, it can become an important element in the strengthening of socialist consciousness and socialist institutions.

Whenever possible, punishment is not alienated from the community. In the same way that there would be collective responsibility for an offense, there would be collective responsibility for punishment. A hierarchy of punishment would still exist, but the lower levels of the hierarchy would be firmly rooted in community control. For a wide variety of relatively minor offenses, some type of "criticism/self-criticism" in a socialist society would be the basic technique of dealing with the offense. For more serious offenses, the central sanction would be some form of community surveillance. Such surveillance would differ from "probation" or a "suspended sentence" in that members of the community would actively participate in the social control of the offender, rather than having that control handled by a probation-bureaucracy. Similarly, if short-term incarceration facilities were necessary, they would be locally controlled and integrated into the general community.

Such community-based punishment would not necessarily be less severe than the bureaucratically controlled punishment of present American society. It could well be that a criticism/self-criticism meeting or community surveillance would be a harsher punishment—harsher in the sense of causing more personal anguish—than a suspended sentence, a fine, probation, or

18. The notion of "criticism/self-criticism" refers to two interrelated processes. On the one hand, the community criticizes the offender and he is expected to examine his shortcomings. On the other hand, the community is supposed to collectively criticize itself as well as the offender and use the offense as an occasion for examining the problems of the collectivity. At its best, such a process provides a mechanism by which the community can evolve and the members of the community can learn how to live and work together; at its worst, this process can degenerate into ritualistic confession meetings in which people accused of offenses have to publicly proclaim their guilt whether or not they actually committed the offense.

even a short jail term in this society. Many individuals would undoubtedly prefer the relative anonymity of a jail sentence to the public censure of community surveillance. The point is not which forms of punishment are the mildest in some abstract sense, but rather, which forms of punishment are most consistent with the goal of constructing a good society.

Punishment is democratic. If the "radically democratic" side of the definition of socialism is to have any substantive meaning, the repressive apparatus of the state—the police, the courts, and the system of punishment—must be democratically controlled. The People's Courts in Cuba are a partial example of this principle. Most criminal cases that affect only a particular community are tried before a community assembly or a popularly elected local tribunal rather than before a bureaucratically organized court.

Of equal importance, the police must be firmly controlled by the people rather than by a centralized, autonomous bureaucracy. It would be possible for police duty to become an obligation of all citizens for a certain period so that a professional police force could be largely eliminated.

Finally, the apparatus of punishment itself must be controlled democratically. Since this would obviously be simplest when punishment is community-based, punishment should be kept within the confines of the community whenever possible. In those cases in which more severe measures such as long-term imprisonment were necessary, it would be important that punishment not be controlled by a self-perpetuating, unrestrained bureaucracy. Some form of strong, democratic surveillance of the prisons would be necessary to avoid the situation of "lawlessness" described in Chapter 11.

The five principles outlined above focus mainly on the broad social ends of punishment in a socialist society. The implications of socialism for the internal operation of prisons is a more difficult problem; any discussion of this issue is necessarily more speculative.

Throughout this book, contemporary American prisons have been criticized as dehumanizing and degrading. It is tempting to say that prisons in a socialist society would automatically be different: that they would respect prisoners as human beings; that they would guarantee prisoners' rights and give them some real measure of power. This will not necessarily be the case. Certainly in the historical attempts at creating socialist societies, prisons and labor camps have often not avoided many of the degrading and dehumanizing features of prisons in a capitalist society.

The problem of the internal operation of penal institutions in a socialist society is closely bound up with the socialist theory of crime. In his essay "Problems Relating to the Correct Handling of Contradictions Among the People," Mao Tse-tung makes the distinction between two different classes of offenders: those who are "enemies of the people," or "class enemies," and those who merely reflect a lack of socialist consciousness. The system of punishment in China is designed to handle these two types of criminals in very different ways. Offenses that reflect false class consciousness are dealt with by criticism/self-criticism meetings, political education, community surveillance, and various forms of mild detention (short-term exile to a commune, labor camps, etc.). "Enemies of the people," on the other hand, are dealt with very harshly. They are placed in repressive labor camps or prisons, and whatever "rehabilitation" is given them is of a coercive, manipulative variety.[19]

The differential treatment of criminals who pose a serious

---

19. It is, of course, not always easy to apply this theoretical distinction in practice. Some criminal acts do not clearly fall into one category or another. If the criminal justice system is controlled by a political elite, the designation "enemies of the people" can become no more than a device for attacking the elite's opposition. This is one reason why radical democracy is so important as a part of the conception of socialism. For a discussion of the criminal justice system in China, see Jerome Cohen, *The Criminal Process in the People's Republic of China, 1949–1963* (Cambridge: Harvard University Press, 1968). His discussion in Chapter 1, "Ideology of the Criminal Law," is especially relevant for the distinction between class enemies and criminals who merely reflect false consciousness.

threat to the social order (i.e., class enemies) and criminals whose offenses are essentially "indiscretions" is not peculiar to a socialist society. As was stressed in Chapter 2, crimes committed by the rich in American capitalist society are handled much less repressively than crimes committed by the poor. Instead of imprisonment, a wide variety of informal and administrative sanctions (especially fines) is used to control criminal or semi-criminal behavior at the top levels of the American elite.[20]

Where a socialist society and a capitalist society differ (aside from the obvious difference in the definition of what constitutes a "class enemy") is that in a socialist society the harsher treatment of class enemies would be an explicit political principle. In liberal-capitalist societies it is often categorically denied that such differential treatment even exists, and it is certainly not part of the formal ideology of punishment. In a socialist society, the criminal justice system would not be mystified by empty notions of "equal treatment for all": there would clearly be one kind of treatment for criminals who pose serious threats to the social order and another for those who simply have not internalized the values of a socialist society. As in other aspects of socialist justice, the political meaning of why certain criminals should be treated differently from others would be made explicit.

As in a capitalist society, imprisonment in a socialist society, especially long-term imprisonment, is likely to be mainly used against people who are seen as class enemies. The internal operations of such prisons could be substantially the same as in the present American society. "Enemies of the people" may well be considered "outlaws"—people outside the law—and

20. There is an interesting similarity between some of the informal and administrative punishments given to the elite in a capitalist society and some of the punishments given to working-class offenders in a socialist society. A court order for a regular audit of the books of a corporation convicted of tax fraud is not unlike "community surveillance" of irresponsible workers in a socialist society. The "transfer" of a corporation executive to an insignificant branch office following some indiscretion is not unlike the "exile" of a worker to a rural commune following some offense in the People's Republic of China.

thus outside the political principles which govern the rest of the society. There is no guarantee that in a socialist society prisoners who are "class enemies" will be considered worthy of respect, humane treatment, civil rights. Improvement of prison conditions and practices in a socialist society will undoubtedly face the obstacles of resource allocation, deterrence, and internal control familiar to prisons in a capitalist order. It is impossible to predict how these issues will be resolved and how prisons in a future socialist society will be run.

The important point in the present discussion is that the issue itself—how repressive prisons ought to be—becomes a much more meaningful question in the context of a socialist society. In a society in which the social ends of punishment are unjustified, even the mildest level of repression is unjustified. This is not to say that simple *detention* is never justified in such a society. Some individuals are so dangerous that it is legitimate to separate them physically from the general population in any society.[21] But repression—punishment which serves as an instrument of social control—is justifiable only when the social ends of punishment are desirable, when punishment serves to protect a just and equitable society.[22] While socialism does not guarantee that prison conditions will necessarily be better than at present, it does create the political and moral context in

21. The obvious necessity to separate from the community the few individuals who are pathologically dangerous—the mad child rapist, the mass murderer —is often used as an argument to justify the entire prison system in the present society. The existence of such individuals may justify involuntary confinement in mental hospitals, but it can hardly justify an elaborate penal apparatus, a court system, and a police system directed at preserving the status quo. And in no way can the existence of such dangerous individuals become a justification for the degradation and oppression of prison life.

22. It is often said that "ends do not justify means." This is a naïve view of the ethical issues involved in the relationship between ends and means. Except in situations in which the means are intrinsically innocuous, it is *only the ends* which can justify them. If the ends are morally intolerable, then no means whatsoever are justified. The imprisonment of a slave because he commits the crime of trying to escape to freedom is unjustified regardless of how decent the conditions of incarceration are, and regardless of how fair the trial of the slave was. The same means become justifiable when they serve the social end of protecting a just and equitable social order.

which the problems of prisons can be constructively resolved.

The United States is far from being transformed into a socialist society. For the moment, the concrete problem that prisoners face is not how prisons can be reconstituted in a future, revolutionary era, but how they can cope with the oppressive reality of their lives today. That oppressiveness is rooted in the internal power relations within American prisons and in the role those prisons play in American society. As the prison movement becomes an element in the internal power struggle within prison, it can begin to mitigate some of the harshness of the prison regime. And by becoming part of a broader radical movement, it can help to create the social conditions in which prisons can eventually be fundamentally transformed.

AUTHOR'S NOTE

In early 1971, a number of lawyers and legal workers came together and formed the Prison Law Project in Oakland, California. The idea of the group was to provide legal services for prisoners and a focus for energies of lawyers and various groups working for change in the prison system. I joined the Project as a writer in order to concentrate my energies on writing *The Politics of Punishment*. It was through the Project that various contacts were made for most of the chapters in the book which I did not personally write.

In November, 1971, there emerged out of the original Project two completely autonomous organizations, the Prison Law Project and the Prison Law Collective. These two groups were characterized by different types of internal organization and differing emphasis on various kinds of activities. The royalties from the book will be divided evenly between these two groups, and used entirely for legal assistance for prisoners.

ABOUT THE AUTHORS

ERIK OLIN WRIGHT graduated from Harvard University in 1968. From 1968–1970 he studied history at Oxford University in England. Upon his return to the United States, he entered the Starr King School for the Ministry (Unitarian-Universalist) and worked as a student chaplain at San Quentin prison. He is currently a doctoral student in sociology at the University of California, Berkeley.

ROBERT BARBER was graduated from Princeton University in 1971. Since then he has worked as a journalist and has covered the trials of various prisoners in California.

BRIAN GLICK is a lawyer with the Prison Law Collective of San Fransisco. He is past Associate Director of the Columbia University Center on Social Welfare Policy and Law. He is co-author of *The Bust Book: What to Do Until the Lawyer Comes,* and several articles including, "The Limits of Liberal Solutions —The Case of Income Guarantees."

THOMAS LOPEZ MENEWEATHER served eight years as a prisoner in the California Department of Corrections. Six of those years were spent in various adjustment centers; three and one-half years were spent without a break in the adjustment center of Soledad prison.

JOHN PALLAS is a graduate student in criminology at the University of California. During 1971 he worked as a Research Associate for the Research Division of the California Department of Corrections.

EVE PELL is a writer with the Prison Law Collective. She first became involved in prison work in connection with the Soledad Brothers case in 1970. Subsequently, she edited a collection of prison letters entitled *Maximum Security*. She is co-author with Paul Jacobs and Saul Landau of *To Serve the Devil: A Documentary Analysis of American Racial History*.

FRANK L. RUNDLE was head psychiatrist at Soledad prison from December 1970 until May 1971. He was fired for "insubordination" when he refused to turn over to the prison superintendent the confidential files on one of his inmate-patients. Dr. Rundle is currently the supervising psychiatrist for the treatment programs in several New York City correctional institutions.

JAMES F. SMITH is a lawyer with the Sacramento Legal Aid Society. In 1970 and 1971 he acted as legislative advocate for the California Rural Legal Assistance program. He was intimately involved in most of the legislative attempts at significant reform of the prison system in the 1971 state legislature.

FAY STENDER is a lawyer with the Prison Law Project of Oakland, California. She was one of the original lawyers for the Soledad Brothers and has been actively involved in prison litigation for the past several years. She is the author of several articles on prison law, including "The Prison as a Lawless Agency" (with David Greenberg), *Buffalo Law Review*, Spring 1972.